ﻢﺳﺑﻣﻣﻣﺳﻳﺳﺳ ﻊﺑﺳﻳ ﺗﻣﺳﺻﻧﻳﺳ ﺳﺑﺳﻳﺳﻳ ﺳﺳﺑﻳﺻ ﺳﺳﻋﻳﺑ ﻟﻣﺑﺳﺑﺳﺳﻣﻳ

ﺳﻣﻳ ﺳﻳﺿ۔ﻊﺑﻳﺿ ﻳﺿﺑﻣ ﻳﺑﺳﺻﻳﺳﺳ ﺳﺑﺳﺗﻟﻧﺳﺳﺑﺳﻳﺳﺑﺳ

ﻳﻊ۔ﺑﻣﻳﺑﺳﺳﺳ ﻳﺳﺳﻳﺳ ﺳﻣﺑﻣﻣﺳﻳﺳ ﻊﺑﺳ ﺳﺳﺑﺳﻳﺑﺳﻳ

ﻳﻳﺳﺳﺑﻳﺳﻳﻊﻳ ﺳﻳﻳﺑﻳﺳ ﻊﺳﻣﻳﺳﺳﺳﻳﺳﺳﺳ ﺳﺳﺑﺳﺳﺑﻳﻊﺑﻳ

ﻳﻳﺳﺳ ﻊﺳ ﺳﻳﺳﻣﻳﺳ ﺳﺳﻳﺑﻳﺳﺳﺑﻳ ﻳﺳﺳﺻﺳﻳﺑ ﻳﺑﺳﺳﺳﺳﺳﻣﻳ ۔

ﻳﻳﺑﺳﻳﺻﻳﺑﺳﻊﻳ ﺳﻣﻳ ﺻﻳﺳﺳﺳ ﻊﺳﺻﻳﺳ ﻊﺳﺳﻳﺻﻳﺳﻳﺑ ﺳﺳﻣﻳ۔ﺳﺳ

ﻳﻳﺳﺳﺳﻣﻳ ﻊﺳﺳ ﺳﻳﺻﺑﻳﺳﻳ ﻳﺳﺳﺑﻳﺑﻣﺳﺳﺻﺑﻳﺳﻣﻳ ﻊﺳﺳﻳﺻﻳﺑﺳﺳ

ﺳﻳﻊ۔ﻳﺳﺳ ﻳﻳﺑﺳﻳﻳﺑﺳﺳﺳ ﻳﺳﺑﺳﺳﻳﺳﺳﺑﺳﺳﺳ ﺳﻳﺑ۔ﻊﺑﻳ ﻳﺳﺳﺳ۔ﺳﺳ

ﻳﺳﻳﻊﺑﺳﻳﺻﻳﻳﺑﺳﺳﺳ ﻳﺳﺳﺳﻳﺑﺑ ﺳﻳ۔ﺻﻳ ﻳﺑﺳﺳ۔ ﺳﺳﻳﺑﻳﺑﺑﺑﻳﺑ ﻳﺳﻳﺑﺑﻳﺻﻳﺳﺳ ﻳﻣﻳ۔ﺳﺑﻳ

ﻳﺑﺳﺳﻳﺑﺳﺳﺻﻳ ﻳﻳﻣﻳﺻﻳﺑﻳﺑ ﺳﺑﺳﺳﺳ ﻊﺳﺳﺳﻳﺑﺳﺳﺳﺑﺳﻳﺑ ﻊﺳﻳﺳﺳﺻﺳﻳﺻﻳﻳ۔ﺑﺳﻳ ﺳﺳﺳﻳﺑ ۔۔

ﻳﻳﺳﺳﺳﺳﻣﻳ ﺳﺳﺳ ﻟﻊﻳﺳﻣﻳﺳﺳﺳ ﺳﻳﺳﺳﺻﻳﻳﺳﺑﻊﻳﺑ۔ ﻳﺳﺳﻳﺳﺳﺳﺳﺳﺳ ﻳﺳﺳﺳﻳﺑ

ﻊﺳﻳﺳﻳﺳﺑ ﻊﺳﻣﻳﺳﺻﻳﺳ ﺳﻣﻳﺳﻳﻳﺳﺳﺳ ﺳﻧﻳﻳﺻﻣﻳﺑ۔ ﻟﻣﺑﺳﺑﺳﺳﻣﻳ۔ﺑﻳﺑ

ﻳﻳﺳﺳﺳﺳﻣﻳ ﺻﻳﺳﺳﺳ ﺳﻳﺑﺳﺳﺻﻣﻳﺳﺳﻳﺳ ﺳﺳﻳﺳﺳﺳﻣﻳ ﻳﻳﺳﺳﺳﺳﻣﻳ ﻟﻣﺑﻳﺳﺳﺳﺳﺑﺳﺳ

ﻳﻊ۔ﺑﻣﻳﺑﺳﺳﺳﺳ ﺳﻳﻊ۔ﺑﻳﺑ۔ ﻳﻳﺳﺑﺳﻳﺻﺳﺑﺳﺳﺳﻳ ﻳﺳﺑﻳﺳﺳ۔ﻳﺳﺳﺳﺳﺳﺳﺳﺳ

ﻊﺳﻣﻳ ﺳﻳﺳﺳﺳﻳﺳ ﻳﺑﺑﺳﺳﺻﻣﻳﺳﺳﺳﺳﻳﺑ۔ ﻳﻳﺳﻳﺿ۔ﻊﻳﺿ۔ ﻊﺳﺳﺑﻟﻣﻳﺳﺳﺳ ﺳﺳﺑﻳﺑﻳﻊﺑﻳ ۔۔

And when you tell me, "with foresight you reach truth," then you give me orders not to be disobeyed. Let me arise before attention comes to me, followed by wealth-granting reward, which will distribute the rewards according to the balance at the (assignment of) benefit(s).

I realize that you are holy, O Mazda Ahura, when one approaches me with good thought to take note of the aims of my wish. You have imparted that to me: (the wish) for a long life that nobody can oblige you to grant, and for a desirable possession which is said to be in your power.

What a wealthy and powerful man would grant to a friend, (grant) me, O Mazda, your support, and the foresight which you have obtained from truth, through your power, so that I may arise with all those who recite your mantras to drive away the challengers of (your) proclamation.

*(Y.43:12–14)*

# ZOROASTRIANISM

*An Introduction to an Ancient Faith*

## The Sussex Library of Religious Beliefs and Practices

This series is intended for students of religion, social sciences and history, and for the interested layperson. It is concerned with the beliefs and practices of religions in their social, cultural and historical setting. These books will be of particular interest to Religious Studies teachers and students at universities, colleges, and high schools. Inspection copies available upon request.

_Published_

*The Ancient Egyptians*    Rosalie David

*Hinduism*    Jeaneane Fowler

*The Jews*    Alan Unterman

*Sikhism*    W. Owen Cole and Piara Singh Sambhi

*Zoroastrianism*    Peter Clark

_In preparation_

*Buddhism*    Merv Fowler

*Christian Theology*    Nora Hill

*The Diversity of Christianity Today*    Diane Watkins

*The Doctrine of the Trinity: God in Three Persons*    Martin Downes

*Gnosticism*    John Glyndwr Harris

*Humanism*    Jeaneane Fowler

*Islam: Faith and Practice*    David Norcliffe

_Forthcoming_    *Bhagavad Gita (a student commentary)*
*Confucianism    Jainism    Taoism    Zen*

# Zoroastrianism

*An Introduction to an Ancient Faith*

## Peter Clark

**sussex**
ACADEMIC
PRESS

***BRIGHTON • PORTLAND***

2 4 6 8 10 9 7 5 3 1

*Published 1998 in Great Britain by*
SUSSEX ACADEMIC PRESS
Box 2950
Brighton BN2 5SP

*and in the United States of America by*
SUSSEX ACADEMIC PRESS
5804 N.E. Hassalo St.
Portland, Oregon 97213–3644

*British Library Cataloguing in Publication Data*
A CIP catalogue record for this book is available from the British Library.

*Library of Congress Cataloging-in-Publication Data*
Clark, Peter, 1957–
Zoroastrianism : an introduction to an ancient faith / Peter Clark.
p. cm. — (Sussex library of religious beliefs and practices)
Includes bibliographical references and index.
ISBN 1–898723–78–8 (pbk. : alk. paper)
1. Zoroastrianism. I. Title. II. Series.
BL 1571.C53 1998 98-27763
295—dc21 CIP

Printed by Biddles Ltd, Guildford and King's Lynn
This book is printed on acid-free paper

# Contents

———

# Foreword

A book of this kind is rarer than it should be. While a seemingly endless series of introductions to the major "world religions" have tripped off the presses, students of Zoroastrianism have had, until recently, only Mary Boyce's ground-breaking 1979 *Zoroastrians: Their Religious Beliefs and Practices* for convenient reference. The appearance of this work by a young and enthusiastic scholar working in an unjustly neglected field could therefore not be more welcome, especially since Peter Clark provides an introductory survey, incorporating the latest academic debate, that is at the same time scholarly and accessible.

It has long been recognized by some that Zoroastrianism played a significant role in the development of both Judaism and Christianity. It is also a tradition that has developed two cultural bases, Iran and India, hence its frequent characterization as "spanning East and West". It would, however, be short-sighted to view Zoroastrianism as interesting mainly because of its interaction with better-known traditions. To paraphrase Bishop Butler, "Everything is what it is, and not something else". And Zoroastrianism addresses, in a unique and compelling way, ethical issues that are still alive in the modern world. Not only does it raise fundamental questions about what it is to be a human being, and the nature of good and evil, it also considers the relationship of humans to the natural world in a vibrantly positive light.

Peter Clark, in providing us with an intelligible and stimulating introduction to this ancient religious tradition, ensures that teachers and lecturers no longer have an excuse to ignore such rich and interesting material. More importantly, he helps to preserve, with sensitivity, that channel of communication between Zoroastrians and other human beings that is periodically in danger of becoming clogged or forgotten, to the impoverishment of us all.

Dr W. J. Johnson
Department of Religious and Theological Studies
Cardiff University of Wales

# *Preface*

---

The purpose of this book is threefold: to introduce the student to what might be considered the main doctrinal features of Zoroastrianism; to demonstrate the continuity between the initial conception of such doctrines, and their subsequent elaboration and development as a result of an increasingly systematic theological approach to the religion; and then to relate these points of doctrine to Zoroastrianism as a contemporary and living faith. The book is thus not primarily an historical survey; historical events are only discussed when they relate directly to doctrine or practice. However, since the book is intended primarily for students who are perhaps more familiar with the Judeo-Christian tradition, an appendix is provided which attempts to show how the Zoroastrian faith was able to interact with post-exilic Judaism in such a way as to exert upon it a lasting influence which was to be felt also in Christianity, and this subject is of course placed within its historical context.

The version of the *Gathas*, the hymns of the prophet Zarathushtra, which I have used throughout this book is the most recent translation to appear, *The Heritage of Zarathushtra* by H. Humbach and P. Ichaporia (Heidelberg 1994). It is recommended that the student acquire or has access to a copy of this book, since it will enable him or her to consider the extracts I use from the individual *Gathas* in their wider literary context. It will also enable students to follow certain arguments as far as the Avestan language is concerned. For example, when discussing the question of the evil spirit in chapter 1, I have stated that his name, *Angra Mainyu*, does not appear in the *Gathas*, though this is the name by which he is most commonly known. This name has been derived from the *Gathas*, however, as a glance at Y.45:2, in its original Avestan form, demonstrates. It is not, though, necessary to be intimate with the Avestan language to understand this book, and all frequently used Avestan (and Pahlavi) words are defined in the glossary.

Frequent use is made of the term *Yasna*, which may be understood in a variety of ways, two of which concern us here. First, it refers to a liturgical celebration which, structurally, pre-dates Zarathushtra and which is now, having been as it were "Zoroastrianized", the high liturgy of the Zoroastrian faith. Secondly, the term (which means "worship/sacrifice") also refers to each of the individual hymns that make up the five collections of Zarathushtra's poetry. It refers also to a number of other hymns, not ascribed to the prophet, collected under the general title of "*Yasna*", and which are those chanted in the celebration of the same name. The *Yasna* collection is incorporated into a larger body of works called the *Avesta* (a term of unknown meaning but which probably means "[authoritative?] utterance"), so called since it is written in the Avestan language.

Each reference to the *Gathas* and other texts from the body of hymns known as the *Yasna* (other than one particular hymn known as the *Hom Yasht*) is indicated by the abbreviation "Y.". Other frequently used abbreviations are: GBd. (*Greater Bundahishen*) and Yt. (*Yasht*).

On the subject of the *Yasna* as a liturgical celebration, in chapter VI I have chosen to discuss this ritual first and then the *Afrinagan* ceremony, before moving on to other rituals and observances, since these two ceremonies are demonstrated on a video recording made by Colorado State University, and which is available by writing to the Office of Instructional Services, Colorado State University, Fort Collins, CO 80523, USA (readers in the UK are advised that this video recording does not come in PAL format and will need to be converted). As a consequence of my own study of the *Yasna* ceremony I have naturally been influenced by the recent work done on it by others, and in particular by Dastur Firoze M. Kotwal, Professor James W. Boyd and Professor Ron G. Williams, whose publications I refer to frequently and whose conclusions I have attempted to synthesize and compress when discussing not only the *Yasna* ceremony but also ritual in general. In drawing on the work of these three scholars, however, I hold myself responsible for any misrepresentation or misinterpretation of their ideas.

Transliterations have been standardized as far as possible and diacritics avoided. The thinking behind this lies in the assumption that this book will be used a resource for students in the study of the religion and for assisting with essays, assignments and so on. It is unreasonable to expect those without any linguistic training to have to come to grips with additional complications on top of the many complexities of Zoroastrianism itself.

Those using this book as a teaching aid may be consoled by the knowledge that from my own experience in this matter, an introduction to Zoroastrianism through its resemblance to better known traditions has often gone some way to easing the passage into less familiar territory. Keeping in mind Dr Will Johnson's pertinent remarks in his foreword, however, it would be unfortunate if the use of the appendix dealing with this subject, intended here partly as an initial taster, were to be interpreted as the *raison d'être* of the entire book. The fact that this subject is confined to an appendix indicates my own view on the subject *vis-à-vis* the study of Zoroastrianism generally. As the plan of the book suggests (pages v and vi), an introduction to the *Gathas* of Zarathushtra, having presented his theological, cosmological and ethical ideas, and having illuminated the vexed subject of his birthplace and time as well as the socio-religious circumstances under which he operated, can lead quite naturally into the more dense field of doctrinal development, which is then seen to be expressed both ritually and in the day-to-day lives of the Zoroastrians themselves. The final chapter examines in a little more detail some of the issues which affect the community today, and which have been mentioned from time to time earlier in the book.

Some tutors and other users of the book, whether because of time constraints or other reasons, may wish to disregard the more technical aspects of parts of this study, such as, say, those dealing with the alleged Platonic parallels to Zoroastrian cosmology, or the more detailed implications of ritual practice as applied to the *Yasna* ceremony. The same applies to some of the notes which, whilst they may assist some readers in appreciating more the connections and similarities between Zoroastrian concepts and non-Zoroastrian philosophies, should in no way be regarded as "compulsory reading".

Bombay, the home of orthodox Zoroastrianism, is now more properly known by its original name of *Mumbai*. Given that much of the activity described in this book took place when that city was generally referred to by its Anglicized name, and aware that the book is primarily intended for use by a Western readership, I have retained the use of *Bombay* throughout.

Writing a book about any living community is bound to be a hazardous task, and an author who attempts such an undertaking runs the risk of making remarks which, taken the wrong way, can easily cause offence. Where I have out of necessity touched upon subjects which by their nature require sensitive treatment, if I have trodden perhaps a little too heavily or seemed a little too judgmental, this is not to be taken as a definitive or even necessarily personal comment on the issue in question. Yet at the same time it would be blinkered of me to deny that certain questions do divide the contemporary Zoroastrian community, and concealing or passing over these problems would be a disservice to my readers. As an outsider looking in, I naturally cannot feel the passion that many of my Zoroastrian friends – on both sides of the debate – feel about the more controversial topics such as conversion or intermarriage. All I can do is lay before a readership the situation as I find it, and trust that my own quest for impartiality will inspire others to approach the issues in the same spirit.

Readers wishing to follow up with the religion's practitioners any areas this book touches upon are referred (in the UK) to *Religions in the UK* produced by the University of Derby, in which official contact addresses are listed (full details are listed in the bibliography); in other countries similar directories should be consulted. I have always found that those Zoroastrians who care about their faith (and, regrettably, there will always be those who do not, as is the case in all religious traditions) are more than willing to offer assistance to students – the acknowledgements refer to the many who have helped me over the years.

My intention in this book has been to present to readers as impartial an account as possible of Zoroastrianism as I have understood it so far in my researches, and yet as I continue to study it there will be conclusions that have been drawn here which I will no doubt wish to revise in the years to come. For the time being, however, I merely offer this book as my perception of the depth and great beauty of the Zoroastrian faith. Yet it is a faith whose history is not without its share of anguish and pain. The opening to chapter V, for example, recounts a particularly distressing time for the Zoroastrian people of Iran, yet without this apparently disastrous episode the great strength that became Indian, or "Parsi" Zoroastrianism, would probably have never been born. The pain the tradition has suffered has, I think, contributed to its extraordinary richness – and beauty – today.

# Acknowledgements

My first, and in some ways deepest, thanks is to Dr Will Johnson of the Religious and Theological Department at Cardiff University. He first introduced me to the study of Zoroastrianism when I was an undergraduate, subsequently supervised my postgraduate studies, and now he has provided the foreword to this present book. His constant help and encouragement have been among the governing factors in the development of my own academic career, and hence his priority in these acknowledgements.

Indeed the department at Cardiff as a whole has supported me in many ways, but I should be failing in both duty and friendship if I neglected to mention the help in this project given by Dr Frank Trombley; he read the entire manuscript prior to its publication and, at his suggestion, I have incorporated a number of revisions which I trust will make the book a more intelligible production and its reading a more rewarding and enjoyable experience than it would have been otherwise. Dr Jenny Rose of Costa Mesa, California, kindly read an early draft of the first two chapters and I have included many of her suggestions, though the faults that remain can be laid at no door other than my own. On this matter I would also like to mention Anthony Grahame, my editor at Sussex Academic Press, who unfailingly responded to my many questions, and Dr Jeaneane Fowler of the University of Wales, Newport, who first suggested that I write this book. On a more general level, other members of the academic community have been unfailingly helpful in my work; Professor John Hinnells of the School of Oriental and African Studies (SOAS), University of London, and Dr Alan Williams of the University of Manchester, deserve particular mention. I also thank Sarah Stewart of SOAS for permission to reproduce her diagram of the Amesha Spentas on page 164. I also acknowledge the enormous influence of Professor Mary Boyce in my studies; the frequent references to her own work throughout this book testify to the debt that I, and indeed all students of this remarkable religion, owe her.

Members of the Zoroastrian community, both here and abroad, have responded with characteristic cheerful generosity to my pleas for help. Chief among these is Malcolm M. Deboo, an almost indefatigable worker for Zoroastrian educational concerns in Britain, who has treated my often impertinent and no doubt naïve questions with customary forbearance; his friendship is also one I have come to value. I have been a frequent visitor to Zoroastrian House in London and have always been made to feel very welcome; Mr Rusi K. Dalal, as president of the Zoroastrian Education Trust Funds of Europe, has extended Zoroastrian hospitality to me on more than one occasion.

Abroad I have received generous and often unrewarded help from friends in India and the United States. My trip to India in 1996 was facilitated by Khojeste P. Mistree, director of Zoroastrian Studies, Bombay, and if I have been remiss in the past in fully acknowledging the help given by him and his team, I gladly do so now. Others in Bombay were also most helpful: Mrs Y. Mama who provided my accommodation; Mr Dinshah Dubash who acted as my protecting *fravashi* when I was there; Mrs H. Modi and the staff of the K. R. Cama Oriental Institute, where I spent many happy and profitable hours doing research; Ervad Dr Ramiyar P. Karanjia, principal of the Athornan Boarding Madressa who has since become a dear friend, together with his wife Havovi; Dastur Dr Firoze M. Kotwal who invited me to his home to discuss aspects of ritual and priesthood with me (and was similarly generous with his time when he visited London); and Dastur Dr K. JamaspAsa, who spent a morning with me in Bombay. Last, but certainly not least, Hilla Pocha and her late husband Piloo, for their friendship and continued interest in my work. In Ahmedabad, Navroze Kanga and his family welcomed me into their home and introduced me to some of the Zoroastrian sites in that region. In the United States, my friend Dina McIntyre, of the Gatha Studies Trust based in Pittsburgh, has corresponded with me for a number of years and has sent me, at her own expense, articles and books relating to Zoroastrianism. She introduced me to three other scholars who have been of help: Ervad Dr Kersey Antia, Professor Gernot Windfuhr and Professor Stanley Inlser, and also, in Britain, to Mr Shapur Captain of the World Zoroastrian Organization, who has ensured that I periodically receive details of that body's activities, and Mr Farrokh Vajivdar, who many years ago, when my Zoroastrian trail was just beginning, wrote to me with an extensive "starters' pack" of bibliographic details. To these I also record my gratitude. Omissions from this list, if there are any, are sincerely regretted.

Leaving the most significant until last, I happily confess to the enormous amount I owe to my wife Maria, whose labours in a field quite outside my own have brought balance and order to a household which would otherwise be dominated by chaos, and in bringing that balance she has done more than can be said to help create and sustain the environment within which this book was written, and who has thus secured for herself the dedication of this small, but I trust competent, contribution to the field of Zoroastrian studies.

Peter Clark,
June 1998

Since He is (the One) to be chosen by the world therefore the judgement emanating from truth itself (to be passed) on the deeds of good thought of the world, as well as the power, is committed to Mazda Ahura whom (people) assign as a shepherd to the poor.

(Y.27:13 – the *Ahuna Vairya* prayer)

Here, I have found Zarathushtra Spitama, the only one who listens to our teachings: he wishes to sing hymns of praise for us, O Mazda, and for truth, to let me enjoy the beauty of his speech.

(Y.29:8)

As a leading priest straightforward in truth, in accordance with the best spirit I am pleased with the thought with which one thinks pastoral works should be performed. With that (thought) I implore your sight and your counsel, O Mazda Ahura.

(Y.33:6)

Hail to us! For he is born the Athravan [*priest*] Spitama Zarathushtra.

(Yt.13 [*Farvardin Yasht*] : 94)

# I

## An Ancient Faith: Zarathushtra – Prophet and Priest

### 1 The *Gathas* of the Prophet Zarathushtra

Zoroastrianism, which can rightly claim to be the oldest of the world's prophetic and revealed religions, has, in common with many younger traditions, evolved over a lengthy period of time. Due to Zoroastrianism's ancient beginnings there are problems with assigning even an approximate date to its emergence, although a figure of roughly 1400 BCE[1] is reckoned by a large number of scholars to be most likely. Since Zoroastrianism began within a pre-literate culture there is a lack of recorded information about its earliest times. All that we know with any certainty about Zarathushtra,[2] the priest-prophet who gave his name to this ancient faith, is that which we can deduce from his *Gathas*. These are seventeen short hymns whose brevity belies their philosophical and theological profundity, and which express what was probably the lifetime's preaching and teaching of their author. We can also use these hymns to build up a picture not only of the world into which the prophet was born, but also of how he thought that world should be transformed in accordance with his own unique vision of God. The *Gathas* introduce to us a number of revolutionary features which are clearly their author's innovations, rich in insight and often startling in originality. Furthermore, to say that Zarathushtra heralded the beginnings of Western civilization is no wild claim, since his powerful message resonated long after his life not only within the religious culture to which he gave new life but, as his descendants expanded their political power a thousand years after, also in the movement that would eventually dominate the west – the Judeo-Christian tradition – where it still continues to be heard, perhaps faintly, even today.

The *Gathas* were passed on from generation to generation, for a long time orally but later in written form, by the priests who recited them as part of their ritual worship and eventually committed them to writing. It is believed that even when their meaning was forgotten or simply ceased to be understood, the mere sounds of the words, being sacred in themselves, were faithfully remembered and taught from priest to priest. Even now the *Gathas* are recited daily by the small but dedicated order of Zoroastrian priests for whom they form the central section of the liturgical *Yasna* ritual,[3] an ancient ritual which knits together heaven and earth and which urges creation on to its renewal, an event which later came to be referred to as the *frashokereti*,[4] when humanity and all that is created will be perfected. Scholarship in the last two centuries has recovered the meaning of these extraordinary poems, resulting in a wealth of modern language translations whose occasional disagreements only serve further to underscore the cryptic and inferential nature of Zarathushtra's thinking.

Zarathushtra's *Gathas* belong to a specific category of ancient poetry, represented in both Iranian and Indian traditions and characterized by defined metrical constraints (which the often untraditional Zarathushtra is not afraid to ignore when the occasion demands it), by an esoteric content and highly allegorical use of language. The technique required for composing this kind of poetry was learnt over many years of study and it presupposes an educated and privileged studentship drawn from the priestly class.

Like the psalms of the Hebrew scriptures, the *Gathas* are deeply personal and often anguished utterances, and at other times they abound with joy. Since the hymns of the *Gathas* are metrical, and grouped according to their metres, it can be supposed that they were conceived within a musical framework and partly intended for use within a ritual context, a notion confirmed by references to ritual practice in the *Gathas* themselves. Although they are not primarily doctrinal treatises, or instructional compositions, they contain much that forms the basis of the Zoroastrian religion, and therefore they can rightly be said to embody the essential truths of Zoroastrianism as Zarathushtra would have understood and taught them. The *Gathas* are, however, first and foremost revelation, and like many revelatory texts they not only contain the revelation itself but also the response of the person to whom the revelation is directed. Thus they are often in the form of a discourse, in which Zarathushtra addresses his god, *Ahura Mazda*, or the Lord of Wisdom, in which Zarathushtra expresses his doubts and questions God, and in which his prophetic vocation unfolds. As Zarathushtra's path becomes more clear to him, he widens it in the hope that it might embrace other followers, inviting his contemporaries to join him on a journey of discovery, the discovery of a new way of living, of a new relationship with God and of a new way of interpreting, understanding and relating to the world.

It is not strictly correct to say that Zarathushtra was the *founder* of an entirely *new* religion. As with other great religious figures who came after him, such as the Buddha, Jesus or Muhammad, what Zarathushtra did was to work within an established religious framework and introduce into it his new, often revolutionary, ideas, transforming it in accordance with his own understanding of the nature of God and the purpose of creation. It is not possible to do this without generating a fair amount of friction, and Zarathushtra was not immune to controversy, as his well-known initial lack of success testifies:

> Where and which part of land shall I go to succeed? They keep me away from the family and the tribe. The community that I wish to join does not gratify me, nor do the deceitful tyrants of the land. How shall I gratify you, O Mazda Ahura? (Y.46:1)

Moreover one can detect impatience and dissatisfaction in the *Gathas*, particularly with the way that religious ritual seemed to have degenerated into drunken and unseemly behaviour. This is not to say, as some have maintained, that Zarathushtra was opposed to ritual *per se*. Since he was a priest (Avestan *zaotar*, literally "one who invokes" or "one who pours"[5]), a fact we know from his *Gathas*, Zarathushtra's own spirituality and deep religiosity would have been underpinned by ritual activity. It is unlikely that he would have identified himself as a priest had it not been of importance to him:

> As a leading priest straightforward in truth, in accordance with the best spirit I am pleased with the thought with which one thinks pastoral works should be performed. With that (thought) I implore your sight and your counsel, O Mazda Ahura. (Y.33:6)

In another place he refers to "the correct uttering of the words" (Y.31:19) which may be understood as an allusion to the injunction (still observed today) to pronounce correctly the prescribed ritual words lest the ritual itself is vitiated. These "fixed" supplications would have been interspersed with extemporary utterances by the celebrant, but the improvised prayers will have nevertheless followed a strict set of guidelines, knowledge of which would have been acquired by the priest during his training.

As if in support of this priestly identity for the prophet, a later tradition, admittedly of a more legendary flavour, relates that it was during the preparation for a ritual that he received his first revelation – or "conference" – with Ahura Mazda in the form of an encounter with *Vohu Manah*, one of the "aspects" or characteristics of Ahura Mazda's creative and caring personality.[6] *Vohu Manah* is the Ahuric aspect of the Good Mind or "good thought". These characteristics, the six personified attributes of Ahura Mazda, are known as the *Amesha Spentas*, the Bountiful or Holy Immortals, and with Ahura Mazda (hypostatically united to his Holy Spirit *Spenta Mainyu*) they constitute a divine heptad. These spiritual entities are developments of the Indo-Iranian deities personifying desirable qualities such as law and piety and so in Zarathushtra's scheme they also denote these virtuous qualities which people must strive to imitate if they wish to be included among the followers and worshippers of Ahura Mazda destined to enjoy the benefits of the world's refreshment (*frashokereti*).

There is therefore no reason to discredit the thrust (if not the historicity) of this tradition concerning Zarathushtra's first glimpse of the divine, since it may be gleaned from the Gathic literature which could only have been composed by one in intimate communion with his God:

> Inspired by good thought and being a witness for Ahura Mazda, I have in mind (one's) soul for (his commendation by my) song, as well as the rewards for (his) actions. For as long as I can and am able I shall look out in (my) search for truth. (Y.28:4)

One can also see in the *Gathas* that Zarathushtra was prepared to adopt and subsume many elements of the religious tradition he had inherited, but he wished to introduce into it a number of new ideas or reforms that were devised to create a more accessible religious environment which was not dependent purely on the ministrations of the priests nor the esoteria of their ritual. In order to do this he acknowledged but redefined the pantheon which had been hitherto worshipped, and established his God, Ahura Mazda, at the head of an Ahuric college, the Amesha Spentas mentioned above. Ahura Mazda was Zarathushtra's name for the greatest deity of an Indo-Iranian divine triad known simply as the *ahuras* (or, in Vedic terms, the *ásuras*), the other two being Mitra (Mithra) and Varuna. It is Ahura Mazda who Zarathushtra exalts above all other beings, and who is the supreme object of his worship. So, although there is no polemic addressed *against* his own religious tradition as such (other than his abhorrence at some of the external practices that had become associated with it and which seem to have been merely the activities of a certain group of priests), there is clear evidence for a *reform* of that tradition, both in its belief structure and in its external expression, particularly, as the *Gathas* seem to suggest, with regard to the behaviour of some of its priests *vis-à-vis* the deities, and in effecting this reform Zarathushtra also redefined the nature and attributes of these deities.

In the Indo-Iranian pre-Zoroastrian religion fire was reverenced, and ritual offerings made to it. We have for example the case of the deity *Agni*, whose name means fire, in the Vedas. Zarathushtra preserved this veneration of fire, saying "O Mazda Ahura, we desire your fire . . . " (Y.34:4), and a passage from the "Younger" Avestan[7] hymn known as the *Farvardin Yasht* hails Zarathushtra as "the *athravan*", a term possibly meaning "fire priest" (although it should be noted that there is no reference to Zarathushtra by this designation in the *Gathas*). Zarathushtra identifies the Ahuric origins of fire:

> The healer of existence, the knowing one who conceives truth, has listened (to your teachings). At will he is in control of his tongue for the sake of the correct uttering of the words, at the distribution of the balances in the good (way), with your red fire, O Mazda Ahura. (Y.31:19)

On the other hand, *Indra*, a warrior god, was seemingly rejected by Zarathushtra, since he may well have been associated in the prophet's mind with some of the less constructive aspects of the Vedic *Soma* sacrifice. *Indra* was invoked before battle, and the *Soma* juice, used in this ritual, was an intoxicant which no doubt encouraged truculent behaviour. Probably because of this association a later Avestan text called the *Vendidad* puts *Indra* at the head of a demonic group which Zarathushtra denounces.[8]

Of great importance is the concept of *rta*, the law regulating the cosmos, which was under the protection of *Varuna* and *Mitra* in the Vedic system. The Zoroastrian notion of *asha*, often rendered as "righteousness", also conveys the meanings "truth" and "order". *Asha*, a concept with which *rta* may be equated, is an empowering force which emanates *directly* from Ahura Mazda and which differs in this respect from the Vedic *rta*, which was essentially distinct from the gods themselves. There is, in Vedic religion, a merely *philosophical* distinction between order and chaos (*nirriti*), whereas for Zarathushtra there is an *ethical* distinction to be made between *asha* and *drug* (deceit). And although Varuna and Mitra seem to have been accessible *only* through ritual, Zarathushtra establishes a link between humanity and Ahura Mazda that is not solely dependent upon the mediations of the priesthood. In the Hindu world *rta* was gradually supplanted by *dharma*, but in the religion of Zarathushtra the significance of *asha* has never diminished. (Indeed *asha* embraces without any difficulty the later Hindu path of personal loving devotion advocated by *bhakti*.) Followers of *asha* are therefore to be called *ashavan*, "possessors of *asha*". *Asha Vahishta* ("best truth") is also identified a member of the divine heptad.

So although it certainly is the case that Zarathushtra exalted Ahura Mazda above the other spiritual beings, there is no evidence to suggest that in doing so he intended to disregard them or deny their existence. An unfortunate misunderstanding of the prophet's use of the Avestan term *daeva* ("demon"), which always appears in a denunciatory context in the *Gathas*, compelled the nineteenth century philologist Martin Haug to suppose that Zarathushtra rejected *all* spiritual beings other than Ahura Mazda, and even the Amesha Spentas were relegated to philosophical concepts (though curiously Haug seemed happy to accord independence to *Sroash*, a Gathic divinity not belonging to the heptad and associated with obedience). *Daeva* was a term with which Haug was familiar from Sanskrit (where it appears as *deva*) in which it denotes divine beings generally, and so Haug carried this interpretation over into its Avestan cognate, resulting in his assumption that, for Zarathushtra, Ahura Mazda was the *only* being worthy of worship. Haug then rationalized the other divine entities mentioned in the *Gathas* and, ignoring any dualistic content in Zarathushtra's verses, also disposed of the demonic references, leaving only a monism, which was no doubt intellectually satisfying to one reared in the academic atmosphere of nineteenth-century post-enlightenment Christianity with its gathering suspicion of anything remotely non-rational, but which was contrary to all that the prophet had taught and the tradition had handed down.

Zarathushtra was surrounded by evidence of evil, and so just as he did not deny the existence of the Ahuric beings, nor did he deny the demonic beings either, or their ability to influence the lives of men and women. Evil was a subject which exercised Zarathushtra profoundly, and the Gathic texts make constant allusions to the workings of an evil spirit who came to be known in the tradition as *Angra Mainyu*, the instigator and promoter of deceit and custodian of the Lie *(drug)*.

The problem this raises, then, is whether to categorize Zoroastrianism as a monotheistic or dualistic religion, and fundamental to this issue is the origin of evil. Monotheism is the term used to define a belief in one supreme exalted God who alone has all the characteristics of a divine being. Dualism has traditionally been understood in a variety of ways in the study of religions. First, it states that reality has a radical twofold nature, and describes the distinction between God and creation in that the two are separate. Second, it says that there are two co-existent and fundamentally opposite forces of good and evil, having neither beginning nor end, which are totally irreconcilable, and thus that the evil in the world cannot be attributed to an all-good God, as is the case with monotheism, but to an adversarial demonic figure who has no dependence on the all-good God, and this leads into an ethical dualism which says that humanity is caught up in this battle between the two forces. Unfortunately the restrictiveness of these definitions has meant that neither is completely descriptive of Zoroastrianism, and indeed the diversity of opinion on this matter which has attended the scholarly study of Zoroastrianism practically since its inception suggests that it may never be possible to say once and for all whether Zoroastrianism is monotheistic, dualistic, or a unique combination of both, and the tradition itself has accommodated without too much difficulty thinkers favouring all three interpretations. One solution has been to say that, since Zoroastrianism does not recognize two gods but two co-existent powers, it is dualistic within an overall context of exalted monotheism.

The starting point for any discussion of this matter is Y.30:3–5 (with Y.45:2):

> These are the two spirits (existing) in the beginning, twins who have been heard of as the two dreams, the two thoughts, the two words, and the two actions, the better and the evil. Between these two the munificent discriminate rightly, but not those who give bad gifts . . . Of these two spirits the deceitful one chooses to do the worst things, but the most holy spirit, clothed in the hardest stones (chooses) truth (as do those) who, with true actions, devotedly gratify Mazda Ahura. (Y.30:3, 5)

Here we are presented with the exalted Lord of Wisdom, Ahura Mazda, his Holy Spirit *Spenta Mainyu*, and the antagonistic or hostile spirit, *Angra Mainyu*. The most important question that is raised is whether the two spirits existed from the beginning or were created. Answers favouring the former interpretation place the religion firmly in the dualistic camp; answers favouring the latter suppose a monotheism. A dualistic interpretation will lead logically to the conclusion that Ahura Mazda and Spenta Mainyu are synonymous to the degree that they are hypostatically united, and that the hostile spirit has always enjoyed an independent existence which owes nothing to the Wise Lord. If, on the other hand, the Wise Lord *did* create the "twin" spirits, the implicit monotheism also suggests that Ahura Mazda is at least indirectly responsible for the evil in the world since in his omniscience he will have known that Angra Mainyu will have chosen to "do the worst things".[9] The dualistic view absolves Ahura Mazda from any such charge, and it is at least implied in, for example, the following passage, which suggests that Spenta Mainyu, as a creative force, may be intimately identified with Ahura Mazda to the extent that the two are, in reality, one:

> Right-mindedness was yours, yours also was the most intellectual fashioner of the cow, when by virtue of your holy spirit you opened ways for her, so that she could join either the herdsman or whoever might not be a herdsman. (Y.31:9)

This would also confirm the independence of the "deceitful" spirit Angra Mainyu by virtue of the opposition he represents in Y.30:3–5.[10]

It is Spenta Mainyu alone who, through the mental faculties that have been given to humans (which will be examined in chapter VII), impels the *ashavan* to recognize Ahura Mazda's claim to be the originator of *asha* and thus all that is true (cf. Y.47:2), and therefore he is the antithesis of all that is false and evil.

Even so it is clearly a problem that will not be solved easily or totally satisfactorily. One solution of course is to say that Zarathushtra's concern was not so much with *how* evil came to reside in the world, but what could be done about it, and that this may account for the apparent ambiguity of the Gathic texts, an ambiguity which was addressed and to a large degree clarified with serious and scholarly vigour by later Zoroastrian theologians. Zarathushtra's aim was not primarily to stimulate speculation as to the nature or origin of evil, but to draw attention to its presence and arouse men and women to fight against it. It is, however, certain that the prophet of Iran would never have considered the Wise Lord responsible for the evil activity he observed around him.

> For then destruction will come down upon deceit through its elimination. The swiftest steeds will be yoked, and they will win good fame (in the race) to the good dwelling of good thought, Mazda, and truth. (Y.30:10)

This would suggest very strongly that the prophet himself advocated a form of dualism, but one weighted towards the eventual triumph of good since he has an unshakeable belief in the power of the Wise Lord over that of the hostile spirit.

Zarathushtra would have believed that evil had to derive from somewhere, it being, in his understanding, not merely an absence of good but a definite force bent on destruction and deprivation, even if, as we shall see in chapter IV, this force came to be understood later as having no material substance and thus ultimately unable to sustain itself. Despite a challenge centuries later by the heterodox Zurvanite movement, which postulated a common origin (*Zurvan*, or "Time") for both Ahura Mazda and the hostile spirit, this uniquely Zoroastrian dualistic position was maintained by the tradition since the later Pahlavi *Bundahishen* states that Ahura Mazda not only knew of the independent existence of the evil spirit (though the reverse was not the case), but also knew of his eventual and unavoidable demise, confirming that evil did not originate with the Wise Lord, but that it was always distinct from him. This dualism, thus formulated, totally denies that the two cosmic principles are equally entitled to worship. Even the ways they are referred to in the literature makes this distinction between them, something to which we shall briefly return also in chapter IV.

Zoroastrianism proposes an *ethical* dualism, implying a radical choice made between good and evil, exemplified by these two spirits, and this cosmically implicative radical choice is echoed in the decisions made by men and women to follow either the Ahuric path or that of the hostile spirit. Since it is the ethical framework which provides the context within which the cosmological elaboration is defined, this primordial dualism is gradually supplanted as creation evolves, via an emerging *pro-cosmic* dualism (that is, one favouring and enhancing rather than rejecting and destroying the Ahuric creation), towards an *eschatological monotheism*, in which the agents of evil are progressively rejected, and as a consequence their influence begins to decrease. So, far from being the cause of evil, Ahura Mazda leaves the choice to humans, since only human activity can cause the increase or decrease of evil in the world as people follow or reject the primordial or prototypical Lie. The human response to good and evil is personified in the two spirits, who, in this hymn, have made their own fundamental choices and thereby established a paradigm for human ethical behaviour. The "choices" made by the two spirits in Y.30 were not made in history as such, but "outside" the normal flow of time as we would understand it, in that mythological era which is not identifiable in the normal historical sense since it does not belong exclusively to the past nor to the present but in a sense to both, even if in chronological terms it belongs to neither.[11] The moment of choice expressed in Y.30, which is no less than the decision to assist or frustrate the renewal of the world, is then seen to be an ever-present reality, transcending temporal constraints and providing an environment within which "myth" and "history" merge. Humanity therefore imitates and simultaneously participates in the scenario described by this passage in the choices that individuals make in this constantly active ethical dualism. The fifth verse of Y.30 supports this interpretation with its implication of continuous displeasure or pleasure directed towards Ahura Mazda since at this stage of the hymn the choices are to be understood as both those made by the spirits and by the individual person. In fact the emphasis of this verse is very much with humanity in contrast to the cosmogonic scene-setting in verse 3. The hymn has shifted from extra-temporal to contemporary and finite concerns, though it retains the connection between the two through its very ambiguity since the prophet never severs the link between the primal, cosmic choice and the human choice. Zarathushtra is therefore further able to suggest that the struggle between good and evil takes place within the individual as well as on the cosmic scale. Thus the universal evolution towards the *frashokereti* is reflected in (and dependent upon) the "fundamental option" that individuals make in favour of Ahura Mazda and the life of *asha*. In contrast to those who follow the Ahuric path, the possessors of *asha*, those who choose to follow the Lie (*drug*) and assist the hostile spirit are called *drugvant*.[12]

In contrast to Haug's claims, this emergent monotheism is not in danger of being compromised by the existence of other good spiritual beings. On the contrary, in offering reverence to a *yazata* (a spirit being worthy of worship) such as one of the Amesha Spentas, or indeed any other Ahuric being, Zarathushtra does not detract from that quality of reverence due to Ahura Mazda alone and nor does he deny Ahura Mazda that worship and veneration which rightly belong to the Wise Lord alone. Worship directed towards a *yazata* is in reality honour and worship to Ahura Mazda, for in honouring these good beings the greater honour is thereby given to their creator. Similarly, the Zoroastrian recognizes the presence of the hostile spirit and associated demonic beings, but chooses to resist their temptations, aided in this by fidelity to the Zoroastrian ethical code of "good thoughts, good words and good deeds", and this is one of the main ways of thwarting the malign power of evil.

We have seen that the name that is commonly given to this hostile or antagonistic spirit is *Angra Mainyu*, but this name does not appear as such in the *Gathas*. Martin Schwartz, who has argued for a multi-level analysis of the literary form of the *Gathas*, and who has considered Zarathushtra's use of proper names, suggests that this is a deliberate omission on the part of the prophet, claiming that the phrase is "tabuistically avoided".[13] In Y.45:2 the two components of this name are separated by six other words (although there may be a more convincing etymological allusion to the adversarial spirit at Y.44:12). A good deal more of the terminology employed by the Zoroastrian theologians and liturgists of the later times is not to be found in the *Gathas* of Zarathushtra. For example, the term *Amesha Spenta* is not seen in the *Gathas* but the concept it embodies is alluded to since all members of the divine heptad are named together at Y.47:1, and the term itself first appears in a text closely related to the *Gathas* but evidently not the work of the prophet (see below). Moreover, the name of the exalted God, *Ahura Mazda*, is hardly even seen in the *Gathas* in that form, though an inversion of these nominal components, *Mazda Ahura*, makes a slightly more frequent appearance. In fact Zarathushtra often addresses his God as merely *Mazda*, or *wisdom* as well as Lord, *Ahura*. It has been calculated that the formula *Ahura- Mazda-* is used 40 times when these nominal components are separated and *Mazda- Ahura-* 48 times under the same conditions. *Ahura-* alone is used 19 times, and *Mazda-* alone 67 times.[14]

Five of the six collections known as the *Gathas* are considered to be the work of Zarathushtra. A sixth, known as the *Yasna Haptanhaiti*, or *Haptanhaiti Gatha*, is reckoned to be the work of another hand, or possibly of more than one author.[15] It is in the same Gathic Avestan dialect as the other five, but it is not metrical. Even so it is believed to have been composed soon after the prophet's death, and it does not contradict any of the theological ideas proposed in the Zarathushtrian *Gathas*. (The fact that it is in prose rather than in the verse form of the Zarathushtrian *Gathas* suggests that an *exclusively* liturgical use may have been envisaged for it, the precedent for this kind of liturgical composition having been set in proto-Indo-Iranian ritual practice.)

The five collections composed by the prophet are as follows:

*Ahunavaiti Gatha* (Y.28–34)
*Ushtavaiti Gatha* (Y.43–46)
*Spentamainyu Gatha* (Y.47–50)
*Vohukshathra Gatha* (Y.51)
*Vahishtoishti Gatha* (Y.53)[16]

The *Haptanhaiti Gatha* comprises Y.35–41. The *Gathas* have been incorporated into a much larger body of hymns for liturgical purposes, such as the celebration of the *Yasna* ritual.

The last of these, *Vahishtoishti Gatha* (Y.53), consists of a hymn which Zarathushtra apparently wrote for the occasion of his daughter's wedding.[17] It contains words of encouragement, and it may be interpreted as being intended for all who heard his message. To please and serve the Wise Lord, one must also please one's earthly lord; thus those to be married are to act in accordance with this, and the daughter of Zarathushtra will fulfil her vocation if she strives to look after her new husband. Care for one's partner in marriage, suggests the prophet, echoes the care that Ahura Mazda has for humanity.

The care of each of the seven primal material creations – stone (or metal), water, earth, plants, cattle, humanity and fire – has traditionally been given to one of the Amesha Spentas. Although this is certainly not dominant among the prophet's teachings, it is without doubt safe to say that Zarathushtra recognized the need to respect and nurture creation, and so out of the attributes of Ahura Mazda enumerated in the *Gathas* there has developed a theology of the universe which reinforces the creator's concern for his creation. It is often remarked that Zoroastrianism is a religion with a strong emphasis on ecological stewardship, and this notion proceeds from the care that Ahura Mazda, through and with his Amesha Spentas, has for the world and all within it. When the Gathic texts became incorporated into the *Yasna* ceremony and its liturgical formula became more fixed – with increasingly less room for improvised interpolations – each of these primal creations was given a definite representation in the ritual. Humanity, Ahura Mazda's special creation, came to be represented by the officiating priest and protected by the Holy Spirit, *Spenta Mainyu*, who is unique in the Ahuric college since he is co-eternal with Ahura Mazda with whom he enjoys a degree of union not accorded to the other members of the heptad, despite their being also intimately united to Ahura Mazda's essence. Ahura Mazda and Spenta Mainyu in fact gradually merge so that the two become completely one and it is therefore probably not coincidental that Spenta Mainyu's name is all but absent from the later Pahlavi texts relating to eschatology.

Just as Spenta Mainyu is unique in the heavenly court in his relationship to the Amesha Spentas, so is humanity in the created order. The elevated status that humanity enjoys in comparison with the rest of creation carries with it added responsibilities and Zarathushtra recognizes this early in his ministry. He is seemingly despondent at the chances of humanity successfully protecting creation having observed the abuse that it was receiving at the hands of humans. Y.29, from the *Ahunavaiti Gatha*, suggests that the cow, a symbol and outward sign of abundance and prosperity in both the Vedic and Avestan traditions, has been unable to enjoy security and comfort. The "soul of the cow" complains to the Wise Lord through his Holy Spirit:

> "For whom did you shape me? Who fashioned me? Wrath and oppression, fury spite and violence hold me fettered. I have no other shepherd (sic) but you. Thus reveal yourselves to me with good pastoral work." (Y.29:1)

As if in response, the Wise Lord reveals Zarathushtra to be the first man to listen to his voice and, therefore, to recognize the need to protect the cow and its guardian, the Good Vision, that is, the correct way of interpreting and behaving towards the world in order to bring in to its renovation:

> Here, I have found Zarathushtra Spitama, the only one who listens to our teachings: he wishes to sing hymns of praise for us, O Mazda, and for truth, to let me enjoy the beauty of his speech. (Y.29:8)

In another passage, Zarathushtra accuses some of his co-religionists of abusing the cow, and of becoming intoxicated during the performance of ritual, presumably though an over-indulgence in the Haoma concoction. This passage, also from *Ahunavaiti Gatha*, relates to the *Haoma* sacrifice which had apparently, in some instances, declined into an orgy of indiscriminate cattle slaughter and drunkenness:

> The Kavis, being a Grehma gang, lay their intellects and their dignities into the fetter day by day. They take their positions (at the sacrifice) in order to assist the deceitful one, and (by obeying) the command "let the (sacrificial) animal be killed" to assist the one who inflames the "fire-resisting" (Haoma, Duraosha). (Y.32:14)

*Haoma* is the name both of a plant and the deity venerated in this ceremony. It evidently has some mood-altering properties.[18] It will be noted that neither in this verse nor a parallel passage (Y.48:10) does the prophet refer to *Haoma*, either as plant or deity, by name. This might imply that he did not wish to dignify it, preferring to mention it only by allusion. Some scholars have interpreted this, together with what appears to be a general condemnation, as Zarathushtra's rejection of the *Haoma* sacrifice in its entirety, yet there is an equal weight of evidence to suggest that his ire was reserved for the unseemly behaviour of the *Karapan* priests,[19] who were from a rival tribe and who clearly did not behave with due reverence during the execution of their public religious duties. No doubt too there were priests of Zarathushtra's more immediate acquaintance who were behaving equally disrespectfully. Since, as we saw earlier, Zarathushtra was himself a priest and therefore intimate with the *Haoma* ceremony, and since he proclaims this priestly identity in these most personal and yet simultaneously public compositions, we are justified in supposing his devotion to the ritual – and he states that he is "in accordance with the best spirit" and elsewhere that he is enthusiastic for "the correct utterance of the (ritual) words". Now, he will have realized that the ritual slaughter of cattle was, at that time, a necessary ingredient in the community's religious life. His concern, therefore, was that the action should be carried out reverently and with true religious meaning.

Bruce Lincoln, in his reconstruction of the "Indo-Iranian priestly cycle",[20] noted the recurrent theme of "reward" in Indo-Iranian religion. In the pre-Zoroastrian sacrifice the slain cattle were presented to the gods who in return for this were expected to provide remuneration. The remuneration would be delivered as it were "through" the patron who paid the priests in "cattle and men"; in this way the sacrificial cycle was maintained. The following verse from the *Ushtavaiti Gatha* seems to suggest that Zarathushtra was familiar with this pattern:

> The person who, through truth, makes real for me that which is most brilliant in value, for Zarathushtra, who deserves a prize providing higher life – two fertile cows along with all imaginable things – through that very person you, O Mazda, reveal yourself to me as the best provider. (Y.46:19)

It is not impossible, either, that the prophet would recognize the thrust behind these words on the subject from Mary Boyce, that

> the old Zoroastrian teaching in this respect is that in the present imperfect world . . . men must kill in order to live themselves; but they must limit the wrong they thus do to animals by slaying them as mercifully as possible, and always consecrating them first – that is, offering them sacrificially to the divine beings – since by this means only the body is killed and the creature's spirit is released to live on and nourish the species. To eat meat other than from a sacrifice – thereby destroying the creature's spirit – was held to be a grievous sin down to recent times.[21]

This echoes Zarathushtra's own recognition of the cow as a gift from Ahura Mazda, but one which must be used wisely and respectfully. The prophet states that

> (t)he best insight, which purifies progeny for mankind, let it also be applied to the cow. Her you breed for us for food. (Y.48:5)

The old Iranian priesthood apparently operated on a remuneratory basis by which patrons would commission a ritual and pay the priests for their services. Zarathushtra sprinkles references to this system throughout his *Gathas*, and he links it with one of his most revolutionary concepts, that of the saviour, the "bringer of benefit" or the benefactor, known in the *Gathas* as the *Saoshyant*. It is this saviour figure – also referred to in the plural – who will bring about the renovation of the world. He uses his familiarity with the custom of priestly recompense to establish his own credentials as one who will bring benefit to the world:

> When shall I know, O Mazda, whether through truth you have control over anything, the fear of which frightens me. Let the pronouncement of good thoughts be told me truly. May the benefactor know of what kind his reward will be. (Y.48:9)

In a direct reference to the renewal of the created order at the end of time, a similarly innovative concept which is inevitably linked with the advent of the saviour figure, Zarathushtra widens the circle of benefactors to include all followers of the path of *asha*, imploring Ahura Mazda not a little impatiently:

> Thus may we be those who make existence brilliant, O Mazda . . . (Y.30:9)

When, though, was this "end of time" to be? The seeds of later Zoroastrian eschatology are contained within Zarathushtra's introduction of the *saoshyant*. It is evident, though, that Zarathushtra was either anticipating the apocalyptic event in the near future or at least that he was hoping for it. Moreover, this concept of saviour (which was later to have such a dramatic effect on the development of the post-exilic Jewish theological thought) is one of the chief means by which Zarathushtra attempts to break from the rigidity of the proto-Indo-Iranian tradition. In a sense he establishes, alongside an "official" sacerdotal class, a preaching vocation of all believers (*ashavans*), who would work with him towards the final event. The exclusivity of priestly access to the world of the divine was maintained in what became Indian (Vedic) religion, and, despite the penetrative steps taken by the earliest advocates of what would eventually flower into the *bhakti* movement, which reached its height some 2500 years later, the priestly class effectively dominated religious practice there until the arrival of the Buddha (*c.*450 BCE). In the Iranian setting, though, Zarathushtra combined a sacerdotal tradition with a more exoteric path. Following the prophet's death the priesthood still occupied a central role in Iranian religious life, and even though now this was beginning to operate from a theological position situated within the framework constructed by the prophet it would be a mistake to imagine that there was at this early stage in the religion's history a uniformity of belief or practice.

## 2  The Transmission of the *Gathas*

The script in which the Gathas came to be eventually written down was not invented until the sixth century CE. Until that time, these holy texts had been passed down orally from generation to generation of priests, whose training demanded the precise memorization of many religious compositions, but especially the ritual texts. This was not merely because writing was unknown in Zarathushtra's day. Even after its discovery, writing was for a long time considered a secular activity, unsuited to higher religious purposes. The sounds of the words themselves were thought to convey power and instil religious experience, a power and experience which could not be captured by the written word. This tradition was maintained long after writing became known to the priests and even today the ceremonies are invariably conducted without the use of service books.

## 3  The Authorship and Integrity of the *Gathas*

One of the features of the *Gathas* that will strike the reader is the number of times that Zarathushtra refers to himself by name in them. There are fifteen appearances of his name in all, as well as the use of the personal pronoun and the occasions that Zarathushtra includes himself in plural designations. Until 1988 no scholar (with the exception of James Darmesteter) had ever departed from the notion that Zarathushtra was the author of the *Gathas*. In 1988, however, a fleeting attempt was made to overturn this long-held belief, when J. Kellens and E. Pirart published a book averring that the *Gathas* were in reality the product of a *"cercle gathique"*, a group of strict ritualists of which Zarathushtra was the president and who was thus enshrined in verse.[22] To do this, this ritual circle (so maintain Kellens and Pirart) commissioned a poet who fashioned the verses we know as the *Gathas* under the impulse and guidance of the circle, in order to express the group's ritual outlook and elevate its head member, Zarathushtra. But, as I. Gershevitch has pointed out in his refutation of this theory,[23] whilst the *Gathas* may express many things, ritual is not high on the list of subjects considered by the figure supposed to be the author, despite the fact that he was a dedicated priest, faithful to his ritual duties. It seems then that this argument falls on the first hurdle, but all that *that* says is that the existence of a ritual circle involving Zarathushtra cannot be argued for from the standpoint of texts which are not particularly ritualistic in content (other than in the few references already noted), even if they are structurally appropriate to ritual use. Of itself it says nothing about the authorship of the texts in question. What we have seen, however, so far in our survey of some of the material in the *Gathas* is that they are concerned with one person's relationship with God and the world, and with a desire to extend that relationship to include all humans. We have also seen that they are coherent, theologically, thematically, linguistically and, it must be added, stylistically. As far as the last three categories are concerned we might turn again to the work done by Schwartz which has demonstrated that the intricate homophonic, anagramatic and acrostic structure of the *Gathas* suggests very strongly that they could only be the *conception*, as well as the work, of one person's mind. This surely disposes of the "composition-by-committee" theory. If we accept this, then it seems illogical also to accept that such a brilliantly imaginative writer would incorporate so many times into his verses a name which is not his, since Zarathushtra is not known for any other compositions and any hypothetical anonymous author would therefore have no reason to adopt a convention of assuming or disseminating these verses under a greater name in order to increase his lesser fame. Obviously we must rely to a large degree on the traditional data regarding the authorship of the *Gathas*, but there being no convincing argument to counter it, and it being attested externally as well as internally, it seems unnecessary to try to establish a contrary theory. Schwartz, who reassured the world of Zarathushtra's authorship of the *Gathas* even *before* Kellens and Pirart presented their controversial hypothesis, should perhaps be allowed to have the last word on this particular subject. He concludes his study of the structure of the *Gathas* with the following words:

Zarathushtra emerges . . . as not only a great religious teacher, but as an outstanding poetic genius, operating in all imaginable hierarchies of sound and meaning, within an ultimately very consistent framework. This, together with his championship of the use of thought, sets him among the more remarkable human paradigms of mind and spirit created by the Wise Lord.[24]

## 4  Dating the Prophet – the Gathic Evidence (and other suggestions)

We have come to this topic only now since it seemed appropriate first to establish the nature of the *Gathas*, their authorship and their content, before attempting to look at their location in history. Satisfied as to their authorship and reasonably familiar with their content and purpose, we can now examine what evidence they offer as to when their author lived; a little later we shall see how similar evidence can be used to determine where the prophet lived.

Some time before 2000 BCE a split had begun to develop between those who would become known as the Iranians and those called the "proto-Indo-Aryans". Bringing their gods with them, the latter eventually settled in the Indus Valley, whilst the former began to move into what is now known as Iran, a word itself deriving from "Aryan", some time later in the second millennium BCE. The common origin of both these waves of settlers has been called "Proto-Indo-European",[25] and the study of shared features in ancient languages has suggested that there was a now lost Indo-European language which forms the basis for languages (and thus cultures) as diverse as, on the one hand, Greek and Latin and on the other Sanskrit and Avestan. This being the case we can now see and account for the similarities between Avestan words and their Sanskrit counterparts. Thus one of our words for "priest", *zaotar* in the Avestan language, is rendered *hotr* in the Sanskrit of the Vedas. *Yasna*, which means "worship" or "sacrifice", is, in the language of the Vedas, *yañja*. The gods, too, though retaining common features, began to be known by different (though obviously related) names, so that in what became the Iranian tradition Mithra was worshipped, and in the Indian context he was known as Mitra.

Our understanding and interpretation of the *Gathas* is going to depend upon where we locate their author in history. Yet there is no agreement as to when Zarathushtra lived. There have been three different periods ascribed to the prophet of Iran. The Greeks dated him to a period 6000 years BCE, a dating which had not commended itself to any contemporary researcher. Modern scholarship has until recently been more or less evenly divided between the second and first millennia BCE, although now opinion seems to favour an earlier rather than more recent time. This second millennium dating, which itself covers a period of some 500 years, has received the most support from those who have argued from philological and archaeological evidence; the first millennium is the favoured time for those who argued from the historical viewpoint. Linguistic evidence has suggested a strong case for placing Zarathushtra at the time of the emergence and compilation of the last text relating to the Vedic religion, that is, between 1750 and 1400 BCE (although the *Rig Veda* did not receive its final redaction until 900 BCE). The dating is approximate and 1200 or the more precise 1080 BCE have also been suggested from linguistic research. The *Gathas* and the hymns of the *Rig Veda* exhibit such a similarity of grammatical style and vocabulary that it is certain that they both derive from a common parent language and thus presume a common cultural and religious heritage. In addition to this cosmetic affinity there are also other significant points of convergence, and so the *Haoma* ceremony, whose abuse Zarathushtra attacks, finds its Vedic counterpart in the *Soma* ritual, and indeed these two terms are related. In further evidence of this early dating, the imagery that Zarathushtra employs in the *Gathas* is that more associated with a pastoral economy than an agrarian one. Just as the cow is a dominant feature of the *Rig Veda*, so she is of the *Gathas*. Humbach dates the prophet to a little later, at 1080 BCE, though he suggests that this agrees with the linguistic evidence, and it still falls within the parameters defined by the Vedic comparison.

Unable to ignore the linguistic evidence, yet wishing to locate the prophet at a later date of around 600 BCE, some have advanced an argument which suggests that since religious language is typically and inherently conservative,[26] Zarathushtra has deliberately employed an archaic style and vocabulary which would have been associated in his intended audience's minds with an earlier period. Whilst this may be true of many religious teachers, the overall practical nature of the *Gathas* argues against their author's use of imagery even remotely foreign to his time and place.

We should also note that in the roughly contemporary *Rig Veda* the idea of a cycle of rebirths – *samsara* – had not been established, and that this idea was not to emerge until the later texts called the *Brahmanas*; it is surely not by coincidence that neither does Zoroastrianism entertain notions of rebirth or reincarnation. Even though the Aryan split had taken place long before, at probably 2000 BCE, there is sufficient reason to think that there must have been some contact between the two peoples, even if it was only sporadic. This reasoning is theological as well as linguistic, as a comparison of the Avestan and Vedic texts demonstrates.[27] If the concept of *samsara* had been a dominant one when Zarathushtra was active, it is feasible to suppose that, given that he evidently did not accept it, he would have indicated this somewhere since he was not inclined to ignore those issues about which he had strong feelings, and this would certainly have been one of them. (This, incidentally, is perhaps why Mithra is not mentioned in the *Gathas*, since the prophet would have found nothing controversial about him. In fact it is likely that Zarathushtra would have been keen on retaining his worship since Mithra and the prophet shared a keen sense of justice). It is probable, then, that he had never actually met with this belief and therefore had no need to condemn it. Given that this idea was a later development in India, and noticing Zarathushtra's obvious familiarity with not only Vedic language and literary technique but also Vedic *religion* it seems that we can conclude that his preaching ministry was one that operated in a pre-*samsara* culture, and this too would place him at an early date. Had he known of the ritual texts called the *Brahmanas*, essentially "supplements" to the Vedas themselves but which presuppose a belief in *samsara*, and which were already being challenged by the sixth century BCE (due in part to the emergence of a prototypical form of *bhakti*), he may have wished to launch some form of polemic against this development. Yet the concept had simply not arisen during his time. How wise it would be to speculate that the prophet actually *prevented* the notion of *samsara* from gaining a foothold in Iranian religion is uncertain. Given that *samsara* could be seen as a natural development within a religious culture which revolved around a continuously turning wheel of sacrificial ritual, and having already seen that Zarathushtra broke into and reformed this sacrificial cycle, we could surmise that in so doing he may well have forestalled the emergence of a cyclical notion of time with its essential component of rebirth. On the other hand, as the example of Vedic religion demonstrates, this very idea was soon to be embraced by the Indian branch of the Indo-European peoples.

Travelling west, we find that a number of Greek writers have placed the prophet at the almost inconceivably early time of before 6000 BCE, writers such as Diogenes who reports earlier attempts to place Zarathushtra at, variously, 6480 BCE (citing Xanthus of Lydia), 6200 BCE (from Hermodorus). Eudoxus suggests some six thousand years before Plato, which would put him at roughly 6300 BCE. Plutarch, who dates Zarathushtra "five thousand years before the Trojan War" (i.e. at 6200 BCE), gives a recognizable if inaccurate account of the twin spirits whom he calls "gods":

> "Now he called the one Horomazes and the other Areimanios; and he showed, moreover, that the former resembled Light more than any other thing perceived by the senses, while the latter again is like darkness and ignorance . . . "[28]

Whilst it is certain that Greek writers were familiar with some of Zarathushtra's ideas, there is no evidence whatsoever to corroborate their insistence on such an early period for the prophet's lifetime.

Lastly, we can permit ourselves a brief look at some later Zoroastrian writings. In the ninth century Pahlavi text known as *Selections of Zatspram*, we read of Zoroastrianism being in existence for 300 years until its "disruption" by the Alexandrian forces, a reference to the toppling of the Iranian throne by Alexander in 330 BCE, and this would give Zarathushtra an approximate date of 630 BCE. From another ninth century text, the *Bundahishen*, we can calculate the year 588 BCE for the prophet, or at least the year in which he first proclaimed his new message.

This text records 258 years from the establishment of the religion until Alexander's conquest. If we read this text together with yet another text, the *Dinkard*, which suggests that Zarathushtra received his first revelation at the age of thirty and made his first convert at forty, we would arrive at a birth date of 618 BCE or 628 BCE, depending on whether the religion was considered "established" with Zarathushtra's first revelation or with his first convert. Unfortunately the calculation from the *Bundahishen*, as with that from other contemporary texts, seems to be one made with hindsight, and it is not impossible that this text was composed in order to bolster a traditionally held belief about the time of the prophet's birth or at least to validate this same view which was obviously held by the author of the *Bundahishen*. Additionally we have no idea of how accurately records would have been kept by the Iranian scribes prior to the Alexandrian invasion, and the argument does lose some of its force particularly when it is remembered that one of Alexander's more devastating achievements was to destroy many of the "holy books" of the Zoroastrians, and to kill off many of the priests resulting in an almost total loss of relevant material. These texts offer arguments, then, that are somewhat circular and ultimately not scientifically satisfying, although one would of course not wish to belittle their value as literary or religious compositions reflecting the sincerely held beliefs of their authors.

It seems, then, that we should accept the earlier dating for the prophet of Iran, though even this is not without its problems since it is impossible to pinpoint exactly when (and where) he lived. The evidence supplied by the Greeks we can confidently ignore. That offered by the ninth century books and corroborating material has a mathematical precision about it which seems initially convincing, but we should not necessarily be seduced by an argument so constructed, no doubt with noble intentions, from within a tradition which, by its own literary evidence, has no recourse to an earlier, contemporary chronology to substantiate it. It seems reasonable to accept a time of approximately 1400 BCE, perhaps even earlier, if the argument from Vedic comparison is sound.

## 5  The Problem of the Prophet's Homeland

As with determining his dates, locating the birthplace of Zarathushtra is also problematic. The literature, other than the *Gathas*, intermingles tradition, legend and what might be historical fact. It can be approached in much the same way as that referring to his date, that is, as later and no doubt well-meaning attempts at a geographical reconstruction which seeks to base tradition and legend in a verifiable historical and geographical context. The content of the *Gathas* themselves has, however, thrown up a few clues. First, the *Gathas* seem to suppose an ethnically insular audience, since there is no mention in these texts of any known groupings other that that reckoned to be Zarathushtra's own. That tribes or clans which the prophet considered to be rivals or even enemies existed within the larger ethnic block is certain, since we have the mention of the *Karapans* (or "mumbling" priests) and *Kavis*, to which the prophet refers with disapproval, but we should also recognize that the religion practised by these denounced priests was substantially that of the prophet, evidently using in its ritual worship materials common to the land in which Zarathushtra was beginning to preach, and we may thus assume a common ethnicity. The society which grew up around what is now north-eastern Iran, and spilling into the central Asian steppes, in the middle of the second millennium BCE displays the conservatism expected of a settled community whose structure had become more or less fixed, and such a structure is reflected in the *Gathas*. Indeed, Zarathushtra's lament that his message has been rejected by his people (cf. Y.46:1) could quite feasibly be an allusion to the stability of family and tribe which he had hitherto enjoyed, and which could be maintained and sustained within a specific geographical area. As we have seen, the prophet makes use of imagery more associated with a stable than a nomadic community, and archaeological evidence suggests that long distance transport was the privilege of the wealthy minority, and not the property of a whole community. Furthermore, the prophet's constant use of the cow as a central figure in the *Gathas* presupposes that his audience would have been familiar with the animal, and such an animal was never destined to traverse long distances. In fact, as M. Boyce points out, when a more nomadic lifestyle began to develop, the cow was the first animal to be left behind,[29] a notion which will have been repugnant to Zarathushtra (and which would have rendered his use of the animal as one of his central metaphors in the *Gathas* redundant). As it was, the conditions encountered there suggest that the cow did not fare particularly well in Iran, a fact which gave added weight to Zarathushtra's use of her as a metaphor, but nevertheless the vegetation and water around the north-east would have provided a passably healthy environment in which cattle could survive.

## 6 Zarathushtra's Death

Prophets, even those of the stature of Zarathushtra, do not ordinarily find it convenient to predict nor easy to record their own deaths. This is normally left to later hagiographers who generally attach to such events a religious significance. Narratives dealing with the death of a prophet are often embellished with legendary details recalling, for example, the violence which attended it (a recurring theme in prophetic demise). In some instances supernatural meaning is attached to a prophet's death so that it gives rise to new levels of revelation and belief. Thus it becomes incorporated into a burgeoning repository of often self-consciously quasi-historical material whose purpose is not to record facts but to support faith.

In the case of Zarathushtra we have no archaeological or historical evidence to corroborate or by which to evaluate the later reports concerning his death. The *Gathas*, being Zarathushtra's own words, are naturally silent on the matter. What we do have, however, is a clutch of apparently conflicting, or at least unharmonious, post-Avestan narratives which suggest that early and contemporary accounts of the violent deaths met by legendary or historical religiously significant figures were uppermost in the minds of those who composed these later texts; and that these authors imagined that their prophet, if his name was to live on in the tradition, required the kind of end which, if previous experience was anything to go by, would be appropriate to and loaded with sufficient *gravitas* for one of his calling and office.

As with his birth, which we shall discuss in a little more detail in chapter III, salutary and instructive stories began to spring up surrounding the prophet's death. Though ratified nowhere outside the tradition and in that sense being merely self-authenticating (which is a problematic notion in itself), these stories do however serve to highlight the significance of a man who occupies a pivotal place in Iranian history, and their dramatic nature ensures that their subject not only stands apart from other, lesser, figures within that history but that he takes his place alongside the great figures of Iranian mythology such as the first created man, Gayomart, who also met with a violent end, but whose death provided the means whereby creation itself as we now know it would be brought into being. Two accounts of the end of the prophet's earthly life particularly illustrate this. They are similar in effect if divergent in detail. One states that he was murdered by a rival priest whilst attending to his ritual duties at the fire altar, whilst the other records that he was killed along with fellow priests during a raid on a fire sanctuary, probably by the rival *Kavis* who had been reviled by him in his *Gathas*. But as Boyce has pointed out,[30] these two accounts bear such a resemblance to similar material from adjacent traditions that their value to theories about the prophet's life, and thus to the nuts and bolts of Zoroastrian history itself, must be questioned. Yet although they have the stamp of neither antiquity nor authority, this is not to deny their value as texts reflecting the continuous endeavours made to retain Zarathushtra's central and unique role in the history of Iranian religion. It could be argued that their purpose was never primarily to provide a record of the historical details of the prophet's life, but to endow it with paradigmatic or didactic meaning suggesting that the struggle between good and evil, and between life and death, passes no-one by, not even the greatest of us.

Not all texts make this claim for a violent death, however, and the Pahlavi *Dinkard* (7.5.1) reports with great sobriety on Zarathushtra's "departure . . . to the best existence, when seventy-seven years had elapsed onwards from his birth".[31]

How reliable are these accounts? Ultimately it does not matter, just as, for example, the details of his lengthy search for truth, involving him journeying through the countryside alone, do not really matter. Literal truth is not what is important, history as such is not the issue, and so versions of such events as his first encounter with Vohu Manah are really to be understood as vehicles of the greater and more abiding religious truths which underlie them.

Zarathushtra lived, he taught, and he died. What is important is that during his time on this earth he breathed into the Iranian religious tradition such a life and spirit that it is as if the fire he so devoutly reverenced would never be extinguished so long as others continue his work – that of ushering in the refreshment of the world. Whether he died in violence during his religious devotions, or in peace asleep in his bed having known again the comfort of family and tribe, the message he left to the world is the same. His *Gathas* are, for us, the living embodiment of his personality. The faith has been kept; the fire has remained burning, and truth and righteousness – *asha* – continue to be diffused throughout the world for which he prayed so earnestly.

The best (manifestation) of this most holy spirit: the action of righteousness (performed) with hands and (inspired) by the utterances (spoken) by tongue in pursuit of good thought, (these) one performs with this realization: "He, Mazda, is the father of truth."

(Y.47:2)

I will worship you, praising you, O Mazda Ahura, along with truth and best thought and by the power with which one can tread upon the path of invigoration ...

(Y.50:4)

We worship the good, strong, beneficent *Fravashis* of the Amesha Spentas . . . who are all seven of one thought, who are all seven of one speech, who are all seven of one deed . . .

(Yt.19:82–3)

# II

# Ahura Mazda, Spenta Mainyu and the Divine Heptad

## 1  Zarathustra on *Ahura Mazda* and the "Divine Relationship"

Although the term *Amesha Spenta*, as we have seen, does not occur in Zarathushtra's *Gathas*,[1] the members of the divine heptad are named together in Y.47:1:

> With *holy spirit* and *best thought*, with action and word in accordance with *truth*, they shall offer Him *integrity* and *immortality*. The Ahura (Lord) is Mazda (wisdom) through (His) *power* (and) *holy devotion*.[2]

What immediately becomes apparent is the link Zarathushtra establishes between the Ahuric wisdom (*mazda*) and "power" (*khshathra*), a link reinforced by Y.45:7 and Y.34:1–2. The two Avestan terms *mazda* and *khshathra* are adjacent in each of the three Gathic passages. *Power*, in this context, can be widened to embrace notions of dominion and this expresses the heart of the Zoroastrian theology of the Amesha Spentas which in turn encapsulates the Zoroastrian understanding of the purpose and trajectory of creation. By living according to righteousness and truth (*asha*), the good dominion of Ahura Mazda will be brought about at the *frashokereti*. It is important to recognize too that the term *frashokereti* is absent from the Gathic literature (it is a coalescence of two Avestan words meaning "to make" and "wonderful"), but Zarathushtra's prayer that he and his companions might "heal the world" leaves us in no doubt that nothing short of a total renovation of the universe is the end to which creation is directed. In this characteristically Zarathushtrian way creation's architect and its ultimate destiny are linked in verse.

Certain of these Amesha Spentas, or "bountiful immortals" as they are sometimes called, can be traced back or otherwise linked to pre-Zoroastrian Indo-Iranian deities. The god Indra, for example, who features extensively in Vedic literature and who is reportedly abjured by the prophet,[3] resembles the Amesha Spenta of the good dominion, *Khshathra Vairya*, though this resemblance is only partial (and substantially etymological). Even Ahura Mazda in his relationship to *asha* of which he is both the originator and custodian seems to have more than a slight similarity, in this attribute at least, to the Vedic deity *Varuna*, and we have seen that "Mazda Ahura" (or variations on this formula) is Zarathushtra's name for the greatest of the three Indo-Iranian *ásuras*.

Spenta Mainyu, the Holy Spirit of God, enjoys in the *Gathas* an inseparableness from Ahura Mazda in the same way as do the others from their particular spiritual qualities; however, since Ahura Mazda is not primarily a spiritual quality as such but the origin of all good spiritual (and material) qualities, and since he is uncreated, neither is Spenta Mainyu created. The passage from Y.30, concerning the "twin spirits", confirms this. The hypostatic relationship of Ahura Mazda and Spenta Mainyu, by which the two are so intimately united that they are to all intents and purposes one being, seems to be an original concept of Zarathushtra, since it cannot be compared to any similar concept in pre-Zoroastrian religion. Nor can it be said to be a relationship summarized by the notion of "necessary and contingent beings". Spenta Mainyu and Ahura Mazda, by virtue of this hypostatic union, can be understood as equally "necessary beings" insofar as they do not owe their existence to any independent agency.

The Amesha Spentas, though they are to be thought of as a group, appear generally in the *Gathas* in pairs, or occasionally in a group of three, and sometimes they appear with other spiritual beings or qualities which Zarathushtra venerated. Theologically however they are usually considered in pairs since they form a logical series of concentric circles, radiating, as it were, from the core which is Ahura Mazda (who dwells there in the most intimate fashion with Spenta Mainyu) to a furthermost rim where the more distant of these *mainyus* reside.

They are generally known as follows:

*Asha Vahishta* (Best Truth; Righteousness)
*Vohu Manah* (Good Mind or Thought; Good Vision)

*Spenta Armaiti* (Holy Devotion)
*Khshathra Vairya* (Power; Dominion or Kingdom of God)
*Hauvartat* (Wholeness and Health)
*Ameretat* (Long Life and Immortality)

The Amesha Spentas of the Good Mind and Truth – *Vohu Manah* and *Asha Vahishta* – make the most frequent appearances in the *Gathas*, and they are considered those closest to Ahura Mazda. It is through these two that the kingdom will eventually be established:

> Him, the Ahura who is heard as Mazda, in my breath, Him I wish to present with the worships (inspired) by our right-mindedness. Let them place for him integrity and immortality, strength and stability in the power that has been committed to him through truth and good thought. (Y.45:10)

Zarathushtra invokes Ahura Mazda through *Vohu Manah* in order that he might understand the purpose of creation, and gain knowledge of the two creations, spiritual (*menog*) and physical (*getig*):[4]

> I approach you with good thought, O Mazda Ahura, so that you may grant me (the blessings) of the two existences, the material and that of thought, the blessings emanating from truth, with which one can put (your) supporters in comfort. (Y.28:2)

*Vohu Manah* and *Asha Vahishta* are followed by *Spenta Armaiti*, the quality of piety and religious devotion and the "royal" *mainyu*, *Khshathra Vairya*, the protector and spirit of the "kingdom of God" or good dominion, and the final pair, most remote from the Ahuric hub (though still united to its essence) are *Haurvatat*, the Ahuric quality of health and *Ameretat*, that of immortality.

When Zarathushtra implores Ahura Mazda for the world to be renovated, he is in effect requesting that the pious and religious conduct of his followers – *Armaiti* – bring about the establishment of the good dominion or kingdom – *Khshathra*. The establishment of this kingdom at the eschatological event will confer upon humanity the two last qualities of wholeness, or perfection – *Haurvatat*, and immortality – *Ameretat*. At the same time these social, ethical and religious conditions can (and should) be prefigured in the pre-apocalyptic age.

## 2 *Spenta Mainyu* and the Individual *Amesha Spentas*: their functions and liturgical representations

### *Spenta Mainyu*

Although Ahura Mazda dwells *in* the divine heptad, he is not simultaneously its members. Each Amesha Spenta retains his or her[5] individual nature and life which was given at their creation. They differ in this respect from Spenta Mainyu who has no existence independent of Ahura Mazda. Creation was accomplished through Spenta Mainyu, the co-existing Holy Spirit. This is also suggested by later, more elaborate creation accounts from the Pahlavi texts in that by the time these texts were compiled Spenta Mainyu had merged so completely with Ahura Mazda that a distinction is often not made between the two.[6] Neither do the eschatological passages from the Pahlavi *Bundahishen* mention the Holy Spirit at all. This can be understood as a legitimate and indeed logical extension of a process of hypostatic integration which Zarathushtra himself sets in motion in the *Gathas* when he intimately and indissolubly identifies the supreme being with his co-eternal spirit in Y.30.

Spenta Mainyu has also been referred to as the augmenting spirit, and that this augmentation is both qualitative and quantitative.[7] *Spenta* can in fact mean "increasing" or "bounteous", suggestive of both unbounded generosity and unlimited growth.

> The Primal one who conceived (the manthra): "Let the free spaces be filled with light," with His intellect created truth. By that spirit with which one upholds best thought you still grow, O Mazda Ahura, you who (have remained) the same until today. (Y.31.7)

He is that part of the divine being which augments Ahura Mazda *qualitatively* by nurturing the divine self-realization, and this self-realization is itself an element of the creative process, since creation is thought of as an extension of Ahura Mazda himself, and it is continuous as it evolves towards the *frashokereti*. It is *quantitative* since through this self-realization Ahura Mazda is able to distribute himself though his creation in a fashion which is inexplicable but which might be suggested (though not adequately defined) by the term "self-replication", and it is an act he also accomplishes through the guardianship and identification that the Amesha Spentas have for and with the world. This must not be taken to imply that, without Spenta Mainyu, Ahura Mazda would be lacking, since the possibility of the two being separated or existing apart from one another does not arise.

In the *Yasna* celebration[8] Spenta Mainyu is represented by the officiating priest (*zot*). At the creation, according to the later texts, Ahura Mazda performed a spiritual *Yasna* to set the cosmos in motion;[9] at the end of time, assisted by other *menog* beings, he will again be the chief celebrant at a *Yasna*, through the celebration of which he will renew the world. Spenta Mainyu's particular protective concern, which he shares of course with Ahura Mazda, is humanity.

## Asha Vahishta

The Amesha Spentas are often named individually in the *Gathas*, and allusions to their characteristics are even more numerous, the most frequently thus identified being *Asha Vahishta*. Indeed it is not always possible to tell whether Zarathushtra is referring to the *mainyu* itself or the principle it exemplifies; the context can assist in deciphering this, but this is not always the case. *Asha Vahishta* is the spirit of the universal law *asha* which should be the choice of all those who wish to be numbered among the company of *ashavans*. This Amesha Spenta is most closely associated with truth and righteousness and, in the *Yasna* ceremony, is represented (or, more accurately, *epiphanized*) by fire. Fire, it will be recalled, played a major part in Indo-Iranian religion, and thus this is an example of Zarathushtra's enthusiasm for retaining elements of his pre-revelation religious upbringing and training. *Asha* is the quality of the divine heptad which most effectively opposes the demonic (or *Ahrimanic*, a term derived from the later Pahlavi name for Angra Mainyu, *Ahriman*) *drug* or "Lie", the instrument of deceit by which the evil spirit attempts to seduce humanity away from the Ahuric path. *Asha* is the opposite of *drug*, for *asha* is the personification, in Zoroastrian terms, of truth, and, being truth, it is the ideal form of the universal Ahuric law by which it is intended the cosmos is to be regulated. In this respect, as we have seen, it parallels the universal cosmic law called *rta* in Vedic religion, but unlike *rta* it can become the common property of all who strive for the Ahuric ideal. To put it another way, and perhaps a little crudely, in Vedicism people live *by* the principle of *rta*, in Zoroastrianism people live *in*, *with* and *through* that of *asha*. When Zarathushtra questions Ahura Mazda as to the nature and purpose of creation, in Y.44, Ahura Mazda is revealed to have created the world through the Holy Spirit (*Spenta Mainyu*) and to have established its order through *asha*. In verse 3 of this hymn, Zarathushtra links Ahura Mazda, as the "primal father of truth", with the establishment of the heavenly bodies and their regular movement through the sky, and in verse 4 the Wise Lord is similarly linked with the natural world.[10] The interrogative technique (which is also found in Vedic literature) used in this hymn allows the poet to supply the answers to the questions he asks in the questions themselves, so we can suppose that Zarathushtra had already worked out in his own mind a coherent theological position on creation by the time he composed this hymn.

This being so, and given the insistence of the hymn (which is made all the more intense in its metrical Avestan version), it seems that uppermost in the prophet's mind, if the final stanza is a guide, was the triumph of righteousness and truth (*asha*) over the deceitful power of *drug*. This is the last issue he addresses in Y.44, the one towards which his questioning was directed:

> This I ask you, O Ahura, tell me truly: How can I deliver deceit into the hands of truth? Let one wipe it out with the mantras of your proclamation, let him place his forceful sword upon the deceitful ones to bring ill and harm over them, O Mazda. (Y.44:14)

Zarathushtra seems to be saying here that *drug* will be overcome by *asha*. So who are Zarathushtra's "deceitful ones"? To understand this, we must recognize that his concern was not only for the future, but also for the present. Zarathushtra had a strong sense of justice and he saw the battle between good and evil as a constant one. There was to be no respite for the *ashavan* since the malign influence of *drug* could be seen all around. The "deceitful ones" clearly included those priests whose activities he so roundly condemned elsewhere in the *Gathas*. The *daevas*, deities of the pre-Zoroastrian Indo-Iranian pantheon who were rejected as false gods by Zarathushtra, are also mentioned in the context of the deceitful ones, as stated in Y.30:6:

> The Daevas do not rightly discriminate between these two spirits, for as they take counsel with each other delusion comes over them, so that they choose the worst thought. In that way they all run to meet wrath, by which the mortals sicken existence.

But presumably just as Zarathushtra widened the circle of *ashavans* to include all who accepted his message, in a typical symmetrical manner he widened the circle of the agents of *drug* to include those who oppose it by word, thought or deed. In addition, then, the *ashavan* will have to contend with assaults not only from other humans, who "sicken existence" (having sided with the *daevas*), but from the demonic forces of Angra Mainyu. The lifetime's work of the Zoroastrian is to distance himself or herself from all Ahrimanic influence, but this is in a sense a negative aim, and somewhat one-sided if it is not balanced by an equally ardent desire to engage with the world in an Ahuric quest to implant righteousness and truth – the qualities which *asha* most clearly expresses – in the hearts and minds of others. It is not, then, a merely passive religious environment which Zarathushtra invites his followers to share. It is one of activity and creativity.

This activity and creativity is expressed in many ways, and importantly by the observance of the code of good thought, good words and good deeds. However, it is also expressed ritually in the *Yasna* ceremony. It will be remembered that Zarathushtra the priest would have been accustomed to performing a version of this liturgy, and would therefore have been involved in the kindling and maintenance of the ritual fire, either directly or in his role as a "leading" priest (*zaotar*) – but whatever his liturgical function he will have been in close proximity to the ritual fire on a regular basis.[11] The attention given to the fire, then as now, protects, cultivates and promotes the principle of *asha*, thereby increasing its influential possibilities. The fire must also be kept free from pollution. For this reason some have understood the smoke that the fire produces as evidence of the Ahrimanic influence even in the most Ahuric of circumstances, a visible sign of the ever-present activity of the hostile spirit. It illustrates and confirms the need for vigilance on the part of the devout *ashavan*, to ensure that on all occasions the presence of evil is deflected.

If *asha* denotes primarily truth, order and righteousness, a necessary concomitant of this triad is justice. In Y.29:2, *Asha* is questioned as to how he will judge the cow, which may, according to G. Cameron, be an oblique reference to the eschatological judgement if the cow in this instance denotes humanity (or at least the community of the faithful[12]) but it is just as likely to refer to the present act of evaluating (i.e. discerning) religious truths, given the cow's association with the Good Vision. However, justice as a concept underscores Zoroastrian eschatology, and a theology developed from the Gathic texts relating to this suggest that punishment and reward will be prescribed in accordance with almost mathematical exactness. However, Zoroastrian eschatology is a subject in itself and a chapter devoted to it follows. For now we merely remark that justice is a concept dear to Zarathushtra, and one which does not allow any half-measures when it comes to evaluating the good and bad deeds of men and women and the eventual consequences of those deeds.

## Vohu Manah

The member of the divine heptad denoting the Good Mind or Vision, *Vohu Manah*, is mentioned a total of 136 times in various forms throughout the *Gathas*, which is a few short of *Asha Vahishta*. Whilst it is probably misleading to construct a theory of importance based *solely* on the number of times each of the Amesha Spentas appears in the *Gathas*, since they all command equal reverence and all have specific roles which are interdependent in Ahura Mazda's plan, the fact remains that *Asha Vahishta* and *Vohu Manah* are mentioned on more occasions than the other four. The importance of *Vohu Manah*, therefore, is not considered to be less than that of *Asha Vahishta*, but on the contrary there is a strong case to make for his seniority since it was through him that Ahura Mazda was able to motivate his creative programme. *Vohu Manah* often appears, together with *Asha Vahishta* and the Wise Lord, as a member of a Gathic trinity, and the following verse demonstrates an important dynamic of that trinitarian relationship. Just as Ahura Mazda activates creation through *Vohu Manah* (cf. Y.28:2 above, and later texts which state that *Vohu Manah* "gave movement" to creation[13]) Zarathushtra reflects that creation back to his God in praise, which is done *for* truth (*Asha Vahishta*), although *through* the Good Mind:

> O approaching ones, I shall now proclaim praises for the Ahura and worships of good thought, worthy of being noted even by Him who (already) knows them, O attentive ones, and for truth (I shall proclaim) the joy which is visible through the lights. (Y.30:1)

A perceptive mind and discerning wisdom, which *Vohu Manah* denotes, are gifts which Ahura Mazda bestows on his followers. Those who live in accordance with his truth, the *ashavans*, are entitled to receive the illumination that comes with and through *Asha Vahishta*:

> May the man obtain the best of all things, comfort in (the domain of) comfort, (and) may he, perceptive though your most holy spirit, O Mazda, (obtain) the blessings of good thought which you grant though truth, all his days along with the joy of long life. (Y.43:2)

*Vohu Manah* enables Zarathushtra to recognize the holiness of Ahura Mazda:

> I realize that you are holy, O Mazda Ahura, when one approaches me with good thought . . . (Y.43:11)

Approaching the issue from a philosophical standpoint, some Zoroastrian commentators have understood this notion of wisdom as two-fold: intuitive (or *noetic*) and acquired (or *received*). This means that through *Vohu Manah* the Wise Lord imparts his own eponymous characteristic in two ways. He may choose to endow someone with knowledge or aptitude irrespective of that person's own efforts to acquire it (provided of course that the person is living according to the principle of *asha*); or he may supplement the person's own efforts to gain perceptive insight or any associated virtue, in which case Ahura Mazda would be conferring on him or her an additional or "augmenting" mental strength. All *ashavans*, being followers of the truth, automatically receive the wisdom necessary to defeat evil simply by virtue of their being *ashavans*. But, as Zarathushtra often suggests, it is through this latter positive application of the Good Mind that Ahura Mazda's help and strength may be obtained in a rather more active and life-enhancing sense than the merely passive way implied by the former. It also suggests that the *ashavan* may advance his or her connection with Ahura Mazda through the quality of the Good Mind, in imitation of Zarathushtra.

In the *Yasna* ceremony *Vohu Manah* is theoretically represented by the sacrificed animal; since animals are no longer sacrificed, this representation has been transferred to the dairy products which are used in the ritual – milk and butter, and a sieve which is made from the hair of a consecrated bull. *Vohu Manah* protects especially cattle, but this is understood to include all animal life.

## Spenta Armaiti

*Spenta Armaiti* (devotion, "holy right-mindedness") is that aspect of Ahura Mazda's personality which denotes fidelity, dedication to the religion and piety. *Spenta Armaiti* is thought of as a feminine spirit.

Zarathushtra invokes her name as he implores Ahura Mazda for happiness:

> Where will joy arise from a pious person? Where will it arise with compas-

sion? Where do people honour truth? Where is holy right-mindedness?
Where is best thought? Where, through your power, are they, O Mazda?
(Y.51:4)

And later in the same hymn the prophet affirms her function as the
divine entity through which the *ashavan* might live a holy and devoted
life:

> By virtue of right-mindedness, this holy man makes truth prosper though
> the utterances (inspired) by his insight, through his action and his reli-
> gious view . . . (Y.51:21)

The care of the earth is given to this divine entity and thus there is
intrinsic connection between the Zoroastrian's religious devotion and
his or her affirmative attitude towards the good creation. In fact
Zoroastrianism has been characterized as being a "pro-cosmic" dualism
which does not reject the benefits of the material world. In recognition
of this protective task, *Spenta Armaiti* is represented in the *Yasna* ceremony as it is now celebrated by the consecrated ground of the area
where the ritual is celebrated. This area is known as the *pawi*. *Spenta
Armaiti* can, in this instance, represent the link between the consecrated
and the unconsecrated, since, having care over all the earth, she tran-
scends the limits created by the boundaries of the sacred arena which
separate it from the outside world. Although the world is essentially
Ahuric, because of the Ahrimanic infection it has suffered special areas
are set aside for the purpose of higher religious services, where purity
can be guaranteed to remain intact, even in the face of the hostile spirit's
onslaughts. This does not assume an indifference or lesser degree of
protective concern for the rest of creation on the part of *Spenta Armaiti*
(or indeed any other Amesha Spenta or Ahura Mazda himself), but it
does suggest that a greater intensity of association between the priest
and the good *menog* (spirit) beings can be experienced in the *pawi*.
Zarathushtra himself, as a priest, will have been accustomed to
performing liturgies in the open air, as was the practice in his day, since
temples were not introduced into Zoroastrianism until around 400 BCE,
possibly as a result of Babylonian influence. It is reassuring, then, to
imagine that Zarathushtra's recognition of *Spenta Armaiti* as the
Bountiful Immortal responsible for instilling, increasing and maintaining religious fervour may have persuaded him to invoke her special
protection over the ground upon which he was standing before
proceeding with his ritual worship. It illustrates that the well known and

much admired concern that Zoroastrians show for the environment may be traced back to the teaching and practice of the prophet of Iran.

## Khshathra Vairya

Although the Vedic god Indra, as one of those who "choose the worst thought", was denounced by the Zoroastrian tradition (as the *Vendidad* has shown us), a residue of his association with temporal conquest and rulership was retained in the Amesha Spenta known as *Khshathra Vairya*, the Good Dominion of Ahura Mazda. This is on the surface an alarming suggestion, since it presumes that, all evidence to the contrary notwithstanding, Zarathushtra somehow approved of the violence and chaos that attended Indra's worship. Indra was, after all, a Vedic god of warriors, invoked before a battle; the drinking of the *soma* juice which accompanied his invocations was guaranteed to exhilarate men into a fighting mood, and Zarathushtra has already condemned the unseemly behaviour which had become all to common in connection with *soma*'s Avestan equivalent, *haoma*. One of Zarathushtra's techniques, however, was to take what he considered the most promising elements of the adjacent religious traditions with which he was familiar and refashion them so that they would harmonize with his own proposed reforms. We have already seen that this was what he did when he introduced the *asha* principle into his religious programme. *Khshathra Vairya* represents another example of this device. It would seem that the related ideals of kingship and social order were never far from Zarathustra's mind, but the establishment of dominion and maintenance of social structure necessarily implied some form of subjugation. There was an ethical price to pay, however, since if Zarathushtra would not sanction the indiscriminate slaughter of cattle, still less would he do so of his fellow humans. So by adapting the structure of the institution of the warrior and superimposing upon it an ethical component, Zarathushtra was able to suggest that the real battle was the one against the forces of evil, and the real prize would not be territory, or even men and cattle, but the realization of the good dominion (*khshathra*) of Ahura Mazda. This eschatological image, then, derives its significance from a pre-Zarathushtrian societal norm which is simultaneously appropriated, inverted and thus denounced.

The word *khshathra* is the Avestan equivalent of the Sanskrit *ksatra*, the Vedic word for Varuna's "kingdom", and it is related to *ksatriya*, the term for a member of the warrior or ruling class in Vedic society, the second class after the *Brahmins*. This etymological connection can further assist in our understanding of the nature of this member of the Zarathushtra's celestial heptad, since in Vedic society the rulers dominated by means of their conquests; in Zarathushtra's way of things, the Amesha Spentas, other good spiritual beings (*yazatas*) and the earthly *ashavans* are the "warriors" who gradually usher in the *frashokereti*, the final expression of the good dominion of Ahura Mazda, by their constant opposition to and eventual defeat of the hostile spirit and his demonic forces:

> When Mazda and the (other) Ahuras are present, as well as truth worthy of invocation, along with reward and right-mindedness, then with good thought I hope to gain for myself strong power through the increase of which we may defeat deceit. (Y.34:6)

Before the kingdom can be fully established, however, later Zoroastrian apocalyptic mythology, rooted in Zarathushtra's Gathic teachings, speaks of a universal trial by molten metal, whereby all men and women will be subjected to a general judgement; men and women who have lived good virtuous lives will be made to pass through the metal and to those people it will seem like "warm milk".[14] Those who have lived evil lives, however, will not be so fortunate, for to them the metal will be agonizing and will destroy them:

> Make clear (to them) in their minds, O Mazda, which (is) the gratification you apportion with your red fire and the molten metal according to the balance. In order to damage the deceitful one you benefit the truthful one. (Y.51:9)

It is believed the molten metal ordeal, whereby molten metal was poured onto the chest of an offender, was a tribal juridical practice with which Zarathushtra will have been familiar (although the *Gathas* do not make clear his approval of the practice, merely suggesting his recognition of its value as an image with which his audience will also, presumably, have been familiar). There is no Gathic evidence to suggest that Zarathushtra envisaged a general resurrection far in the future; his poems strongly suggest that as far as he was concerned the refreshment of the world or *frashokereti* was to be within his lifetime. The modifications which occurred within Zoroastrian eschatological mythology were a result of Zarathushtra's vision being unrealized, an issue we shall examine in chapter III.

In the *Yasna* ceremony, *Khshathra Vairya* is represented by the metal implements used by the officiating priest and his assistant. *Khshathra Vairya* is responsible for the protection of the sky, which was originally thought to be made of stone but later came to be thought of as metal. *Khshathra Vairya* suggests to the *ashavan* the need for prudent authority in the temporal sphere, an authority which is clearly illustrated by this notion of trial by molten metal. This authority must be visible in every stratum of society, and so the head of a family is just as bound by the necessity of a fair exercise of justice and rule as is the king, priest or any other person in a position of power.

Indra's rulership, once wielded in fear and domination, is replaced by one exercised in faithfulness to Ahura Mazda and the good religion, and it is one that sets its sights not upon the ephemeral glory of worldly rule obtained in violent struggle but upon the renovation of the universe, brought about by justice and truth.

## Haurvatat and Ameretat

These last two Amesha Spentas are invariably grouped as a pair, and they are thought of as the members of the heptad most distant from Ahura Mazda. This sense of remoteness is not to be interpreted as implying any inferiority on their part, but it is rather because the qualities they exemplify are only fully realized after death, when the soul of the pious Zoroastrian has been judged and has entered heaven, the House of Song. *Haurvatat* personifies wholeness, perfection or integrity and *Ameretat* personifies long life which leads, for the *ashavan*, to immortality. If praises are directed towards *Haurvatat* and *Ameretat*, the best of all benefits shall be granted:

> The best (part) shall be for him the Knowing one, who may pronounce for me the true manthra concerning integrity and immortality of truth. (Y.31:6)

Since *Ameretat* is the entity personifying immortality, it is appropriate that she is represented in the *Yasna* ceremony by the sacramental *Haoma* preparation. It will be remembered that an epithet for *Haoma* is *duraosha* – the "bestower of immortality", so the *Yasna* ceremony confirms this association. Her particular concern in creation is vegetation (of which the *Haoma* plant is an example), an essential ingredient for ensuring long life. *Haurvatat* has the responsibility for water, an equally important contribution to a healthy life, and it is by water that she is represented in the *Yasna* ceremony. This connection with the healing and preserving properties of food and water is evoked in his *Gathas* by Zarathushtra who, in linking the two *mainyus*, also identifies them as a source of augmenting "food" upon which Ahura Mazda himself can be nourished:

> Both integrity and immortality serve you as food. (Y.34:11)

## Other significant Gathic entities

In addition to Ahura Mazda and the divine heptad, Zarathushtra invokes or otherwise makes reference to a number of other divine beings in the *Gathas* which did not come to be included in this "inner circle" of heavenly beings but which share the title of *yazata*. *Geus Urvan*, the "soul of the cow", appears in Y.29, where she is in dialogue with *Geus Tasha*, the "fashioner of the cow". The former is also mentioned in Y.28, where she may be understood as denoting the good vision of the world informed by proper religious belief and behaviour. The latter figure may be understood as that aspect of Zarathushtra's own spirit which impels him to recognize his emerging religious vocation, the promotion of the good vision, which he must protect and nourish. In this sense the whole of Y.29, in which these divine entities figure most prominently, can be seen as a metaphor for Zarathushtra's own "calling" by Ahura Mazda to become his prophet. Yet there is sufficient reason to believe that Zarathushtra also recognized these two beings as discreet spiritual entities whose nature and function were much the same as that of the Amesha Spentas – that is, they are personifications of religious qualities worthy of worship and honour in their own right. Both divinities are related to and draw their impact from the notion of the reverent and courteous treatment of all animals, but especially the cow, in matters of sacrifice and their consumption as food, a theme to which Zarathushtra refers elsewhere in his *Gathas*.

*Ashi* and *Sroash* have also been identified as beings of particular significance to Zarathushtra, who alludes to their qualities in the same manner as he does to those of the heptad.[15] M. Boyce argues that this is due to their liturgical connections.[16] *Sroash*, the divine being personifying obedience and devout attention to God, is represented by the *Yasna* itself since performing this liturgy is the way that Ahura Mazda is best honoured, and *Ashi*, the goddess of recompense, by the payment the priest would have received for his ritual services, a practice Zarathushtra links not only with his priestly function but also to his status as *Saoshyant*. We have already established that the prophet attached considerable importance to his priestly office, and so, Boyce's argument states, his familiarity with its duties and the way of life it demanded would have formed a framework around which his personal devotional practices were structured, and it was these devotional insights, elaborated upon in his mind and then compressed into verse by the prophet's visionary genius, that evolved into the hymns comprising the *Gathas*. *Sroash's* value to Zoroastrianism was maintained and he will be seen to have an important role in eschatological mythology; *Ashi*, on the other hand, faded somewhat as other texts came to be composed though this must not suggest that she was conceived of by the prophet as anything but a *mainyu* exemplifying the desirable and laudable religious quality of reward demonstrated by the stipendary system. No doubt this too, as with certain ritual procedures, was subject to abuse, another reason for accepting Zarathushtra's enthusiasm for interpreting it on an ethical level as being a divinely sanctioned practice.

*Atar*, the divinity of fire, is also invoked in the *Gathas*. In his association with fire he clearly has a special relationship to *Asha Vahishta*, and this seems to be a Gathic concept. At Y.43:9, a ritual allusion is made by the prophet, acknowledging the particular importance of fire in the liturgy, and verse four of the same hymn suggests that fire is strengthened by truth. At Y.46:7, a connection is established between fire and the good mind by which truth is nourished, and a similar link between the spirit of Ahura Mazda and fire is established at Y.31:3 where truth is said to be transmitted through *Atar* and Spenta Mainyu. Later Avestan texts (for example the *Haptan Yasht*) refer to him as the "Son of Ahura Mazda". The putative etymological connection of the Avestan *atar* with *athravan* (Vedic *atharvan*) now seems unlikely.[17]

The figure of the *daena* presents certain problems in an analysis of Gathic divine entities, not least of which is that, unlike other *menog* beings, she seems in the *Gathas* to be ethically neutral, aligned with neither Ahura Mazda or Angra Mainyu.[18] Her name has been variously rendered as "conscience" or "religious view" and she is charged with the eschatological function of directing the souls of men and women to their fate; a later tradition concerning her changeable appearance – she is perceived as being beautiful or ugly, depending respectively on the accumulated virtue or demerits acquired over the lifetime of the person who encounters her – seems to reflects this neutrality. We shall meet her again when we come to consider Zoroastrian eschatology. A more general usage of the term *daena* denotes "religion".

## 3  The Divine Heptad and the Individual Zoroastrian

The Amesha Spentas and the qualities they exemplify, as expounded in the *Gathas*, offer a clear and concise map to the *ashavan* as he or she journeys through life, providing theological and ethical signposts which both direct and assist the *ashavan*'s progress towards the dual goal of individual sanctification and universal renovation. At each point and for each circumstance of life there is an attribute or characteristic of Ahura Mazda to invoke, to implore or to serve as a fortification and an encouragement. In striving for fidelity to the Zoroastrian injunction to care for creation, the *ashavan* need only contemplate the examples of the great mainyus of the divine heptad, for each of the Amesha Spentas, in addition to having a protective function, is also worthy of worship in his or her own right and each is given praise when his or her creation is nurtured. Moreover this praise and honour amplifies the absolute greatness of Ahura Mazda. Thus careful management and custodianship of fire is respect and devotion given to *Asha Vahishta*; honouring the just and lawful temporal authorities of one's country, one's place of work or one's family is honouring the Amesha Spenta of the Good Dominion, *Khshathra Vairya*. Since Ahura Mazda is the author of all creation, humanity, the Wise Lord's greatest achievement, is a reflection of Ahuric benevolence, and thus it is considered a religious duty to care for one's own physical and mental health, since Ahura Mazda and Spenta Mainyu are honoured by this. Therefore there is in Zoroastrianism no place for of asceticism and self-deprivation, such as that found in the monasticism or celibacy associated with some other traditions. The denial of the benefits offered by creation is not an ideal entertained by the devotees of Ahura Mazda since the world and all in it is to be celebrated. A rejection of the good creation is a rejection of Ahura Mazda; a rejection of Ahura Mazda is an open invitation to the forces of evil. In similar vein there is no concept of inherited guilt or original sin in Zoroastrianism; if there were it would imply an imperfection in Ahura Mazda. On the contrary, the complete perfection of Ahura Mazda is demonstrated in the college of Amesha Spentas and reflected in the inherent goodness of creation. The qualities denoted by the great mainyus of the heptad are not only aspects of Ahura Mazda's own perfect status, but the relationship that exists between the members of the heptad is itself perfect in its indissolubility. Although *ashavans* are constantly under threat from the Ahrimanic Lie (*drug*), the example and support offered by the Ahuric college impels the devout Zoroastrian on to the *frashokereti*, when all will be made perfect. Thus the Amesha Spentas can be considered multivalent figures whose multiple functions within the tradition are themselves reflections of the one exalted being of which they are attributes.

## 4 Ahura Mazda and the Amesha Spentas in the Later Literature

### The Yashts: Ahura Mazda, the Amesha Spentas and the Development of the Avesta

The familiarity with which Zarathushtra addressed the Lord of Wisdom and the intimacy of relationship that it suggests was not to last beyond the Gathic period. The evidence of the hymns known as the *Yashts* is that following Zarathushtra's lifetime a more formal approach towards Ahura Mazda was adopted by the priest-poets, who, as we shall see, were unable to imitate the prophet's style or reproduce his insight.

The *Yashts* are fragments of a larger body of literature which had been composed over a long period of time. Later *Yashts* may be dated to the Achaemenian period (550–330 BCE), but many pre-date that era by hundreds of years, if not in form then certainly in thematic material. Many are obvious reconstructions, put together in an attempt to maintain a liturgical and theological tradition which had been handed down orally by the priests. The nature of the oral tradition, as far as these hymns are concerned, granted the priests considerable freedom to add new material to existing compositions. This is clear from the mixture of pre- and post-Zarathushtrian matter that makes up the majority of these works.

A *Yasht* is typically a hymn in honour of a less significant good *menog* being, though the first two in the collection chiefly concern Ahura Mazda and the Amesha Spentas respectively. Many of these hymns are appointed to be recited at the specific times appropriate to the beings they honour in the liturgical calendar. Other *Yashts* may be recited at any time. It is clear from the content of the final form of many of these hymns that they represent the culmination of a period of consolidation between Zarathustra's own ideas and other concepts which may have been superimposed onto the Zarathushtrian reforms, or that may have been seen as logically arising out of them. Also, since they retain elements of pre-Zoroastrian Iranian religion, these hymns depict, in many commentators' eyes, an attempt to secure a continuity of tradition between what existed *before* the prophet and what he had proposed. The hymns exhibit the varying degrees of success with which this venture met. In some of these *Yashts* the names of the members of the divine heptad are intermingled more or less indiscriminately (and without concern for priority) with those of less important mainyus. In others there is an obvious and sometimes clumsy attempt to lend the authority of history to popular belief, and to present ideas as if communicated directly by God to Zarathushtra by the use of a formula such as "Ahura Mazda spoke to Zarathushtra ... ". The distance in time covered by the composition of these hymns, and the multiple authorship their analysis reveals, testify to the intensity of theological activity which prompted their preparation, and these factors might be a partial explanation for their apparent departure from Gathic thought.

In chapter I we saw that the phrase *Ahura Mazda* was not the common form of address used by Zarathushtra when he spoke with his God. Zarathushtra in the *Gathas* is seemingly comfortable with a familiar and even intimate style, whereas a more formal mode of address, in which the term *Mazda* is practically always preceded by the honorific *Ahura*, is established in the later Avestan works. In these texts Ahura Mazda becomes a figure more talked *about* than talked *to*, since even when he is addressed it is as if the author was merely reporting a dialogue in a formulaic fashion, hardly with the passion of Zarathushtra in the *Gathas*. There are certainly none of the heartfelt outpourings to which we had become accustomed in those earlier texts. By the time these Avestan compositions were formalized, then, Ahura Mazda had undergone a change of personality. In the *Gathas* he is the noble but benign all-wise ruler of creation, who dwells in transcendent intimacy with his holy immortals but who is, at the same by virtue of his simultaneous immanence, relevant. The later Ahura Mazda, as seen in so many of the *Yashts*, has lost something of this vibrancy. He is no longer spoken of in the imploring terms that Zarathushtra uses in his *Gathas*, but in a merely academic or regulative terminology evoking function rather than personality, often suggestive of an abstract distant creator who has no desire to interact with his creation. The sense of respect tinged with familiarity which Zarathushtra so often displays in his *Gathas* is missing from these later Avestan hymns. Attempts to show Ahura Mazda and Zarathushtra engaging in passionate discussion promise more than they deliver. Ahura Mazda's towering majesty had absorbed his personality, which had become buried in an explosion of abstract epithets. As an example of this, we might examine briefly the first of these hymns (not the first to be composed, but the first in the collection). This hymn, the

*Ohrmazd Yasht*, is substantially a litany of Ahura Mazda's attributes, and is fairly representative of the flavour of many of these hymns:

> Ahura Mazda replied to him [i.e. Zarathushtra]: My name is the one of whom questions are asked, O holy Zarathushtra!
> My second name is the Herd-giver.
> My third name is the Strong One.
> My fourth name is perfect holiness.
> My fifth name is All good things created by Mazda, the offspring of the holy principle.
> My sixth name is Understanding.
> My seventh name is the One with understanding.
> My eighth name is knowledge.
> My ninth name is the one with knowledge. (Yt.1:7)[19]

Although some of these epithets (e.g. "perfect holiness") may resemble the attributes exemplified by the Amesha Spentas as found in the *Gathas*, Ahura Mazda is now, more often than not, understood *only* in this kind of deferential terminology, no doubt conceived in imitation of the *Gathas* but lacking their intimacy.

What happened, therefore, is that other, more accessible deities replaced Ahura Mazda as the objects of popular devotion, since Ahura Mazda was now too far away to identify with everyday life, and it is these deities which are the subject of many *Yashts*. At times the devotion offered them seems excessive. From a *theological* point of view Ahura Mazda's centrality to the tradition remained unthreatened, but this is not the same as recognizing his attractiveness as a focus for religious fervour. Ahura Mazda was still honoured and praised through his spiritual creation; the direct line of communication, however, was now more rarely used. M. Eliade sums up what is in fact a not uncommon phenomenon in religions, and although he is not thinking particularly of Zoroastrianism when he writes that "the Supreme Being seems to have lost *religious actuality*; he does not figure in cult and the myths show him as having withdrawn far from mankind, he has become a *deus otiosus*",[20] he could very well be describing what happened to the figure of Ahura Mazda.

The collection of *Yashts* in honour of other deities, then, though no doubt gradual in formation, can be interpreted as a response to the need to fill the gap created by Ahura Mazda's equally gradual departure from the centre of Iran's devotional stage. With this there came a challenge to the unique position of the Amesha Spentas, since they are now joined by a host of other celestial beings. Even though the *Gathas* speak on occasion of other *menog* entities, the priority is always given to the Amesha Spentas, whereas these later texts do not always suppose such a hierarchy.

Two such *menog* beings, both of whom are celebrated in *Yashts*, are *Haoma* and *Mithra*. It is claimed by a number of writers that the *Hom Yasht*, the hymn to *Haoma*, shows a definite attempt to reconcile Zarathustra's harsh words about the use of the preparation which bears the deity's name in ritual with the long-established practice of *Haoma* veneration. The hymn recounts how *Haoma* approaches Zarathushtra who, after the customary attention to the fire and reciting the *Gathas*, asks who it is, "the most beautiful thing he has ever seen", that is coming towards him. *Haoma* identifies himself by name (and by function as the "averter of death"), and continues to instruct Zarathushtra in his worship, upon which Zarathushtra greets the deity with the cry "reverence to Haoma!". Significantly the hymn does make reference to the Kavis and Karapans, the very same people denounced by Zarathushtra in connection with a Haoma cult, and the hymn more or less repeats Zarathushtra's imprecations, linking these people with all manner of evil doers. The character and thrust of the hymn change halfway through, suggesting that this might be an earlier section of the hymn; it makes no further reference to Zarathushtra but it contains formulaic petitions repeating Haoma's function as the "averter of death", and it concludes in this fashion, the prophet, it would seem, having quietly disappeared from the scene. Quite possibly there was a danger of the ancient *Haoma* cult being lost, and it is equally possible that it was the intention of the composer(s) of this hymn that no such thing should occur. In creating a text fashioned from elements of the pre-Zoroastrian *Haoma* cult and introducing, in such a positive way, the figure of the prophet Zarathushtra who is seen to be in awe at his encounter with *Haoma*, the cult itself is authenticated and guaranteed a place within the developing Zoroastrian tradition whilst the author can identify himself with Zarathushtra's condemnation of its abuse. Some scholars have satisfied themselves on this point by arguing that Zarathushtra never intended to do away with *Haoma* worship in the first place but that he wanted to reintroduce its chief ingredient in a non-intoxicating variety since it was this that he complained about. In doing this the cult could continue but the drunkenness and abhorrent behaviour which Zarathushtra associated with it would be avoided. As his priesthood was never denied but actually *affirmed* in the *Gathas*, we may believe that he will have maintained the practice in some form which suited his purposes, and we would be justified in arguing that the *Hom Yasht* was composed to emphasize this point, and to guard against the relevant Gathic passages being interpreted too literally.

The *Hom Yasht* is the only hymn of its category to be accorded a place in the *Yasna* ritual, where it accompanies the consumption of the presanctified *parahom* mixture[21] and immediately precedes the recitation of the profession of faith, the *Fravarane* (Y.12). In consuming the holy food and drink the priests call upon and assume the strength of *Haoma* in imitation of Zarathushtra's reverence and veneration of him as recounted in the hymn.

This desire to preserve continuity is also attested in the Avestan hymn in honour of *Mithra* (*Mihr Yasht*). In this hymn, which may well be a fusion of elements from three different periods,[22] not only is pre-Zoroastrian *Haoma* shown in a positive light, but *Mithra* is also accorded such a status. *Mithra*, a major deity in the Indo-Iranian pantheon (he appears as *Mitra* in Indian texts), as well as (possibly) a significant figure in a Roman military religious cult,[23] comes to be associated in Zoroastrianism with judgement, so he has an eschatological function. He is also identified, as he is in the Vedic context, with the notion of "contract" and, by extension, friendship. As far as "contract" is concerned, *Mithra*, it has been suggested in sources dating from the Sasanian era, is the figure responsible for "mediating" between Ahura Mazda and Angra Mainyu but this is hardly in keeping with his almost universally accepted image of championing good and opposing the Evil Spirit.[24] In the Avestan hymn it is stated that even Ahura Mazda worships Mithra, an extravagant claim but one which may possibly be explained by the fact that *Mithra* is spoken to by name and not title (whereas the Wise Lord is *always* addressed by title in post-Gathic literature), an adoption of a conventional form of address which in this instance maintains Ahura Mazda's claim to pre-eminence.[25] It is also a way of ensuring that veneration of *Mithra* is validated at the highest possible level. In typical fashion the hymn announces Zarathushtra by name, identifying him in the opening verses as if to endow the text with revelatory status from the outset. The formality of address, as discussed earlier, both reinforces Ahura Mazda's supremacy and, at the same time, distances him from the more accessible *Mithra*.

*Mithra* has always enjoyed a prominent status in Zoroastrianism, and evidence of his durability and his significance to the tradition is found even today. The month of *Mihr* (September/October[26]) is dedicated to him, and a Zoroastrian fire temple, where major or higher ceremonies are performed, is often referred to as a *Dar-I Mihr*, a "Court of Mithra".

The Zoroastrian priests, at their ordination, are given the Mithraic mace to ward off evil, since it was by this that *Mithra* was said to thwart the Evil Spirit.

In summary, although we seem to have dealt with a number of issues here, there is a connecting thread which runs through them all. First, the desire to hold on to old ideas, itself perfectly understandable, must be linked with a need to maintain social order and control. Before the coming of Zarathushtra the priesthood had exercised control over the religious tradition, and thus to a large degree the social activity which centres around religious practice, and it would, naturally, be reluctant to relinquish its authority. Nor must it be forgotten that the priesthood was a position which was stipendary, an equally important considera-tion for the priests, and families of priests which would have been dependent upon their expertise to maintain an income. Second, proclaiming Ahura Mazda and then elevating him to such an exalted position was running the risk of locating him at a point outside the orbit within which most people operated. Without the guiding genius of Zarathushtra, the abstract nature of Ahura Mazda, though manifest in a spectacularly effective and wholly accessible fashion in the *Gathas*, became too distant. The later priests (which would include those responsible for the *Yasht* in his honour) were unsure of what to do with him, and they had no means of reproducing the prophet's vision. They also had no earlier point of reference, for Ahura Mazda, despite his superficial resemblance to the Vedic *Varuna*, was essentially an original concept in Iranian religion. Third, and because of this, there was a resur-gence of the attention given to other divine beings. These beings could be much more easily identified as sharing human traits, and could occupy the vacuum created by Ahura Mazda's gradual departure, which was, it must be emphasized, a *psychological* vacuum rather than a *theo-logical* one. The needs of society were met by providing access to the many gods of pre-Zoroastrian Iranian religion, who now sat comfort-ably alongside the great beings of Zarathushtra's heptad. The theology was satisfied by maintaining Ahura Mazda's status as creator and supreme being, who still presided over all the world, but now in a fashion more akin to an absent landlord maintaining his controlling interest through his agents.

In the *Gathas* the members of the divine heptad are presented as exemplifications of what might be termed the ethical and theological qualities or virtues – righteousness, immortality, piety, the kingdom of God and so on. As a general rule, when they are solely examined in the Gathic context, only secondary, often metaphorical associations with the material world are made. In the *Yashts* however the associations are by and large dominated by those relating to the created order.

The *Yashts*, then, present us with a fairly lively mixture of Zarathushtrian thinking and later ideas (together with some re-worked from an earlier period). They are full of references which link the old and the new. The Amesha Spentas who, in the sense that Zarathushtra conceived them can justifiably be called his innovation, are accorded a prominent place in them, but this is an honour they must now share with other *menog* beings, many of which can be traced back to pre-Zoroastrian times. Whereas Zarathushtra in his *Gathas* offers a vision of a simultaneously immanent and transcendent Ahura Mazda surrounded by the bountiful immortals, with the occasional glimpse of other celestial figures (such as *Sroash*, the divinity who impels us to hear the word of God and urges us to be obedient to it), the literature from post-Zarathushtrian times suggests that the heavenly court might be somewhat more populated than we had first imagined. We also see in the *Yashts* a definite blurring with regard to the order of importance of the heavenly beings, since other *menog* beings are named side by side with the Amesha Spentas, often with no clear distinction between the two categories.[27] Once again this may be due to no more than the desire to retain the veneration of the earlier entities, and by suggesting that they might have a more or less equal status with the Amesha Spentas, by effectively *exaggerating* their importance, they could be drawn into and *kept within* the round of ritual and praise. The deity *Haoma* is possibly a case in point (though his association with a major rite might put him in a distinct category). It is equally certain that in parallel with this was the gradual shift in how Ahura Mazda was perceived and how, as discussed above, he changes from the god who almost walks amongst his people – certainly one who addresses them (through his mouthpiece, Zarathushtra) without recourse to formulae – to one who is almost purely transcendent.

And although this gave the Amesha Spentas the opportunity to emerge (along with other *menog* beings) with a more sharpened sense of independence, it is still apparent is that they had not been given a definite history.[28] For this we must turn to still later works.

## The Bundahishen: Ahura Mazda, the Amesha Spentas and Cosmogony

This ninth-century Pahlavi text exists in two recensions, the Greater (because longer) *Bundahishen* and the Iranian *Bundahishen*. Much of what follows is based on the understanding that although some of the material may be dated to Avestan times, its use by scholar-priests, whose *lingua franca* was Pahlavi, and who were accustomed to a degree of theological sophistication not always evident in the (post-Gathic) earlier works, substantially defines it as a late piece of often speculative writing, drawing its content from more than one source, even reaching as far back as some features derived from a pre-Zoroastrian cosmogonic mythology which had evidently been incorporated into the steadily crystallizing doctrinal core of the faith.

The *Bundahisen*, meaning "creation" (although it also has much to say on eschatology), is thus a complex document which serves many purposes. In addition to its cosmogonic and eschatological content it deals with topography, geography, history, the life of Zarathushtra and the lives of a number of other priests. Reaching its final redaction at some time in the ninth century, it is composed of Avestan material (the *Damdat Nask*, no longer extant) as rendered into Pahlavi, into which has been interspersed commentarial material.

In order to appreciate the background to this text and others like it, we should bear in mind that an intense consolidation of apocalyptic thought had taken place at the time of the Alexandrian invasion during the fourth century BCE.[29] This was no doubt a response to what many scholar-priests will have believed to have been the signal of the end of the world, and for many it was indeed the end of the world as they had come to know it. Prior to that, contact with the Babylonians during the Achaemenian period resulted in the formulation of a "world year". This concept of a "world-year", with the movement of history reflecting the change of the seasons and the lunar cycle, and thus suggestive of a cyclical nature of time, can be identified in a variety of religious traditions. A residue of the concept survives in the retention of a liturgical cycle or calendar, common to many religions. The Zoroastrian understanding of the world-year consists of a division of history into four equal 3,000 year segments, perhaps influenced by the seasons. It thus spans a period of 12,000 years, or one thousand years for each lunar month. It is based on a similar Babylonian concept, but with an important difference. The Babylonians were astronomers and astral determinists; that is, they related what they observed in the skies to what happened on earth, in a manner similar to astrology. As well as being astral determinists, the Babylonians were also believers in the continuous repetition of events, a notion that they had gathered from the apparently endless repetition of the movement of the heavenly bodies; and here is the major difference between the Babylonian and

Zoroastrian interpretations. Although these Zoroastrian scholars were unable to accept the cyclical notion of time (Zarathushtra of course having established for them that the movement of time is linear), the idea that history could be divided into pre-determined stages was an attractive one. It was an idea that was to find its way into Zoroastrian tradition and it is dealt with in a number of texts such as the *Bundahishen*. These texts, whilst not always agreeing on the nature of the divisions, nevertheless agree on the general principle. The *Bundahishen* presents the subject with an almost mathematical conciseness. In a wider sense the *Bundahishen* seems to represent a convergence of at least three traditional sources: the Zarathushtrian celestial court and apocalyptic vision, the modified Babylonian world year and also a pre-Zoroastrian creation mythology. These three strands have then been woven together in the one text.

Furthermore, it is from the *Bundahishen* that we receive a clear and coherent picture of the concept of Ahura Mazda as creator of the Amesha Spentas and the purpose of their creation. Whereas the *Gathas* merely allude to the creation of these divine beings but presume their existence and are more concerned with assigning to them the qualities most beneficial to humanity, and the *Yashts* implicitly maintain this position, although from a considerably more *liturgical* standpoint, the *Bundahishen* introduces them at a fixed point in the creation narrative.

The opening chapters of the *Greater Bundahishen* (GBd.)[30] concern the creation, and offer a complex but disciplined account of how and why the universe came into being. In these accounts Ahura Mazda has continued his distancing from the world of mortals which we noted in the *Yashts*. He is known by the Pahlavi name of *Ohrmazd*, and in the *Bundahishen* has become so remote in the minds of its authors that it is established at the beginning of our text that he dwells in isolation. The Holy Spirit, Spenta Mainyu, has merged so completely with him that he is not mentioned separately. Angra Mainyu is known in these later texts as *Ahriman*; in chapter IV we shall see how he too has changed.

In an eternity without beginning, in a boundless time that exists outside our own, Ohrmazd dwells in isolation in a realm of pure light and the evil spirit in a realm of utter darkness. In this fashion the *Bundahishen* sets the pattern for a subsequent series of mirror images designed to accentuate the contrast between the domains of Ohrmazd and Ahriman. The symmetry is not perfect, however, for the text states that whereas Ohrmazd is omniscient and knows of Ahriman's existence, the reverse is not the case. Moreover the evil spirit only has "backward knowledge", that is, he can only know what has happened, not what will happen. Because of this Ohrmazd is able to make advance preparations, and he fashions his immaterial (*menog*) creation, which remains static for 3000 years. It is only when Ahriman becomes aware of Ohrmazd's realm of light that he rises up from his place of darkness, jealous of Ohrmazd, and conceives his destructive plan. He returns to his domain and begins to fashion his own demonic creation.[31] Ohrmazd and Ahriman confront each other (cf. Y.45:2) and Ohrmazd, because of his knowledge of what will occur in the future, tells the evil spirit that his quest is hopeless; he cannot ultimately win the battle. He advises the demons to switch allegiance and worship him, but this they will not do.[32] So Ohrmazd offers Ahriman a compromise. For a fixed period the final battle between the forces of good and the forces of evil will be postponed. This period is set for a further 9,000 years, and for 3,000 years Ohrmazd will be in control of the cosmos; for the next 3,000 years there will be a state of "mixture" (Pahlavi *gumezishen*) during which time Ohrmazd and Ahriman will have equal control; and during the last battle the defeat of Ahriman will be secured. Ahriman, unable to see the future, agrees to this. It is only when Ohrmazd allows him a vision of what is to come that he sinks back into despair and, as the text recounts, "lies prostrate for 3,000 years" (cf. GBd. 1:32). Thus, according to this scheme, 12,000 years later the battle will be won by the Ahuric forces. A later passage states that it was during this time (when events will go "according to the will of Ohrmazd") that the material world was conceived, though nothing is said about it at this point.

In fact so far in the narrative there is no mention at all of material creation; all that has been done so far has been in the spirit or *menog* realm. Since Ohrmazd knew that the only way Ahriman could be defeated was on a physical level, he began his material creation while Ahriman slept, in order eventually to "tempt" the evil spirit onto a plane where he would meet his downfall. Ahriman, it should be added, is incapable of material creativity, a fact which Ohrmazd knew. From the unlimited time in which he moved, Ohrmazd created first a period of limited time, or the "time of the long dominion" (cf. GBd. 1:39), which would house the material (*getig*) creation. It was during this period that Ahriman's creation too was able to develop. Having already established the "essence" of an order of spiritual beings (in effect, a prototypical template upon which to base the *menog* entities), Ohrmazd was now in a position to bring "from his own self, from the realm of light" an army of *yazads*, those beings who will come to be reverenced by *ashavans* and who will aid Ohrmazd and humans in the forthcoming struggle. Picking up again the technique of the creations mirroring one another, Ahriman creates an equivalent army of demons which will invade the spatio-temporal domain that Ohrmazd was in the process of establishing. Zarathushtra in the *Gathas* does not clarify his understanding of the demonic creation, other than to acknowledge its existence and its capabilities. Since, according to Y.30, the *daevas* have made a conscious decision to choose the evil path, they may be considered as having the same status as humans as far as their ethical nature is concerned (which is no doubt why Ohrmazd presents them with the opportunity to worship him, a chance they can accept or reject).

Ahriman creates "lying speech" (cf. *drug*), the exemplar of his wickedness and of course the opposite quality to the Ahuric truth (*asha*), created by Ohrmazd from the substance of light.[33] It is worth noting that for the Zoroastrian the words "lie" and "sin" are practically synonymous, but through the exercise of truth "the Creator is manifest" (GBd. 1:50).

It is at this point in the narrative, at 1:53, that the *Bundahishen* first mentions the Amesha Spentas (*Amahraspands*). We learn that Ohrmazd "parted himself among them", confirming the fact which we have already gathered from the *Gathas*, that he shares their essence but does not disturb their individual autonomy. Vohu Manah (*Vahman*) heads the list, as, by implication, he does in the *Gathas*. The heptad is named; a non-Gathic demonic equivalent is also enumerated.

Now, according to the next portion of the text, it was while Ahriman was prostrate that the material world was formed, and the primal creations are named in order: sky, water, earth, plant, animal, the "just man" and fire. It is not without significance that fire is the last creation. It will be recalled that *Asha Vahishta*, the mainyu who protects fire and is denoted by it in the *Yasna*, is also the mainyu identified with cosmic order, and thus may be understood as regulating the cosmos. So one way of looking at this portion of the text is to say that this task is given to *Asha Vahishta* once the rest of creation is in place Ohrmazd then appoints the Amahraspands to look over and protect each of the creations, and "takes for himself Mankind" (GBd. 2:11). The physical creation is in a state of perfection at this point. As if in preparation for the battle to come, the other Amahraspands are also assigned their material creations, corresponding to those we have already seen in our discussions on the *Yasna* ceremony.

They are, in their Pahlavi forms, with their creations (their Avestan forms are given in brackets):

| | | |
|---|---|---|
| *Vahman* | *(Vohu Manah)* | cattle |
| *Ardvahist* | *(Asha Vahista)* | fire |
| *Sharevar* | *(Khshathra Vairya)* | metals |
| *Spendarmad* | *(Spenta Armaiti)* | earth |
| *Hordad* | *(Hauvartat)* | water |
| *Amurdad* | *(Ameretat)* | vegetation |

The text continues to recount the creation of a countless host of other spirit beings, many of which correspond with the entities adulated in the *Yashts*. These lesser beings exist to serve the Amahraspands and to guide the *ashavans*; particularly important is the group known as the *fravahrs*, or *fravashis*. These beings are celebrated in the longest of the *Yasht* texts, the *Farvardin Yasht*. A *fravashi* might be defined as the indwelling presence of Ahura Mazda or Ohrmazd in each thing that exists. Even Ohrmazd himself is said to have his own *fravashi* (though Spenta Mainyu does not). In a verse loaded with ethical significance the text says that the fravashis were given a choice as to whether they would go into the world to take up their duties, which they did "for the sake of freedom" (GBd. 3:23–24).

The perfect state of the *getig* creation was only to last until the Ahrimanic assault began. One by one the material creations of Ohrmazd are attacked and destroyed by Ahriman's forces. Finally Ahriman comes to "the Bull" (the Gathic *Geus Urvan* seems to be Zarathushtra's own extension of this myth) and the Just Man (*Gayomart*), intent on destroying them. Why and how the Amahraspands are powerless to stop this destruction is not dwelt on, but this is almost certainly because had they successfully intervened, the myth would have been brought to an abrupt and inconclusive end. It is, however, recounted that Ohrmazd eased the suffering of the Bull and of Gayomart by administering a narcotic and thereby inducing in them sleep. In a scenario reminiscent of Vedic creation mythology,[34] from the killing of the just man, there sprang not only the entire human race but all manner of minerals. In a curious variation on the Vedic scenario (which states that the "cosmic man" provided the materials for the structure of the universe and the pattern of society from his dismembered body during the prototypical sacrifice), as Gayomart died, his seed entered the ground where it was guarded for forty years; from this seed came plant life which eventually produced the first pair of the new human race. Therefore in destroying creation and slaying the Primal Bull and the First Man, Ahriman was unknowingly laying the foundations for his eventual destruction. The temporary victory of Ahriman, we now realize, had to be permitted without any hindrance from the Amahraspands to enable the greater good, the birth of humanity from Gayomart's seed, to occur. As fire was the final creation, so it is the final object of the Ahrimanic assault. Unable, it seems, to destroy it entirely, Ahriman mingles "smoke and darkness" with it as a lasting sign of his malevolent presence in all things, and secures his goal of defiling all of the Ahuric creation.

The *Gathas* do not go into any detail about these events. The Amesha Spentas and their qualities are given there a high profile but their relation to the material world is left unconsidered in any depth, since for Zarathushtra the heptad first and foremost represents the ethical and theological qualities with which a person must identify to be counted amongst the *ashavans*. The *Yashts* equivocate between on the one hand the might and glory of an increasingly remote but still uniquely important Ahura Mazda and on the other the need to create and validate a theological environment for the emerging significance of the other *menog* beings, an equivocation which is addressed and to some degree rectified in the *Bundahishen*. It is not, however, until the eschatological passages of that text are read that we can judge how successful this rehabilitation has been, and how successfully Ahura Mazda and the Amesha Spentas, only at that point in cosmic history, are finally restored to their rightful places.

## 5  Some Other Important Ahuric References

### The Visperad

The *Visperad* ("lords of ritual") is a small collection of hymns clearly intended for liturgical use, composed and compiled during the later part of the Avestan period. When combined with hymns from the *Yasna* it forms a separate liturgical ceremony, though it is never used as a liturgy on its own. It is replete with references to Ahura Mazda, to the Amesha Spentas and many other *menog* beings. As with the *Yashts* which we have seen, the *Visperad* shows a tendency to ignore whatever celestial hierarchy may have been conceived by Zarathushtra since the great mainyus of the heptad and other *menog* entities are once again indiscriminately intermingled. There are in this collection a number of references to the prophet himself, as well as to the eschatological "saviour" figure, the *saoshyant*, a figure who is introduced, though in an uncertain, undefined, and, some would consider, shadowy form, in the *Gathas*, with whom the prophet identifies himself and his followers, and who was to assume a more solid identity and increased importance in other post-Gathic literature, and particularly in the closing chapters of the *Bundahisen.*

## The Achaemenian Inscriptions, and other texts of that period

Some secular and non-Zoroastrian writings also make reference to the Amesha Spentas or otherwise allude to them. Although they do not have as much to offer to the study of theological development in Zoroastrianism as the Avestan and Pahlavi texts, they nevertheless help to confirm the importance of the Amesha Spentas to the tradition.

Little is known of the details of the religion of the Achaemenian kings Cyrus, who conquered Babylon in 539 BCE, Darius the Great (522–486 BCE), and their successors other than that gathered from the inscriptions dated to their reigns which have been found in and around Persepolis; we can be confident, however, in stating that this was an essentially Zoroastrian faith that was maintained. These inscriptions, written in the cuniform script associated with south-western Iran, devote much space to the god *Ahuramazda* (sic) but say nothing about the divine heptad as a homogenous group. From this we can deduce that the religion, though rooted in Iranian tradition, had in some features departed from or even developed separately to the priestly religion of the north-east Iranian Avesta. There are no references to Zarathushtra himself in these inscriptions, but there are important references to the deceit-promoting *druj*, a number of abjurations of the *daevas*, and frequent allusions to *Ahuramazda* in such terms as "greatest of the gods", which of course indicates an acceptance of other divine beings, and "creator", which denotes *Ahuramazda's* supremacy. Certain texts suggest a more recognizably Avestan religion being observed. In these texts the divine heptad is not enumerated in its entirety but there is evidence for the worship of individual members such as *Asha Vahishta* and *Khshathra Vairya*, the latter possibly being venerated due to his connection with kingship. There are also references to Mithra and to the goddess Anahita.

Although there is no explicit mention of the heptad in these cuniform inscriptions, there is what might be an important allusion to it in the Hebrew scriptures dating to approximately the same time, at Ezra 7:14. Ezra (*fl* 458 BCE) was a legal expert, a priest-scribe and worshipper of Yahweh, who was attached to the court of the Achaemenian ruler Artaxerxes, and included in his duties was the inspection of the re-established temple at Jerusalem. The benign rulership of the Achaemenian empire, established by Cyrus when he overthrew the Babylonian

Empire (and returned stolen religious objects to their rightful places), encouraged indigenous religious custom. It is also possible that the Yahweh of the Hebrew peoples may have been identified with *Ahuramazda* by the Achaemenians, but even if that is not the case, for it cannot be proved, there is sufficient reason to believe that Yahweh was respected, at a distance, by Artaxerxes. Ezra 7:14 refers to the "the king and his seven counsellors", and it is not impossible that this advisory chamber within the royal court was a remnant of an earlier monarchical structure, perhaps set up in imitation of the divine heptad, with the king representing Ahura Mazda and the seven counsellors representing Spenta Mainyu and the Amesha Spentas.

This, together with the references to individual Amesha Spentas found on these inscriptions, would suggest that the religion of the Achaemenians had retained, possibly without realizing it, many of its ties with that of the Avesta. However its orthodoxy is questionable in view of the fact that such practices as burial, which on the evidence of Cyrus's mausoleum suggests entombment, do not seem to be in keeping with the Zoroastrian custom which in this particular matter required, as it still does today, exposing the corpse to the elements.

It was during the Achaemenian period that another important departure from the practice of Avestan Zoroastrianism occurred, one that was to have a lasting effect on Zoroastrianism's liturgical life until the present time. The building of temples to various deities, and to house the ritual fire, a custom hitherto unknown to the Persians, began in earnest during this time. The construction of such buildings was almost certainly a result of the Achaemenians having observed the Babylonian tradition in this matter, and the significance and value of buildings set aside for the purposes of divine worship was clearly not lost on Artaxerxes II, as his concern for the recently re-established temple at Jerusalem indicates. The prophet Zarathushtra would not have considered the construction of buildings to house representations of deities, or even the sacred fire itself, not because he would necessarily have been ideologically opposed to such a practice, but simply because it would never have occurred to anyone reared in the religious tradition of north-eastern Iran. The Achaemenians, on the other hand, were seemingly keen to subsume and adopt, where appropriate, the prevailing religious habits they encountered as a result of their conquests, and their eagerness to appear as benign rulers no doubt impelled them to modify at least the external customs of their subjects and in doing so to acknowledge some of their practices.

Thus may we be those who make existence brilliant . . .

(Y.30:9)

O Mazda Ahura, whosoever, man or woman, gives me those
things which you know are the best of existence: reward for truth
and power through good thought, and whom I stimulate to glorify
those such as you, with all those I will cross over the Account-
keeper's Bridge.

(Y.46:10)

May the benefactor know of what kind his reward shall be.

(Y.48:9)

# III

# Zoroastrian Eschatology

―――

## 1 The Eschatology of the *Gathas*

### The Saoshyant

Zarathushtra's references in his *Gathas* to a figure known as the *saoshyant* ("bringer of benefit" or "benefactor", also sometimes translated as "saviour") suggest a man who wishes to proclaim an eschatological message.

It would be well first to examine the term that Zarathushtra most commonly employs. The Avestan root *sav-*, which appears in various forms ten times in the *Gathas*,[1] means "to be useful, profitable, to produce the benefit".[2] In Y.48:9, when the prophet refers to himself as "the benefactor", he uses the form *saoshyas* which, being a future participle, denotes one who will come later to bring benefit – a future benefactor. In Y.48:12 he uses a future *plural* form, *saoshyanto*, to refer to the "benefactors", the ones who will be "removers of wrath".

It is generally believed that its use in the singular form (*saoshyant*) denotes Zarathushtra himself.[3] This indicates Zarathushtra's promotion of himself as a figure of eschatological significance. When it is used in the plural, however, it can either mean all those called *ashavan* – the followers of truth – or it could refer to specific "saviour" figures who are to come after the prophet, in a "messianic" fashion. Given Zarathushtra's apparent belief that the renovation of the world was to be within his lifetime, since his entreaties would make little sense if not accompanied by a belief in the imminence of the *frashokereti*, it is almost certain that the first interpretation is the one which Zarathushtra would have intended, and that the second is a later theological reflection, probably prompted by a fading, over time, of the prophet's own eschatological vision. We shall explore the second possibility and its ramifications later; for the time being we should confine ourselves to the prophet's words and try to establish what he was saying.

When Zarathushtra uses the term in its plural form, then, it is not used in the sense of a succession of prophetic figures who will follow on one from the other as time progresses, but rather it refers to a group of *asha-vans* – awaiting their commission, as it were – who, so Zarathushtra believes, will usher in the *frashokereti*. This being the case, we should note that there is no evidence that Zarathushtra believed, as later Zoroastrianism does, in the resurrection of the body. The *frashokereti* is to be brought about, as far as Zarathushtra is concerned, in the near future, so although he uses future forms of the word this must not be taken as to suppose he meant that the end of time was to be a far off event. Those who live in accordance with the qualities exemplified by the Amesha Spentas deny the adversarial spirit his chance of increasing his evil dominion, and so as soon as all walk the Ahuric path the onslaught of creation will cease, the Ahrimanic *drug* will no longer be able to deceive and the good dominion will be established. The prophet's use of the future forms of *sav-* implies his own hope in the realization of this event.

Despite his willingness and even insistence that all *ashavans* are responsible for the renewal of the world, it is fair to say that Zarathushtra believed himself to have a unique role in the process. We may link this with his recognition of his task to protect the good vision – the cow – which we will remember from Y.29. For Zarathushtra, eschatology begins with himself, since the first step in the renewal of the world is the recognition of its condition, with which must be coupled a passionate desire to do something positive about it. Given that the truth of Ahura Mazda's religion inspires its act of proclamation, the "bene-factors" are those who bring it to its realization. It is not enough merely to know the teachings of the religion, but they must also inspire acts of religious duty, chief among which is preparing for the renovation and creating the conditions within which it becomes a possibility. Assuming that Zarathushtra saw himself as a teacher and therefore a leader, which we can deduce from his complaint about his message being rejected (Y.46:1), we can further assume that he would want to lead by example.

Since Zarathushtra is, in this context, the paradigmatic human being, he also signals the beginnings of eschatology, but with the under-standing that this is a function in which all his followers will share. That the evolution towards the refreshment is a gradual process does not detract, any more, from its imminence. If the world is in a degenerate state, which the prophet seems to believe, this does not mean that it cannot be wrenched back into a state of perfection swiftly. Yet this will not be an abrupt event, coming without warning. The signs of it are already here, gathered in the person of the prophet, manifested in the qualities exemplified by the heptad, and shared in by the *ashavans*. For Zarathushtra, all that is required is a turning away from the path of the *druj* to embrace *asha*, and the rest will, as it were, fall into place. Does this suppose a simplicity, or even a naïveté, on the prophet's part? On the surface it may seem to, but it would be wrong to imagine that the apparently child-like innocence of what Zarathushtra was proposing – reject the lie, follow truth – was not built on a complex and ancient religious heritage.

The structure within which the *frashokereti* might be realized has been in place for a long time, and Zarathushtra is faithful to this structure, for it provides him with a theological (and liturgical) framework which he can modify and into which he can introduce his new ideas, ideas which have been revealed to him by Ahura Mazda and encrypted in the *Gathas*. What Zarathushtra did was to reinterpret this entire structure and inject into it an ethical element demanding personal responsibility, an element which had been previously all but absent. This absence of a dominant ethical component was, of course, not impossibly compensated for by the emphasis on ritual, an activity which is essentially corporate, and which to a large degree obviated the need for what might be termed personal commitment since the mere fact that ritual is performed could, in Indo-Iranian terms, ensure the tradition's survival. *Asha*, however, unlike the Vedic law of *rta*, implies the individual's entry *into* the Ahuric life, and it involves a relationship which, as we have seen, had hitherto been the prerogative of the priests to mediate. Without dissolving the priesthood, Zarathushtra suggested that the way of *asha* also demands a response to the creator *in addition* to that made possible through ritual.

It is the *ashavan* who is entitled to lay claim to this relationship, and, in so doing, is permitted to participate in the function of the *saoshyants*, those who will "make existence brilliant". Certainly Zarathushtra is the first *Saoshyant*, but by including himself amongst the larger body of *saoshyants* he assumes the status of first among equals. Are, then, the "benefactors" and the *ashavans* one and the same? One cannot be a benefactor without first being an *ashavan*; that much is certain. Perhaps the question is best answered by discounting those whom Zarathushtra excludes from the *ashavans*. The first requisite of the *ashavan* is that he or she should be human. Thus the good *menog* beings – for Zarathushtra first and foremost the members of Ahuric college – are not *ashavans*, since they already dwell in unity with Ahura Mazda and therefore are indissolubly connected to *Asha Vahishta*. The role of the good *menog* beings in the *frashokereti* is different in kind to that of the human *asha-vans*, since the adversary can only be tackled on the material (*getig*) plane by humans co-operating with the will of Ahura Mazda though the end result which both classes desire is the same.. Presumably neither then the *daevas* can become *ashavans*. They have rejected the opportunity to join the Ahuric realm, as Zarathushtra points out in a hymn which mocks their attempts to gain control of the world by appropriating the gifts offered to Ahura Mazda:

> You, Daevas, cheat the mortals of good life and immortality in the same
> way as both the evil spirit, (associated) with evil thought, (cheated) you,
> the Daevas, and the action (inspired) by evil word by which a ruler recog-
> nized a deceitful person. (Y.32:5)[4]

But the role of the human is specific and consciously chosen. The encounter of the two spirits in Y.30 exemplifies the tension encountered in the struggle which leads up to the *frashokereti*. Although it is a struggle between the unseen forces of good and evil it is also a struggle which demonstrates itself in the opposition between the *ashavans* and those who follow the *druj*, those who, like the *daevas*, have been deceived. This radical dualism is gradually supplanted by the eschatological monotheism we touched upon in chapter I, since the tension between the opposites which the two spirits exemplify cannot sustain an equality as individuals cease to follow *drug* in favour of *asha*.

The message of Zarathushtra is that the *ashavans*, who are also *saoshyants* by virtue of their Ahuric disposition, will bring about the brilliant existence which is the *khshathra*, the visible sign of the *frashok-ereti*, since the *drug* cannot withstand the forces of good. This is despite Angra Mainyu's presence in the world, since Angra Mainyu can only survive when men and women allow him to. Deceit, for Zarathushtra, is destined for no lesser fate than obliteration:

> And truth, O Mazda, has been implanted in this (our) choice to benefit
> (us) but deceit (has been implanted) in false teaching in order to harm
> (people). Therefore I request the shelter of good thought, and I banish all
> the deceitful from (our) fellowship. (Y.49:3)

But the *ashavan*, the person who lives by truth, will enjoy the benefits of the *frashokereti*. It is significant to note that the ethical dualism underpinning human experience is constantly alluded to by Zarathushtra in his verse:

> Brilliant things instead of weeping will be (the rewards) for the person who comes to the truthful one. But a long period of darkness, foul food, and the word "woe" – to such an existence your religious view will lead you, O deceitful ones, because of your own actions. (Y.31:20)

## The Bridge of the Separator

One of Zarathushtra's most striking eschatological images concerns the individual's judgement and his or her arrival at the *Bridge of the Separator*, or the *Account-keeper's Bridge* (Avestan *cinvaot peretu* – the *Chinvat Bridge*[5]). This is a much older myth which is now presented with Zarathushtrian modifications. Chief among these is that whereas in the earlier version only men were capable of attaining salvation, now in the prophet's more egalitarian vision both men and women are equally entitled to enter a state of bliss if their lives have warranted it. We must therefore assume Zarathushtra's familiarity with this earlier myth. He also states that he will accompany the souls of the virtuous dead across the Bridge:[6]

> O Mazda Ahura, whosoever, man or woman, gives me those things which you know are the best of existence: reward for truth and power through good thought, and whom I stimulate to glorify those such as you, with all those I will cross over the Account-keeper's Bridge. (Y.46.10)

The actual process of judgement receives little attention in the *Gathas*, and it is not until the later texts that we shall encounter it in a more systematic form. In the *Gathas* we have the idea that at death the person's soul is presented at this bridge or "crossing"; the crossing can either lead to the House of Song (heaven) or the House of Lies (hell). The "separator" itself may have been the enormous chasm that may be supposed to exist between the House of Song and the House of Lies, for some versions of the myth state that the soul destined for damnation will find that the bridge contracts to such a degree that it is impossible to remain on it; and so the soul will fall off and plunge down to hell.

It seems that as far as the prophet is concerned, this was to be the final judgement passed on the individual. Once again, Zarathushtra chooses the Karapans and the Kavis, those who worshipped false gods, as his example of those most obviously doomed to the House of Lies, and in doing so provides a frightening picture of what happens at the Bridge:

> Through their power the Karapans and the Kavis yoke the mortal one to evil actions in order to destroy existence. When they reach the Account-keeper's Bridge their own soul(s) and their own religious view(s) will make them tremble, and they will be guests in the house of deceit for all time. (Y.46:11)

Because this scenario sets out a vision of final banishment, some translators have called this place the *Bridge of Judgement* or the *Bridge of the Separator*. The phrase "for all time" does not evoke notions of remission, particularly as the prophet tells us elsewhere (Y.51:9) that the trial by molten metal will not be purgative but final (see also above in chapter II in the section dealing with *Khshathra Vairya*). In the later books the House of Song and the House of Lies become temporary places, where men and women wait in bliss or agony until the final judgement.[7] In Zarathushtra's teaching, however, this development had not taken root. For him, it seems that the fruits of the cosmic renewal would only be tasted by the *saoshyant-ashavans* – those who had brought about the *frashokereti*. Life after death meant either complete happiness or complete misery. There is, therefore, a finality in Zarathushtra's eschatology which is completely in keeping with his sense of justice. It also has a spatial dimension, since good and evil cannot occupy the same space simultaneously. This is as true of the spirit domain as it is of the physical, but it is on the physical plane that evil will be defeated.

This harmonizes with the emergence of an eschatological monotheism which we have already seen implied in the *Gathas*. The destruction, not just of wicked people, but of the spirit that lures them into wickedness (since he can only survive in any productive form *in* those people), leaves room only for the power of good, Ahura Mazda, and the good dominion.

Judgement, though, as part of Zarathushtra's eschatological package, begins in the here and now:

> If the way better to tread is not seen by the (faithful), then I approach you all since Mazda Ahura knows the judgement on these two shares (a judgement), through which we can live in accordance with truth. (Y.31:2)

In other words, judgement has already begun, and the *ashavan*, in anticipation of the judgement that Zarathushtra envisions for all, must exercise discernment, for the discernment which the *ashavan* exercises in this earthly life will determine his or her behaviour which will in turn decide his or her fate. Eschatology is not merely a once-and-for-all event in the undefined future, but a present reality with which individuals must reckon. The Avestan term which Zarathushtra employs in this passage – *ratum* – is rich with juridical associations. In the society which flourished at the time of Zarathushtra it denotes one who has the ability and authority to discern, or judge, in religious matters. It is a concept with which the prophet will have been familiar and with which, he will have been aware, his intended audience too will have had some acquaintance. In enjoining his followers to discern between the path of *drug* and that of *asha*, he forges, by his use of juridical imagery, an association in their minds with the culmination of the ongoing judgement, which awaits them all at the Bridge of the Account-keeper, where the good and the wicked are separated for ever.

## 2 The Eschatology of the Later Literature

*The Saoshyant*[8]

That the term *saoshyant* was one Zarathushtra happily applied to all his followers – the *ashavans-* was a consequence of his belief in an impending apocalypse. There is no evidence from the *Gathas* that Zarathushtra maintained a belief in future prophet-like figures who were to take over or continue his task; certainly there is no indication that such figures would come centuries after his lifetime. The approaching end was, for the prophet, a determining factor in his relationship with the world and with Ahura Mazda. There is an urgency in his vision which impels him to gather as many people as he can into his family of co-workers in order that the hostile spirit might be defeated and the *frashokereti* then brought about speedily. We find ourselves referring again to that Gathic text in which Zarathushtra prays that "may we be those who make existence brilliant". This expectation, however, was one which was not fulfilled during Zarathushtra's time, though the terminology associated with it has remained firmly established as part of Zoroastrian religious vocabulary. References to the *Saoshyant* are scattered liberally throughout the post-Gathic literature, but the figure now takes on a new and more exclusive meaning.

It is clear that these later writings are partly an attempt to reconcile the apocalypse that Zarathushtra had prayed for with its apparent failure to transpire. One way around this was to recast the *saoshyant* figure not as a general representation of all those who worked towards "the end" – a innovative concept in itself which was to become increasingly elaborate as it became more distant – but as a specific figure within history. History was now clearly not going to end yet, and so there was considerable room for the theologians to manoeuvre within the tradition as they tried to account for a change in its trajectory.

There arose out of this a doctrine which taught that there was to be a succession of *saoshyants* (of which Zarathushtra was the first), who would, over succeeding millennia, be born of virgins from the seed of the prophet, which will be miraculously preserved in the lake *Kayansih*, as told in the *Bundahishen*. Since the *Gathas* do not define a number, it is difficult to say when the figure of three was determined; three, though, is an auspicious number in Zoroastrianism (as it seems to be in many other traditions). These *saoshyants*, now three in number following Zarathushtra, were to appear at intervals in the history of the world when it was in danger of such a moral degeneration that it might seem that it had fallen finally to the forces of evil. But from the moment of the first of these saviours' appearances there will be a reversal of the trend towards evil and all the qualities associated with the Ahuric way – justice, peace, piety and so on – will prevail. The next period of decline will precede the next of these saviours. The last of the world saviours will be the one to begin the final work that brings about the *frashok-ereti*.

Accommodating such a doctrine required the construction of a timescale within which these events could occur. This was necessary since the time-scale that Zarathushtra had envisioned had long been superseded. We have already seen, in chapter II, how the *Bundahishen* sets out a period of 12,000 years from the beginnings of the *menog* creation, through the confrontation between Ohrmazd and Ahriman, the Ahrimanic assault on creation, to the period of the Mixture until Ahriman's eventual defeat. The last three thousand of these years, as the *Bundahishen* states, will be the period during which the battle between good and evil will be most intensely fought, and according to this scheme, Zarathushtra heralded the beginnings of this final era which begins with the prophet's thirtieth birthday. This was the age when, according to the *Selections of Zatspram*, he received his first revelation. Zarathushtra then, both in his *Gathas* and in the later texts, can be said to represent the beginnings of eschatology.

The final 3000-year period of the world year is further divided into three 1000 year periods. These three millennia are known by the names of the *saoshyants* who appear at their beginnings. Each period begins with its respective *saoshyant's* thirtieth birthday, in obvious imitation of Zarathushtra's first revelation with which has been combined an elaboration of the notion of cyclical repetition. We have seen that the year 9000, according to the chronology of the *Bundahishen*, will have been the start of Zarathushtra's millennium. The year 10,000 will see the start of the next saviour's period, the period of *Ukhshyad-ereta*, the name of the first of the three great *saoshyants*. Then, one thousand years later, the second saviour, *Ukhshyad-nemangh*, will arrive to rally once more the forces of Ohrmazd to fight against the forces of Ahriman. The final world saviour, the "true" *saoshyant*, *Astvad-ereta*, will arrive in 11,943[9] and begin the process which will draw history to a close in the year 12,000. We shall return to this last character later, for he has a far greater role than the previous two – even, arguably, greater than that of the prophet himself in this eschatological aspect of Zoroastrianism – but for now we should look at the *purpose* of the legends surrounding these saviours, and the new identity which they confer upon the prophet.

Tradition recounts that each *saoshyant* will be born of a virgin, as we have seen. However, the hereditary nature of the priesthood meant that Zarathushtra himself could not have been born of a virgin, since he would require a priestly father, for in the Iranian tradition priesthood is only open to members of a priestly family and transmitted through the male line, passed on from father to son, and so we may assume that Zarathushtra had a priestly father even if this is not attested in the *Gathas*. But as the prophet moved further away in time, legendary accounts and mythological elaborations began to develop. (In fact a series of legends containing details of supernatural or at least unusual occurrences surrounding the prophet's birth and infancy did evolve. Book 7 of the *Dinkard*, a Pahlavi version of a now lost Avestan text, often known as the "Marvels of Zoroastrianism", records that three days before his birth the village of Zarathushtra's father Porushaspo was illuminated; that the three characteristics of his being, his heavenly glory, his protecting *fravashi* and his bodily nature, were united in his mother's body before he was conceived; that he laughed instead of cried at his birth, that at birth he was protected from danger by a bull standing over him.[10] The *Farvardin Yasht*, Zoroastrianism's great treatise on the *fravashis*, states in verse 93 that "the waters and plants grew" at his birth.[11] It is not impossible that versions of these legends began to circulate fairly soon after the prophet's death.) It seemed important that Zarathushtra was elevated from a merely human status, but if a virginal conception could not be accorded to Zarathushtra, since the prophet's priesthood had to remain intact, there was no reason why a miraculous birth could not be predicated for his successors. Then the need to elevate the prophet above ordinary mortals could be met by exalting him *through* these successors. And so, because of the belief that Zarathushtra's seed was preserved in the lake, awaiting the time when it would be impregnated into a succession of virgins, these *saoshyants* had a connection with Zarathushtra which was no longer just scriptural, or even ideological: it was now biological. It is probably no coincidence that the evolution of this semi-divine status for Zarathushtra occurred when heterodox and other rival religious groups would have been emerging, and when the expansion of Zoroastrianism as a religion, involving encounters with other religious traditions, occurred as a natural consequence of political expansion. In a sense, the establishment of the good dominion, now believed to be an event which would take place in the distant future, could at least be anticipated in the temporal domain.

Zarathushtra's new position as a *saoshyant* as understood in the post-Gathic Avesta as opposed to the Gathic sense, is amplified by a number of other titles given to him which serve to underline further his status. One of these, a priestly title, is that of *athravan*, and it comes from another text which is almost certainly composite, containing as it does elements from ancient pre-Zoroastrian religion – material verging on ancestor worship, since in many instances no distinction is made between "soul" and *fravashi* – which have been incorporated into this Zoroastrian hymn of praise. The *Farvardin Yasht* greets the prophet's birth with an air of expectant jubilation unsurpassed in any other text, and it also connects him, by the use of this title, to a class of priests from pre-Zoroastrian times, confirming the Iranian religious tradition's continuity whilst simultaneously setting the prophet above that priestly class. The texts recounts that "all the creatures of the good creation" welcome the prophet with these words:

> Hail to us! For he is born the Athravan Spitama Zarathushtra. Zarathushtra will offer us sacrifices with libations and bundles of *baresma* . . . (Yt.13:94)[12]

The passage effectively creates a super-*athravan* in Zarathushtra, and hints at his *saoshyant* role since because of him "the good Law of the worshippers of Mazda" will spread over the earth (see Yt.13:94), suggesting the implementation of the kingdom of God and confirming Zarathushtra as the first eschatological sign.

It is interesting to note that the *Farvardin Yasht* had evidently been completed *after* the legend of the lake had become established; in verse 62 we read how a *fravashi* will "watch over the seed of the holy Zarathushtra". We also learn (v.19) that the *saoshyants* who are to come have *fravashis* to protect them, so the eschatological content of this hymn is not inconsiderable; the fact that *fravashis* are appointed to ensure the success of the *saoshyants'* work demonstrates the importance that the concept had acquired.

## Resurrection, Judgement, Immortality

Just as he had connected the primal choice made by the two spirits and the human's choice to follow the path of *asha* or that of *drug*, Zarathushtra had also made a link between the judgement between good and evil that all who wish to become *ashavans* must exercise and the eventual (and final, as far as he was concerned) judgement that awaited them at the Bridge of the Account-keeper. But by the time the *Bundahishen* had received its final redaction, the finality of Zarathushtra's vision had given way to a much broader understanding of eschatology, and it prompted some modifications to the prophet's original message. One of the most significant changes that was required concerned the fate of the individual after death and the nature and consequences of the judgement he or she had received. Zarathushtra had implied that the trial by molten metal would result in either salvation – which in this context must mean enjoying the benefits of the world's "healing" which the *ashavan-saoshyants* would bring about – or destruction for the individual, depending on the accumulation of good or bad deeds. He had not indicated that there would be a final resurrection in which the living and the dead would be required to submit to a further judgement.

Dealing with the individual judgement first, the mythology that developed from this speaks of the individual soul being met at the Bridge of the Account-keeper by a maiden figure, the *daena*, a personification of "religious attitude", who was evidently retained from the pre-Zarathushtrian version of the myth. If the soul was one of virtue, having lived a good life, the *daena* would appear as a beautiful maiden to accompany it into the House of Song; if, on the other hand, the soul belonged to a person who had been wicked, the beautiful maiden would appear as or transform herself into an ugly hag, the bridge would shrink and the "soul", unable to remain on it, would fall into the House of Lies. This figure, either beautiful or ugly, is said by Zoroastrian commentators to be the personification or reflection of the person's own soul. It is not clear whether this formed part of the prophet's original teaching. The *Gathas* are ambiguous on the figure (and therefore the nature) of the maiden. The term itself is value-free. and has also been rendered as "conscience",[13] and so possibly has connections with the concept of free will, and thus with the "choice" of Y.30 which was discussed in chapter I. Possibly the prophet did intend to personify the human attribute of conscience or religious inclination in this way, although given the ethically neutral nature of the term this would not be representative of Zarathushtra's usual way of identifying *menog* personalities with abstract concepts. M. Boyce has drawn to our attention a suggestion that the word is used in two related ways (possibly denoted by two pronunciations), both deriving from the Avestan root *di-* to see, which may even denote two distinct *menog* beings. It this case, one would be the maiden at the bridge who "sees" the good or bad deeds the individual has committed, the other would be the religious spirit of the individual who has "seen" the truth of the religion proclaimed by the prophet. However, it is equally feasible that the maiden who meets the soul represents the conscience of the person presented for judgement.[14] *Daena* is a feminine noun, and although it has no aesthetic implications, it is almost certainly derived from the earlier myth in which it appeared as a representation or foretaste of the sexual fulfilment which would be one ingredient in the totally blissful existence awaiting the souls who were permitted to enter the House of Song. This is because in the earlier version of the myth the maiden would only greet the souls of *men* destined for heavenly reward; women, it would seem, were denied this passage into the afterlife.[15] It is all the more significant, then, that if the prophet did choose to retain this element of the myth, it underlines the importance he attached to the notion of individual judgement. It is also true, however, that if this is the case he must have rejected the myth's sexual associations, given that, as Y.46:10 suggests, the souls of women were also met by this maiden at the Bridge of the Separator.[16] Furthermore there is no suggestion in Zoroastrianism that the *daena* constitutes part of the reward for good behaviour.

The *daena* also figures in the later Avestan writings, and in such books as the *Vendidad* she appears, accompanied by dogs and finely dressed, to assist the fortunate souls destined for the House of Song, although her appearance as an ugly woman does not occur in this text. Instead, the dammed, in this account, are dragged down to the House of Lies by demons. Among the Pahlavi books, Chapter 21 of the *Dadistan i-Denig* ("Opinions on the Religion"), composed by the ninth-century priest Manuschir, provides a much more systematic if concise picture of individual judgement including the role of the maiden, but the eschatology of the Pahlavi texts is also considerably widened to enable a universal judgement to be incorporated into Zoroastrian teachings.

We have seen how at crucial stages in the world's history saviour figures will be born to once more preach the good religion and instil the Ahuric qualities in men and women. The role of the third and final *saoshyant*, however, will be somewhat different. Born fifty-seven years before the *frashokereti*, his task is to begin the resurrection of the dead in preparation for judgement and, for those who require it, cleansing. Those still living at this time will also be required to undergo a judgement.

As recounted in the *Bundahishen*, the final *saoshyant's* first act will be to raise *Gayomart*, the first man, who was slaughtered by Ahriman and from whose body plant and human life sprang. For the next fifty-seven years the souls all of humanity will be recalled from their places, and they will be reunited with their bodies. Whether they have been languishing in the agony of the House of Lies, or rejoicing in bliss of the House of Song, or merely existing in the Place of the Mixed Ones, they will be presented for a final judgement. At the judgement, which seems to be the concern of the *saoshyant*, since there is no mention yet of Ohrmazd's role in the apocalypse, "fire and the yazad *Airyaman* will melt the metal in the hills and mountains, and it will be upon the earth like a river" (GBd. 34:17). When people are made to pass through this metal as part of the universal judgement, the just will be unaffected by it, but to those who have lived wicked lives, those who have been in hell as well as those still alive during these last times, it will be purgative, and after this ordeal all people will "come together with the greatest affection". There is a marked shift towards leniency, then, in this doctrine from the Pahlavi books. There is here none of the Gathic final destruction of the evil-doer. The House of Lies, it seems, is now to relinquish its captives so that they might pay for their wrong doing in a most tortuous way, but only in order that they might be able to join their fellow humans in the perfection of the good dominion when Ohrmazd's creation will be restored. Perhaps here is a hint of the nature of that Ahuric perfection which must be total – that is, not one human must be lost when the restoration takes place, for if that happens the completeness of creation will also be lost. To effect this task, we are told that the *Saoshyant* will begin to perform a *Yasna* ceremony, as did Ohrmazd at the beginning of creation when, with his *Amahraspands*, he solemnized the ritual at noon and commissioned the *fravashis* as the final act in preparing the world for the battle with Ahriman (GBd 3:23f). Now, at the apocalypse, Ohrmazd will enter the arena and complete the *Yasna*.

So the Gathic and later eschatologies do have significant differences, particularly with respect to the fate of the wicked and the second judgement, which does not figure in the prophet's verses. The original teaching concerning the trial by molten metal has certainly been retained in that particular element, though its purpose has now changed. This conflict of eschatological detail M. Boyce explains by agreeing with J. H. Moulton that Zarathushtra was not bound to be consistent in his eschatological teachings, since eschatologies are by their nature inconsistent, and furthermore that Zarathushtra would have been quite capable of modifying his own teachings on this subject (as with any other) over his lifetime.[17] Boyce suggests in the same place that the later teaching also reflects the leniency of a more urbane age, but, given the Gathic evidence, it can be argued with equal conviction that this modification is a result of the eschatological horizon being much more distant than it was in Zarathushtra's time (a fact which must have become obvious quite soon after his death), rather than necessarily attributing it to a change in the prophet's eschatological outlook brought about by the failure of the apocalypse to materialize during his lifetime.

Parallel to this, the figure of Ahura Mazda, as we have seen, also underwent a change – that is, he was understood differently by the priest-poets of the later Avestan writings. But now, in the final stages of the world's history, he is able to reclaim his position, along with the Amesha Spentas, as the focal point for religious devotion. There is an almost visual technique which the *Bundahishen* employs to ensure Ohrmazd's rehabilitation.

The *Bundahishen* recounts that when the *saoshyant* begins his *Yasna*, he will slay the "Hayadans Bull" from whose fat, mingled with the "immortality-conferring" *hom* derived from the *haoma* plant, a preparation will be made and distributed to all humanity. The first animal to die, we will recall, was the Bull, when Ahriman began his assault on the good creation. This bull of this apocalyptic narrative will be the one who has to die so that all people can become immortal. The *hom* preparation will confer immortality on the bodies of men and women. The text then states that the Amahraspands will be set against the demonic heptad of Ahriman, and the demons will be defeated. Ahriman has yet to meet his downfall, even though his forces are now severely depleted. It is only now that Ohrmazd himself enters the scene. This is the most dramatic moment in the narrative, and it has been carefully prepared by the author. The psychological tension that had been created as the events of the apocalypse unfold is now resolved with Ohrmazd's appearance as the central actor in the drama. The text has paved the way for the moment that he finally "unveils" or reveals himself (the meaning of "apocalypse" derives from the Greek verb meaning *to reveal* or *unveil*) as a series of increasingly powerful figures – the *saoshyant*, the Amahraspands and Sroash, and finally Ohrmazd – is introduced into the narrative.

The passage detailing these events is worth reproducing here in its entirety for it gives some idea of the expansiveness of the scene that the writer is attempting to communicate:

> The Soshyant (*Saoshyant*) with his helpers will perform the *yasna* for restoring the dead. For that yasna they will slay the Hayadans bull; from the fat of that bull and the white haoma they will prepare ambrosia and give it to all mankind; and all men will become immortal for ever and ever . . . Ohrmazd will himself come into the world as celebrating priest, and the just Sroash as serving priest; and he will hold the sacred girdle in his hands. And at that Gathic liturgy the Evil Spirit, helpless and with his power destroyed, will rush back to shadowy darkness through the way which he had entered. And the molten metal will flow into hell; and the stench and filth in the earth, where hell was, will be burnt by that metal . . . and there will be Frashegird (*frashokereti*) in the world. (from GBd. 34)

With this final *Yasna*, Ahura Mazda/Ohrmazd, is now re-established. The other *menog* beings, their importance not denied, nevertheless defer to the Wise Lord. Mary Boyce has suggested[18] that the appearance of these two *Yasna* celebrations at the beginning and the end of human history ("limited time") formed part of Zarathushtra's original teaching, since the *Yasna* ritual was clearly of great importance to him. Though we have no suggestion of this in the *Gathas*, it is not impossible that, given his priestly identity, he would have envisioned *some* kind of liturgical framework within which history would be played out; if this is so he would presumably have anticipated the final *Yasna* as an event to occur in his lifetime. This being the case, we still must reiterate that Zarathushtra's original projection was greatly modified, either, as Boyce suggests, by the prophet himself, or by the later scholars, to accommodate the now deferred apocalypse.

As the narrative indicates, as a result of the final act of Ohrmazd, before the kingdom is brought about, the evil spirit and evil *as a concept* will be banished for ever into the depths of hell. There can be no place for it in Ohrmazd's renewed ordering of the world. The molten metal which had been the instrument of judgement now becomes the instrument of destruction. It had been used to purge evil from the hearts and minds (and *bodies*) of women and men; now it is used to remove evil from existence. Evil is removed entirely from this plane, and locked into the inner depths of the earth from where it can never again wield influence. The entrance to Hell is covered over with the metal, as if to ensure that there is no chance of even a reminder of the evil spirit's malignant power surfacing again.

There are two important points we must also recognize. First, that the *saoshyants* are not considered to be divine beings, and nor are they of the *menog* realm. Despite the fact that they are born miraculously, they are still creatures of the material creation. The co-operation of humanity has always been a fundamental tenet of the Zoroastrian teaching concerning the *frashokereti*. Secondly, the good dominion is to be established on the *physical* plane, though one free of Ahrimanic disfiguration. In Zoroastrianism the *getig* (material) is always superior to the *menog* (immaterial) for it is the latter endowed with the former, although it is recognized that the two states form two parts of the one ontological whole. The only way Ahriman can work his evil is on the superior *getig* plane. Because of this the *getig* is always in more jeopardy than the *menog*. Another text recounts how Ahriman, aware now of this, attempts to destroy all the immortality-conferring *haoma* in the world, since immortality itself can only be conferred in the physical realm:

> It is manifest that Ahraman (*sic*) speaks to the 'Divs' (*Daevas*) every night: go into the world; and first go to the sea and dry up the sea; and go to the white Hom and dry it up entirely, for they will revive the dead bodies of men thereby . . . [19]

Ahriman is clearly aware of the power of the *Yasna*. Deficient in creative power himself, he thus attempts to stifle Ohrmazd's; deficient also in a priesthood, he attempts to remove from the world the necessary equipment of the priesthood that honours Ahura Mazda, and in so doing prevent the resurrection of the dead.

But this can never be. The eschatological teaching of the Zoroastrian faith is one of hope, a hope which shades into the certainty of Ahura Mazda's triumph and in Ahriman's defeat. It is also one of profound morality and intimate co-operation, since its success depends on the concerted efforts of humans – the *ashavans* – to observe the threefold injunction of good thoughts, good words and good deeds. With this final event the limited time that Ohrmazd had set in the beginning[20] comes to an end, space and time are transfigured, and taken up into eternity. History is now over. The world and all creation has been renewed and freed from Ahriman's influence, and the new and endless age of the Separation (*wizarishen*) has begun.

I approach you with good thought, O Mazda Ahura, so that you may grant me (the blessings) of the two existences . . .

(Y.28:2)


May that man attain what is better than good, who could show us the straight paths of benefit of this material existence and that of thought, the true (paths) to the possessions where the Ahura dwells, the one such as you, zestful, bound (to us), and holy, O Ahura.

(Y.43:6)

# IV

# The Two Existences and the Problem of Evil

## 1 Menog and Getig

Just as Zarathushtra seemed unconcerned with the details of creation, so he leaves us little in the way of his ideas about the cosmos. Despite the fact that he makes two allusions in the *Gathas* to the immaterial and material realms of existence,[1] *menog* and *getig* (although these are not the terms he uses), it is not until the later Pahlavi writings that a more developed theological position on this matter is met.

Zoroastrian eschatology posits that the fullness of creation, which will be realized at the *frashokereti*, will be on the physical plane. This is certainly a vision original to the Iranian prophet himself and one which is maintained in the Pahlavi writings, though in its more elaborate form it is not without apparent contradictions. For example, we have seen that evil can only be defeated on the physical plane, and that Ohrmazd (Ahura Mazda) himself is unable to venture into the physical *getig* realm as such (which is why his manifestation through his attributes personified in the Amesha Spentas assumes such an importance, for it is in this way that he interacts with his creation). He has thus fashioned humanity as the pinnacle of his creation in order that the men and women who so choose – the *ashavans* – may act as Ahuric agents to bring about the ruin of evil and the end to Ahrimanic influence. Yet we also know that Ohrmazd will in fact enter the world to celebrate the final immortality-bestowing *Yasna* ritual. How Ohrmazd is able to enter the world in this way whilst Ahriman is still permitted to be active, and why, if he is so able, he did not do so earlier, is not explained. We may confidently categorize this particular passage (GBd. 34) as belonging to that typically hyperbolic style characteristic of the mythological imagery found in many eschatological writings, though this does not successfully explain away the apparent discrepancy as far as the *theology* is concerned. On the other hand a dramatic presentation of future events in such a graphic literary form, as a glance at, say, Christian scriptures demonstrates, is not always bound to be theologically consistent.

Simply put, Zoroastrianism recognizes two states or planes of existence: the *menog* (immaterial) and the *getig* (material). A derived nominative use of the terms denotes immaterial and material beings respectively.[2] The *getig* plane is that which we now inhabit; the *menog* plane is that inhabited by the spirit beings. Once again this is a generalization, since *menog* beings can (and do) inhabit the *getig* realm, and at times particularly significant figures (such as Zarathushtra himself) are said to be able to "see" *menog* beings. Staying with this general definition, however, we note that for both classes of being the present conditions within which they operate and exist is temporary, for at the end of time the good kingdom of Ahura Mazda will be established in the *getig* world, but it will be a purified and flawless world, free of Ahrimanic assault. The *getig* plane, as we know, was brought into being to provide the battleground where the fight between good and evil would occur, the idea being that Ahriman would be "tempted" out of the *menog* realm and into the *getig* where the physical army of Ahura Mazda – headed by the *ashavans* – could defeat him. This has the temporary drawback that the Wise Lord would be limited in his ability to operate in the cosmos. The limitation is self-imposed in that the Wise Lord permits the Evil Spirit to wield his influence in the *getig* sphere.

It has been suggested that a *menog*, or immaterial, creation can be understood as a prototypical *getig* creation and because of this attention has been drawn to a conceptual similarity between the Zoroastrian and the Platonic notions of "physical" and "spiritual" realms. Both Plato and Zarathushtra advocated a dualistic view of the universe, though their respective forms of dualism are only superficially related as we shall now discover. Plato taught that the things we perceive on this earth are imperfect "shadows" of perfect prototypes, or "Ideas", and that this is as true for abstract qualities as it is for the physical world. To explain this concept, Plato, in his *Republic*, uses the example of a bed which a craftsman constructs (*Republic* 596 ff). In constructing this bed, argues Plato, the craftsman is merely following the pattern of an "ideal" bed which exists on a metaphysical level, so that every bed which exists (and has existed, and will exist in the future) shares in the nature of the "ideal" bed, though without having the sum of its qualities. Thus J. J. Modi writes that "the Fravashis of the Avesta remind us . . . of the ideas of

Plato; . . . just as, according to the Avesta, the Earth has its Fravashi, according to Plato it has its Idea . . . ".[3] This is an initially useful but, as we shall shortly see, somewhat limited analogy, since a superimposition of Platonic thought onto Zoroastrian cosmic speculation suggests a common Graeco-Iranian metaphysical dualism in which the particulars (in Zoroastrianism the things of this *getig* realm, for Plato the earthly bed) share in the universals (in Zoroastrianism the things of the *menog* realm, or the Platonic "ideal" bed) but in an imperfect or incomplete manner. However this cannot be the case in Zoroastrianism which teaches that created things are essentially Ahuric (because Ahriman cannot create material things) and thus cannot be inherently imperfect since if they were it would imply that Ahura Mazda is also imperfect.[4] Things *do* participate in Ahura Mazda's essence in the sense that they are derived from it, but this participation is no more imperfect than Ahura Mazda's own temporary self-limitation which is itself a result of his creation of the *getig* realm, intended to lure Ahriman into a position where he will be destroyed. Imperfection on the part of *getig* creatures is not a result of any diminished or partial resemblance to an ideal *menog* form, but it is due to Ahrimanic attack. This can be (in the case of humans) something which is *chosen* and accepted (resulting in a turning away from the Ahuric life). In the case of non-human creations, it can be due to an appropriation by Ahriman of their matter (with which is linked the Zoroastrian insistence on stewardship of *all* creation which must be protected from the Ahrimanic assault). In addition to this, the ultimate expression of Ahrimanic activity is death itself, introduced with the slaughter of Gayomart, as recounted in the *Bundahishen*. In Zoroastrianism, unlike Platonism, there is an ethical struggle to make the *menog* accessible through the *getig* on the basis that the more good there is in a spatially and temporally finite world the less evil can reside there, whereas the Platonic view tends towards the eventual rejection of the *entirety* of the mundane, allowing the "ideal" world of forms to be realized and experienced in its totality. Plato illustrates this in his famous analogy of the cave (*Republic* 514 ff). In this cave, the only light is that cast by a fire, which causes shadows to dance about on the cave's walls. To the people who live in the cave, and who have never seen the "outside" world, these shadows are their only experience of reality; yet Plato argues that the flickering and unstable shadows that the cave's inhabitants see are merely unstable representations of the "ideal world" which they are unable to perceive. He does not deny that the shadows have reality, merely that they have durability, and so they must eventually make way for the ideal forms from which they borrow their existence. Zoroastrianism in contrast to this is progressively epiphanic since the manifestation of the *menog* in the *getig* is understood as a fulfillment of the former; thus the durability of the physical *getig* realm is essential to Zoroastrianism. It is, however, a gradual manifestation which will not be accomplished fully until the *frashokereti*. F. M. Kotwal and J. Boyd point out that it is thus wrong to think of the physical and the spiritual as different *in kind*[5] whereas this is the precise nature of the Platonic distinction, since for Plato the things of the mundane realm are substantial but ultimately transient and ever-changing shadows of the perfect, eternal and unchanging ideal forms. There is still a parallel, however, to draw between the two world views since both offer archetypal or exemplary forms from which the contingent beings proceed and upon which they depend, and it is hoped that the comparison might prove helpful in introducing Zoroastrian metaphysical dualism to those more familiar with western modes of thought.

The process of identifying ethical or religious characteristics with divinities does not necessarily presume that the latter were those first thought of, even by Zarathushtra, despite his adoption and modification of some of the characteristics belonging to certain figures of the Indo-Iranian pantheon. Since the entire language of Zoroastrianism, from the *Gathas* onwards, permits interpretation of these terms on at least two levels, it is feasible to suppose that Zarathushtra's recognition of the supreme importance of these qualities would lead him to suggest that they might owe their origins to "proto-qualities" (which is one reason why the Platonic comparison has been so compelling to many writers), and such a recognition is but a short step away from the personification of these qualities. And since Zarathushtra was preaching to a people accustomed to dealing with a multiplicity of divine beings, each with his or her demands and attributes, the theological structure was, as it were, merely waiting for the Iranian prophet to appear so that he might introduce into it an ethical component. Isolating individual qualities and attributing to them discreet personalities, whilst maintaining their union with the supreme godhead, was an invaluable way for Zarathushtra to inculcate into his intended followers the qualities that the good *menog* beings express, since by presenting them not merely as abstract qualities but as real beings they were accorded a means whereby they might be accessed, on both a ritual (public) and a private level. In other words the introduction of this ethical component implies some form of reciprocity, and this need could be met by acknowledging that the desirable qualities that an *ashavan* should strive to obtain are qualities emanating from the Lord of Wisdom, both as abstract concepts and as beings worthy of worship. Yet the fact that these qualities reside within human beings means that they also interact with the *getig* world but in a way dependent on it. This means that there are limitations imposed on the divine heptad itself since, though of the *menog* realm, it operates through the medium of the *getig*.

Although it is traditionally held that the material *getig* realm is superior to immaterial *menog*, since the former is the latter endowed with the added quality of physicality, *menog* is nevertheless pre-existent and therefore necessary whereas *getig* is (in this sense) derived and thus contingent. Furthermore *menog*, in its "eternal" form, requires no explanation or justification since, according to the texts, Ohrmazd and Ahriman, as archetypal *menog* entities, have always existed, whereas *getig* has not always existed and therefore does require explanation and justification. It is explained and justified by its created purpose which is that it is the means whereby the evil Ahrimanic influence might be defeated and destroyed. Yet *getig's* dependence on *menog* for its existence is balanced by the need that *menog* has for *getig* if evil is to be defeated. That is to say that evil, though present *conceptually* in the *menog* realm can only meet its defeat on the *getig* plane. But we know that evil *of itself* has no physical form, since Ahriman is unable to match Ohrmazd's material creation with one of his own. Unfortunately the texts throw up what might be seen to be a contradiction here, for the Pahlavi text *Dadistan i-Denig* suggests that certain *menog* creations are indeed Ahrimanic in concept. The text speaks of "scorpions, porcupines and vermin"[6] as being of Ahrimanic origin, and, in effect, doing Ahrimanic work. This being the case might not Zoroastrianism's pro-cosmic dualism lose some of its integrity since evil evidently resides within the *getig* realm as an essential constituent of creation, as well as outside it? These creatures are not merely susceptible to Ahrimanic influence, as is the case with humans, but they are *inherently* tainted. Yet Zoroastrianism states that evil cannot have corporeal form. This apparent paradox is resolved by saying that evil of itself does not assume corporeality, but merely "clothes" itself in a material substance which is in reality foreign to its essence. A. V. Williams has suggested that it might therefore be permissible to think of evil as an "anti-body", since "it has itself no physical, only a parasitic, destructive presence in the world".[7] Thus those creatures which are viewed as Ahrimanic in Zoroastrianism – frogs, scorpions, snakes and so on – are the "shells" in which evil walks upon the earth. In other words, Ahriman, as part of his assault upon creation, uses elements of that creation against the creator, but unlike the good creation which is manifestly Ahuric, cannot attain corporeality. It therefore becomes the religious duty of the devout Zoroastrian to destroy such creatures through which Ahriman manifests his evil plan, just as it is to resist the demonic forces which attack directly from the spiritual realm.

This does still not account satisfactorily for the presence of Ahriman in the world. Since, unlike Ohrmazd, he can have no corresponding *getig* or material form,[8] how can we with any certainty speak of a "mixture"? Is the implicit dualism of GBd.1:28 ("3,000 years, in the Mixture, will go according to the will of both Ohrmazd and Ahriman") not compromised since the "will of Ohrmazd" is clearly destined to prevail? Whereas, as we have seen, the *Bundahishen* recounts Ahuric and Ahrimanic *menog* creations paralleling each other, there is no Ahrimanic *getig* creation corresponding to that of Ohrmazd. We know that the Ahuric creation proceeded from the light of Ohrmazd himself, so his creation is in the most intimate sense derived from his essence. But there is no notion of Ahriman imparting his essence into a physical form, since we are merely told that he "shaped his creation from the substance of darkness".[9] S. Shaked has pointed out[10] that we have no indication of where this darkness received its substance, and it is clearly not sufficient to say that this darkness received its substance from Ahriman himself. But, given the emphasis placed on the "light" of the Ahuric creation, it seems likely that "substance of darkness" is another way of saying that there was no substance to the Ahrimanic creation, since light indicates a physical presence whereas darkness suggests a lack of it. Thus Ahriman's *menog* creations are not entities as such, but rather the reverse: where Ohrmazd produces, Ahriman merely provides a negative environment in which destruction and deprivation may occur in an invasive fashion. This, incidentally, also seems to be the position taken by Boyce in her remarks on the "twin spirits" passage of Y.30, in which she suggests that the "non-life" (*ajyati*) that the evil spirit created was a deprivation of something positive rather than a negative entity in itself which exists independently.[11] We will also remember the central position of fire in Zoroastrian spirituality, both in various texts which we have seen and in a liturgical context. Fire, which produces light, was a very real and very physical element to the world into which Zarathushtra came, and it has never lost its significance in Zoroastrian theological thought. There thus being no material from which Ahriman was able to fashion his own corresponding demonic creation, the only valid conclusion seems to be that he appropriates the Ahuric material creation and turns it into a vehicle for his own substance-lacking creation.

## 2  The Problem of Evil Creatures in the *Vendidad*

This foregoing being the case, how then do we explain the first chapter of the Avestan text called the *Vendidad*, in which Angra Mainyu performs counter-creations to Ahura Mazda's good creation of the various lands? It is, frankly, not an easy task to reconcile this passage with what we have just discussed. It might help if we were to examine briefly the nature and character of the *Vendidad*.

The *Vendidad*, which according to M. Boyce reached its final form during the Parthian period of Zoroastrian history (141 BCE–224 CE),[12] is principally a book of laws regulating certain practices of the Zoroastrian religion and particularly those concerning purity. This forms the bulk of the material and is the central section of the book. This "legal" section of this text is flanked by material of a more mythological nature, and additional passages on medicine. It is thus clearly a composite book since the outer sections do not always relate thematically to the central main section, though the second chapter recounts how the law was transmitted to humankind. The *Vendidad* is also incorporated into the official liturgical life of Zoroastrianism. Its preoccupation with purity would imply a need to expatiate upon the cause of impurity – Angra Mainyu – so the apparent discontinuity between certain sections of the text is perhaps explained by an editorial desire to contrast purity with impurity.

According to the *Vendidad* for each of the good lands – *getig* creations – fashioned by Ahura Mazda there is a work of evil created by the adversarial spirit. These works of evil may be a noxious creature (e.g. the "stained mosquito"), or a sinful attribute (e.g. "pride"), or what was understood by the compilers as a physical aberration (e.g. "abnormal issue in women", a reference to the menstrual cycle). That such disparate entities and characteristics are bundled together in the one chapter may give us some clue as to the nature of these Ahrimanic inventions, and how they may have been understood in the mind of the authors. Since the later *Bundahishen* makes it clear that Ahriman is incapable of *material* creation, but not that he is incapable of influencing the lives of men and women, such characteristics as "pride" can be understood as a rejection of the Ahuric path.

The same might be said of his manipulation of matter resulting in the "abnormal issue in women". But the *Vendidad* also clearly states that, for example, the serpent and the mosquito were created by Angra Mainyu. This is obviously not the same as that which we have just discussed whereby the Evil Spirit appropriates matter and cloaks himself in it.

The answer may lie in the recognition that Angra Mainyu, as he appears in much of this Avestan literature (with the notable exception of the *Gathas*) and the Pahlavi figure Ahriman are not in fact totally one and the same. This is the contention of S. Shaked, whose work on later Zoroastrian theological thought has led him to notice subtle (and not so subtle) differences between Avestan and Pahlavi texts. He notes that in certain Avestan texts Angra Mainyu is a creating divinity, as witnessed in the *Vendidad* (as well as Y.57:17). This differs from the picture of Ahriman gathered from the Pahlavi texts. We should not be disturbed by this gradual shift in emphasis, however. It was part of the process of the evolution towards eschatological monotheism, a process which would naturally involve diminishing the powers attributable to the Evil Spirit. Thus, as Shaked indicates, just as the *Bundahishen* can state that Ahriman creates his own creatures *in the form of* (for example) a frog, so it can be argued that, rather than create matter himself, he manipulates existing substance. This distinction illustrates the shift in emphasis from the later (post-Gathic) Avestan *creative* to the definitive Pahlavi *appropriative*. In the latter, Ahriman deprives a creation of its Ahuric characteristics by infecting it and manipulating it for his own evil ends. The *Bundahishen*, being a later text and the product of lengthy theological reflection, whilst it certainly contains material dating from centuries before its final redaction, can be viewed in this instance as the final statement on the Zoroastrian belief in the powers of the adversary as would be understood today. This development is consistent with the modifications we have so far seen taking place between the religious tradition inherited, transformed and promulgated by the prophet, and the theological notions propounded by what are regarded as the later parts of the so-called Younger Avesta and subsequent texts. It is in fact probable that Zarathushtra's understanding of the existence he called that of the "mind" – which we have learned to call *menog* – was at best a recognition of the entities and laudable attributes (Amesha Spentas) of his God, rather than a compressed allusion to the cosmology of the Pahlavi texts, which no doubt owes as much to external – particularly Babylonian – influence as it does to the prophet's own utterances.

It is stated elsewhere in the *Vendidad* that killing a noxious creature is in effect killing Angra Mainyu, but killing a good creature is (at least symbolically) killing Ahura Mazda. We must assume, however, that the latter is a reference to non-sacrificial animal slaughter. Even so, there can be no doubt that in killing a noxious Ahrimanic creature the power that the Evil Spirit is able to exercise over the Ahuric creation is lessened. Killing an Ahuric creature, on the other hand, increases Ahrimanic power since a struggle for space is being fought in the *getig* realm. The Zoroastrian tenet of eschatological monotheism, which we have touched upon at various points in the previous discussion, determines that, despite appearances to the contrary, Ahura Mazda's power, with the co-operation of the *ashavans*, is guaranteed to overcome that of Angra Mainyu/Ahriman. This of course is because the good *getig* creation – wholly Ahuric in origin according to the later tradition – is the means by which Ahriman and his army of evil *menog* beings meet their downfall, an outcome predicted and guaranteed in the *Bundahishen*.

As far as their own natures are concerned, Ahura Mazda (Ohrmazd) and Angra Mainyu are completely opposite to the extent that whereas it is appropriate to say that the former has life, it is more correct to say that the latter has "non-life" and that his "creations" are in fact "anti-creations" or deprivative incursions into the Ahuric. Thus although we can characterize Zoroastrianism as a dualism of sorts, this must be qualified since we cannot say that the religion recognizes two gods in Ahura Mazda and Angra Mainyu precisely because of the radical distinction in their natures. This distinction is confirmed textually. The term for "Lord", for example, is never applied to Ahriman (Angra Mainyu) in the Pahlavi books, and both the Avestan and Pahlavi languages have curious double vocabularies in which certain terms are inherently Ahuric and others inherently Ahrimanic. Even seemingly neutral terms like "leg" and "hand" have different words in Avestan, depending on whether they are used with reference to Ahuric or Ahrimanic entities.[13]

## 3 Eschatological Considerations: The Stages of History and the Human Journey

The evolution of creation towards the *frashokereti* can thus be formulated as a three-stage process, as follows: from (a) *menog* (Ahuric and Ahrimanic creations) into (b) *menog/getig* (Ahuric *menog* creations endowed with *getig* substance but with the capacity to be polluted by Ahrimanic *menog* influence – the *Mixture*) and thereafter to (c) *getig/menog* (Ahrimanic *menog* "creation" destroyed, Ahuric perfection restored in perfected *getig* creation endowed by *menog* – the *Separation*). It is the material or *getig* bodies of men and women, united with their souls, which will be given immortality at the final *Yasna*. The distinction between *menog* and *getig* is also seen here to be ethically neutral since denizens of both realms can be either Ahuric or Ahrimanic, though why they are so is due to different factors. Therefore, following on from this, *menog* must not be exclusively identified with the Ahuric and nor, of course, must *getig* be so identified with the Ahrimanic, despite the corruption it suffers. In fact such qualitative distinctions are foreign to Zoroastrianism generally. This is a natural consequence of Zoroastrianism's insistence that the material and the immaterial are not the totally separate conditions that some traditions assume them to be (though obviously characteristics of *getig* are not found in *menog*), but rather that *menog* finds its fulfillment in *getig*, and this is one of the main characteristics of the present limited time of Mixture which sees the emergence of *menog* not as a replacement of or substitute for *getig*, but as a gradual unification of two modes of what is ultimately destined to become one nature, and this will be accomplished at the eschatological event.

Just as Zarathushtra, especially in Y.30, drew a parallel between the struggle of good and evil which takes place in the individual and the cosmic struggle which takes place as it were "out there", by identifying abstract qualities possessed by humans (truth, piety, immortality and so on) with *menog* realities (the Amesha Spentas and other *menog* beings), so the three stages of history later came to be seen as embodied in the life of the individual, from birth until death and beyond. Birth is entry in to the *getig* state, in which material form is given to *menog* reality but in which the integrity of neither is surrendered, and nor does one subjugate the other since they are complementary. At death, when body and spirit are separated, the individual moves into a *menog* existence. At the general resurrection the *menog* individual returns to the *getig* state where once again it assumes corporeal form, and the two forms of existence are united indissolubly for eternity (having enjoyed the benefits of the *hom* preparation), but this new *getig/menog* state of existence is now experienced without the malign pull of Ahriman's influence. Death, once the mightiest of the Ahrimanic weapons, is defeated and in its place the bliss which comes with immortality is guaranteed.

(Tell us about) the gratification which you grant with (your) spirit and (your) fire and which you assign through truth . . .

(Y.31:3)

O Mazda Ahura, we desire your fire, strong through truth . . .

(Y.34:4)

To your fire, I will think the offering of reverence for truth as long as I am able.

(Y.43:9)

# V

# *Zoroastrianism and Fire*

## 1  Zoroastrianism in Exile

In the seventh century CE, as part of an extensive Islamic military campaign which included a policy of proselytization, the Arabian forces invaded Iran. Although it took three hundred years for Islam to become established as the country's dominant religion, life for Zoroastrians under the new rule grew increasingly difficult. The *Qur'an* stipulates that those who do not acknowledge Islam but yet are monotheistic – a "people of the book" – should be subjugated ("humbled") and made to pay taxes but not forcibly converted.[1] Technically speaking, Islam recognized only Christians and Jews (and probably Sabians) as "people of the book" (*dhimmis*) since these are mentioned in this context by the *Qur'an*,[2] and these were given the choices of death, conversion or payment of a heavy tax (*jizya*) in what was perhaps an over-enthusiastic interpretation of their own scriptural injunction. Zoroastrians were initially given the choice of death or conversion, since their status as a *dhimmis* people was not acknowledged. But when they were able to demonstrate that they too should be recognized as a "people of the book", they received a measure of toleration. However, they were still required to pay the onerous poll tax which was levied on all non-Muslims if they wanted the protection of the state, and were forbidden, along with other non-Muslims, to build places of worship. Many Zoroastrians converted to Islam, but many others refused to submit and faced economic or physical persecution and even death. Slavery was more often the option, and many Zoroastrians found themselves serving a Muslim household in this capacity. Conversion provided one way out of this situation too, but by the tenth century conditions had become crushing for a large proportion of the practising Zoroastrians in Iran, who saw no immediate solution to the injustice and intolerance to which they were being subjected. Even those who escaped physical harassment and worse were still required to pay heavy taxes to the many local rulers who had sprung up, and who now wielded an even fiercer power than before due to their independent status which may have enabled them more or less to create and implement their own laws regarding the non-Muslims within their sphere of jurisdiction. And so a small group of devout yet anxious Zoroastrians decided that it was time to seek a new home.

The story of the journey from Iran to India, where these Zoroastrians eventually found a society in which they could live and worship unthreatened (at least, for a while), is told in the epic narrative poem written by a priest in the seventeenth century, the *Qissa-i Sanjan* . This document was written some seven centuries after the period it describes; it also has a certain bias due to its authorship (and intended readership), and there have therefore been doubts expressed as to its reliability, though it is probably safe to say that it reflects the general train of events it claims to narrate. Sasanian rule in Iran, an empire rooted in Zoroastrianism, had come to an end in 651 CE when the reigning king, Yazdegird III, was overthrown and killed. Despite pressure from the new power, though, Zoroastrianism continued to be practised throughout the country. However the increased opposition from the Islamic rulers convinced one "learned Dastur" (senior priest), as the *Qissa-i Sanjan* puts it, to leave Iran, and so a small band, originating in the north-east of the country, left by sea in 917 CE, setting off from Hormuzd, a town in the south where the Persian Gulf meets the Arabian Sea. According to the *Qissa-i Sanjan*, this group of travelling Zoroastrians first landed on the island of Div, where they remained for nineteen years and where they learned the language of Gujarati. After this time, at the prompting of the same learned Dastur, they set sail again, but met with violent storms on the way. They made a promise to Ahura Mazda that, if their journey was successful, they would build a magnificent fire temple in thanksgiving for a safe arrival.

Sanjan was the name the emigrating Zoroastrians gave to the place where they landed in India in 936 CE, naming it after a town they had left behind in Iran. Upon arrival in Sanjan, in the Gujarat region of north- western India, they were allowed, by the tolerant Hindu ruler of the area, to retain their own religious faith and customs. A few conditions were imposed upon the new immigrants: they must assume the local traditions as far as dress and marriage regulations were concerned; they must not arm themselves and they must respect and not interfere with the lifestyles of their new hosts. This local prince, Jadi Rana, also requested that the new members of his region explain to him their religion, and we may assume that he found their explanation satisfactory since they were granted permission, under the previously mentioned conditions, to settle if they wished. Having met these conditions, and having been granted a plot of land, the band of Iranian exiles set about constructing a fire temple at Sanjan. The text recounts that ritual objects (*alat*) eventually arrived from Iran, having almost certainly been brought overland (since the tradition forbids the carrying of these sacred items over water) and so they had no difficulty in establishing a sacred fire.[3] Indeed, Jadi Rana was eager to make life as easy and convenient as possible for his new subjects, supplying them with all the materials that they required for establishing a familiar religious and social lifestyle, and it seems that the Zoroastrians were relatively untroubled for a number of generations.

Unfortunately for the Zoroastrians their new found peace and relative prosperity was eventually shattered. The Muslim armies finally reached India, and with this a new period of persecution was inaugurated. It was envisaged that Gujarat would come under the control of the Muslim sultanate which had been established at Delhi, and in 1297 Gujarat was forced to surrender to the power at Delhi. Many Hindus and Zoroastrians alike were slaughtered in the wake of the conquest. A new and severe tax was imposed on all non-Muslims, which once again served to encourage conversions to Islam, and this political climate continued for about 150 years. The Indian Zoroastrians – *Parsis*, as they came to be known – were not new to this kind of persecution, but in 1465 they joined with their Hindu neighbours in mounting a resistance to the Islamic conquerors. The sacred fire, which was the focal point of religious devotion and a visible sign of the Indian Zoroastrians' links with the land of their faith, Iran, was removed for safe keeping to a secluded location in the countryside, a place called Bahrot, where it remained for twelve years until more settled conditions permitted its return to a more populated area. The fire was then taken to a small town known as Banshda, which fell within the Sanjana Zoroastrian ecclesiastical jurisdiction. During this time it was reverenced and honoured as it had been when it was more publicly situated. Due to the upheaval that had taken place it was necessary that a new permanent home be found for the fire, and that would require sizeable funding. Two years were to pass before a new benefactor arrived on the scene, one this time from within the Zoroastrians' own fold.

According to the *Qissa-i Sanjan* money was forthcoming from a wealthy Zoroastrian layman called Changa Asa. Changa Asa was a philanthropist whose largesse was uninfluenced by the religious allegiances of those he saw to be in need, and it was he who provided the funds for building a fire temple in the town of Navsari. The fire that was enthroned in Navsari was kept burning until the eighteenth century, when it was translated to Udvada, a little further south along the western coast. (It was this Changa Asa who was also the inspiration behind the *Persian Rivayats*, a series of exchanges between Iranian and India-based Zoroastrians on theology, ritual and related matters.)

In the meantime of course some Zoroastrians had stayed in Iran, still subject to persecution but nevertheless fiercely clinging to what they considered their birthright. During this period, after the initial wave of Arab invasions had ceased and many Zoroastrians had fled to India, the Iranian Zoroastrians too were suffering persecution, but this time from the threat came from the east in the form of the Mongols who seized the caliphate at Baghdad in the thirteenth century and carried out the indiscriminate slaughter of men, women and children, Zoroastrian and Muslim alike. Some time in the later part of the thirteenth century a group of Zoroastrians retreated to the desert territories towards the central south of the country, setting up communities in places such as Yazd, where a strong Zoroastrian presence has been maintained to this day. We have, for example, the well-known report from the seventeenth-century French traveller and trader Chardin who writes that

> their principal temple is near Yazd . . . This is their greatest 'atesh-gah' (*fire temple*) . . . This place is also their oracle and academy. Their high pontiff lives there always, and without quitting it. He is called the 'dastur-dasturan' (*high priest*). The pontiff has with him several students, who form a kind of seminary. The Mahometans allow it, because it is inconspicuous, and generous presents are made to (their) officials.[4]

They were able to survive in such regions as this due to their relative inconspicuousness, and so, by exercising the discretion which had been forced upon them by circumstance they were able to keep the sacred fires burning in the land of the prophet, whilst their emigrant co-religionists were planting the seeds of the faith afresh in their new home.

## 2 Sacred Fires, Holy Places

It is significant that the first task of the Zoroastrians in their new land was to build a place where the sacred ritual fire, duly consecrated, could reside, and it is equally significant that in times of danger the fire should be taken to a place of safety. We have also seen that during the turbulent period when it appeared to the Gujarat Zoroastrians that their religious identity and freedom were once again about to be erased the fire continued to be visited and honoured. This total and absolute respect and concern for fire, and the intensity of devotion that fire instils, which is no better illustrated than in this brief survey of its life in the early centuries of Zoroastrians in India, is clearly attested in the *Gathas* but it can be traced back to before the time of the prophet. Before Zarathushtra's arrival it was recognized that fire's simultaneously destructive and beneficial properties required that it be propitiated at regular intervals; in these characteristics it resembled or reflected the personalities of many of the gods associated with the pre-Zoroastrian Iranian and Vedic pantheons who could be alternately creative, destructive, beneficial, malicious or merely capricious. But in his *Gathas*, despite the fact that Zarathushtra venerates *Atar* as a god associated with fire, he does not worship fire itself, since worship must mean, in this context, that quality of reverence and devotion due to Ahura Mazda alone.

It is therefore a common misconception that Zoroastrians are "fire-worshippers". This is a misguided notion that has been promulgated by a variety of observers, including the earlier Greek-speaking commentators and reporters such as Herodotus and Strabo, and it is one that is, unfortunately, maintained by many to this day. It is true that fire is honoured and reverenced, in much the same way that an altar is reverenced in many Christian churches, or icons and saints' relics are honoured and treated with special care. Fire is even "addressed" in certain Zoroastrian liturgical contexts, for it is a "sample" of the divine life of *asha*, the attribute of Ahura Mazda denoting righteousness and truth. It has a genuine sacramental quality since although it is not Ahura Mazda himself, it points the way to him and even participates in Ahura Mazda's life in an iconic fashion. But fire is not of itself thought of as "a god", as Herodotus once erroneously claimed, although it is true, as that same writer remarked, that Zoroastrian tradition strongly discourages the burning of dead bodies in cremation since, as we shall see later, fire must not be allowed to come into contact with corrupt and polluted matter.

We have already seen in this chapter the importance attributed to fire by the Zoroastrians whose attachment and devotion to it meant that they were unwilling to leave their homeland of Iran unless there was a guarantee that the sacred fire could be enthroned in their new home; and that the first thing they did in thanks to Ahura Mazda for his blessings and protection on their perilous journey was to establish a fire temple in which he could be ritually honoured and worshipped through the fire, and so one of their number was commissioned to go to Iran and bring the *alat* objects back to India. This fire at Udvada, which is uniquely known as the *Iranshah*, was, and still is, one of the most important fires that has been cherished by Zoroastrians throughout their history, and it is given the highest honour. Zoroastrians from other countries who visit India make a point of visiting this particular fire in order to pay their respects to it.

The highest grade or class of ritual fire, such as the one at Udvada, is called *Atash Bahram* ("victorious fire", so named after the deity of victory, Bahram, who offered protection to the pioneering Iranian Zoroastrians on their sea journey[5]), and this is also the name most commonly given to the temples in which it is housed. There are a number of these in Bombay as well as in other parts of India, and also, of course, in Iran.

This fire first and foremost denotes *asha*, righteousness. We have spoken already of the "enthronement" of the fire, and indeed such a fire is treated regally, a crown being placed above it in many of these temples. A fire such as this cannot merely be "lit". Chapter 8 in the ritual text of the *Vendidad* lays down specific instructions on how the fire should be established, stipulating that it requires the amalgamation of a number of other fires (now fixed at 16), including the fire from a "burning corpse" which, as J. C. Heesterman suggests, "has to be rescued from its tormented condition and made part of the cult fire that integrates all fires on the transcendent plane of absolute purity",[6] as well as such fires as that of a brick maker, a fire of a goldsmith, and a domestic fire.[7] Nor can such a fire, once created, ever be permitted to die, and the conscious act of extinguishing a consecrated fire is, in Zoroastrian understanding, a grave sin.

Devout Zoroastrians, recognizing its regal status and in imitation of the courteous and respectful behaviour towards earthly rulers, will never turn their backs on a sacred fire, and they will always ensure that it is kept free from anything that might pollute it, such as waste matter. In particular corpses are to be kept away from the fire, and specific measurements are given to ensure that there is no danger of the fire coming into contact with anything that might defile it. This is because one of the most powerful weapons that Angra Mainyu uses against the good creation of Ahura Mazda is impurity and his most powerful of all is death; we shall see in chapter VI that purity is the noblest condition to which a Zoroastrian can aspire, since death is the ultimate expression of impurity.

According to F. M. Kotwal and J. Boyd, the fire that burns in the Atash Bahram is "metaphysically linked to the fire that will purify all impurities at the end-time of the resurrection",[8] a mythological concept developed from the cathartic use of fire as suggested in such texts as the *Zamyad Yasht* (Yt.19), which speaks of *Atar*, a divinity of fire (invoked by Zarathushtra in the *Gathas*), battling with and overcoming the "three-mouthed" demon *Azi*. Thus in addition to fire being the sign of Ahura Mazda's personality-aspect of *asha* operating in this world it also has an eschatological dimension, offering a glimpse of the world to come which will follow the *frashokereti*. In this consecrated form, that is, within the sacred confines of the Atash Bahram and after the requisite ceremonies have been performed to sanctify it, the fire makes present the divine light of Ahura Mazda not only through a symbolic or signifying process but by virtue of its physical identity *as* fire, and so it is entitled to be addressed as the "son of Ahura Mazda". Once again it must be emphasized that this does not mean that it is offered that quality or category of worship due to Ahura Mazda alone. It does however mean that the divine characteristic of Ahura Mazda known as *asha* is made present in a particular way inside the area within where fire is housed, since fire is the ritual expression through which *asha* is made accessible as the exemplar of the Ahuric aspect it both represents symbolically and epiphanizes actually. Thus fire has multiple functions and meanings in Zoroastrian liturgy and theology.

As to the physical nature of the ritual fire, Kotwal and Boyd have also addressed the question of whether the "(ritually induced) unity of *menog* with *getig* (in the fire temple) . . . changes (the fire's) substance".[9] Noting that the subject is not given great attention in any relevant Zoroastrian text, the authors conclude from an analysis of Zoroastrian rituals that the fire is viewed as an animate being which deserves the respect due to all living creatures but that it maintains a *getig* form, rather than one in which *getig* and *menog* converge to the degree that the fire of itself becomes a recipient of the devotion reserved to a divine being of the highest order.

Other uses and treatments of fire, outside the confines of the temples, reinforce the sacred nature of fire to the Zoroastrian community. Fire is one of the chief ways by which the malign activity of Angra Mainyu is combated, since the hostile spirit operates most successfully and intensely on the physical plane. Thus a fire, which even of a "lower" grade is sufficiently Ahuric to have power against evil, is kept burning in any house where someone has recently died, in order to discourage demonic activity in the house. A small flame may be lit at the beginning of such activities as lectures (since the presence of the good *menog* beings is always invoked during Zoroastrian gatherings), or other non-liturgical pursuits – a constant reminder and recognition of the presence of *asha*.

In one sense, then, those brave but possibly frightened Iranians who journeyed to India and established their sacred fire on the shores of Gujerat were doing nothing unusual in directing their initial efforts towards this task for, just as a devout Christian making a journey would ensure the availability of a Bible or other devotional objects, so the sincere Zoroastrian would not want to be far, whenever possible, from a ritually consecrated fire. And in the western world, where fire temples cannot be constructed, the devout Zoroastrian will make petitions and offerings to Ahura Mazda and the other divine beings in the presence of fire either in the home or in one of the many buildings which Zoroastrians have established there for social, educational and liturgical meetings. But it is the fires that burn constantly in the great fire temples of India and Iran that possess the most power, and it is only in these temples, the Courts of Mithra, in the presence of this fire, that the most powerful and intricate ceremonies may be held.[10]

In reverence for him, with hands out-stretched at first I entreat (you) all, O Mazda . . .

(Y.28:1)

The healer of existence, the knowing one who conceives truth, has listened (to your teachings). At will he is in control of his tongue for the correct uttering of the words, at the distribution of the balances in the good (way) with your red fire, O Mazda Ahura

(Y.31:19)

I shall declare myself your praiser, O Mazda, and I will remain so for as long as I can and am able through truth.

(Y.50:11)

# VI

# A Living Faith – Zoroastrian Worship, Rituals and Other Observances

## 1 The *Yasna*, an "Inner" Ceremony

The rich and complex *Yasna* ceremony is the highest of the Zoroastrian liturgies, one of three major "inner" ceremonies that have much in common, the other two being the *Visperad* and the *Vendidad*. We shall examine only the first of these three in any detail, in order to get the flavour of the higher rituals of Zoroastrianism. A *Yasna* is traditionally celebrated in honour of a specified deity, though the veneration and praise is directed towards all the prescribed *menog* beings, most important of which is Ahura Mazda himself, who join the ceremony at the "invitation" of the celebrant.

The *Yasna*, which consists of 72 chapters of text, can only be performed in the morning, when the sun is rising, since this is said to represent the fire of *asha* scattering light and heat over creation, dispelling the darkness of the Ahrimanic forces and instilling truth and righteousness over the world. It is an "inner" ceremony, which only Zoroastrians may attend, and is only celebrated in the Iranian and Indian fire temples by suitably qualified and ritually purified priests. The entire 72 chapters of the *Yasna* are recited from memory, and the actions that make up the ritual are performed without reference to a liturgical book. The *Yasna* takes two and a half hours to celebrate, much of which is taken up with reciting these texts, which include the *Gathas* of the prophet, in the Avestan tongue.[1] The ceremony takes place within a sanctuary, the *pawi*, often one of many such sanctuaries inside the Fire Temple, and only ritually purified priests may enter the *pawi*. This rectangular sanctuary is demarcated by furrows, also called *pawi*. The two priests required for this service are generally known as the *zot* (the main celebrant) and *raspi* (his assistant). The purpose of the *Yasna* is to purify the world (the chief celebrant is also known by the Avestan term *yazdathragar*, or the "one who purifies creation"), to strengthen the bond between the *getig* and *menog* realms by creating an environment within which they might form a unity, and to give praise and glory to Ahura Mazda and his good *menog* beings. As a consequence of this, the Ahrimanic forces are weakened and the Good Dominion (*khshathra*) can gradually increase. Thus the *Yasna* is a ceremony replete with eschatological meaning and potential.

The *pawi* is set out in a prescribed manner, with the consecrated fire in its silver vase (the *afargan*) elevated on a marble table (*afarganyu*) at the south end of the sanctuary, where it is constantly attended by the *raspi*. At the north is a stool from where the *zot*, at specified intervals, presides over the ceremony, and immediately to the *zot's* south is a table (*alat-khwan*) upon which are laid many of the ritual instruments and requisite substances, including a cup containing a presanctified libation known as *parahom* (prepared by the *raspi* in a prior ceremony called the *paragna* or "pre-worship"), a cup of libation water, a cup containing bull's hair, a saucer of goat's milk and a saucer with *hom* (*haoma*) and pomegranate twigs in it. There is also a portion of consecrated bread (*dron*) with clarified butter (*ghee*), which will be consumed by the *zot* as part of the ceremony. Also on this table are a bundle of twenty-one metal *barsom* wires[2] which will be tied together with a date-palm cord. To his right, as he faces south, is a round metal basin containing a pestle, a sieve-like saucer and some additional cups.

Water also plays an important role in the *Yasna* ceremony. Every fire temple is provided with a well from which the water is drawn, and this is used in purifying the ritual objects and the priests themselves. Respect is also paid to water in much the same way as the ritual fire, with offerings being made to it and appropriate prayers directed towards it. One of the benefits of the *Yasna* is good physical health, signified here by the water which in creation is presided over by the Bountiful Immortal Haurvatat (the Amesha Spenta denoting wholeness and health).

The *Yasna* is an exclusively priestly activity, and neither requires nor permits any participation from the Zoroastrian laity, though lay members of the community may attend and witness the ceremony from an area outside the *pawi*. The ceremony begins as the *zot* enters the *pawi* (the *raspi* having performed some preliminary purifying rituals) and recites the *ashem vohu* prayer, "righteousness is good (for the pleasure of Ahura Mazda)", and the two priests each place a face mask (*padan*) over their mouths and noses. This prevents any defilement from their saliva and breath infecting the purified (*alat*) objects. It also creates an impression of anonymity and presents us with a dramatic image of, as R. Williams and J. Boyd have remarked, "a being who sees but does not speak".[3] This anonymity is appropriate in view of the fact that the priest both represents Ahura Mazda, and, without losing his own human priestly identity, "brings upon himself and the *getig* world the manifest, bounteous and righteous spirit of God"[4] in the *Yasna*; in this way his own personality becomes subsumed into that of the Wise Lord (but without that sense of self-abandonment which often traditionally accompanies mystical experience). Other impurities, both physical and spiritual, are prevented from entering the sacred area by the furrows which surround the sanctuary. To cite once again Williams and Boyd, these furrows suggest "invisible walls" which "constitute a volume rather than a plane",[5] in effect enclosing the priests not only horizontally but also vertically, visually registering the *pawi* as an exclusive and privileged area in which *menog* and *getig* may unite. The fire is then honoured with incense, the first of many such acts of veneration.

As the service proceeds, the two priests will chant the Avestan texts, paying attention not so much to their meaning as to their correct pronunciation,[6] since the words are believed to be inherently sacred and are "no longer bounded by the conceptual distinctions predetermining ordinary experience".[7] A portion of the consecrated bread with the *ghee* is consumed, as is the *parahom*, the libation prepared in the earlier ceremony by the *raspi*. After this the *fravarane*, or "creed" is recited. Then the date-palm cord with the *barsom* wires is introduced into a mixture of goat's milk and the consecrated water. The water represents the presence of the Amesha Spenta Hauvartat in the *Yasna* and thus signifies health, and the milk, a dairy product, is the presence of Vohu Manah, the Good Mind, protector of the animal kingdom. The *hom* twigs and the pomegranate leaves, mixed with consecrated water (essentially the ingredients of the presanctified *parahom*), are pounded with the pestle, the milk is added to this and the resultant mixture, as a final act, is taken to a special well outside the *pawi* and poured out to the whole of creation to strengthen it. In fact so important is this section of the ritual, the final act of the *Yasna*, that some of the preparation is held back in the sanctuary in case, as it is taken from the *pawi* to the well, there is spillage or some other accident. After the *hom* has been poured successfully into the well, from where it will flow out into the world, the residue is then offered to the "patrons" of the *Yasna*, that is, those who have commissioned the priests to perform the ceremony for a special intention or purpose, and it may be also offered to any other observers who have attended the celebration.[8] This small rite is called *chashni*. A final prayer is offered to the ritual fire, and the *Yasna* comes to an end.

An essential prerequisite for a successful celebration of the *Yasna* is purity of mind and body. The celebrants' theological orthodoxy, though presumed, is not prescribed, whereas a priest cannot approach the *menog* realm within the confines of the *pawi* without first preparing himself mentally and undertaking specific rituals to ensure that he, and the sacred place where he will celebrate his liturgy, are free from Ahrimanic defilement. In practice this means that in order for a priest to celebrate successfully and correctly any liturgy he should be in a state of both moral and physical purity, but it is the latter which seems to be the basic requirement if the liturgy is to be efficacious at all, for if a priest has an imperfect moral intention but is physically clean "the *yazads* and *amahraspands* will listen to him ... but they will not come down and be one with him in the ceremony"; if, however, he is physically unclean "the ceremony is vitiated altogether",[9] since Ahriman is able to use even the smallest amount of impure or unclean matter for his destructive purposes and thus the absolute purity required for the ritual's success is potentially destroyed. So an inadequate moral or mental preparation guarantees at the very least that the good *menog* beings will recognize the performance of the *Yasna*, even though its celebration is unlikely to have any beneficial effects, but a priest who is in a state of physical impurity might just as well not be celebrating the holy liturgy at all, since it will have no meaning, purpose or result. This applies equally to the *pawi*, which should be ritually prepared before the *Yasna* is celebrated.

To this end, each *Yasna* is prefaced by a shorter service we have already touched on, the *paragna*, in which the ritual objects and other materials are made ritually pure, and in which the milk is obtained from a goat, and the *parahom* prepared for use in the *Yasna* proper, and it is the responsibility of the *raspi* to carry out these duties. However, continued exposure to the *menog* realm in the daily celebration of the *Yasna* is itself a powerful instrument in maintaining a state of purity, so in Zoroastrian understanding ritual not only requires purity but also simultaneously creates the conditions within which it becomes a possibility.

As W. Darrow has written, the Zoroastrian priesthood is adamant that without the *Yasna*, "the world would collapse".[10] What this means in effect is that the link between the *menog* and *getig* realms will be severed, the world will degenerate into irretrievable chaos and the

Ahrimanic forces will gain complete control, preventing the *frashokereti* from ever happening. It is therefore a great responsibility to maintain the daily celebration of the *Yasna*. The *zot* and *raspi*, if they are attentive to their duties, and lead pure and godly lives, will reflect this not only by their flawless performance of the *Yasna* ceremony (and other rituals) but also by their physical appearance. Dastur Kotwal has remarked that a good priest possessing ritual purity and power (*'amal*) "has glory on his face".[11] It is not, though, the priest's own glory of itself which is displayed, but that of Ahura Mazda and the good denizens of the *menog* realm, who are indescribably and unfailingly glorious and pure, and yet in whose life the priest participates and whose perfection shines through him. The devout priest visibly prefigures the bliss of the *frashokereti* by the radiance of this reflected glory since through it the perfected fusion of *menog* and *getig* which will characterize the *wizar-ishen*, when all created things will have been made pure, can be glimpsed in the present age.

Yet despite the sense of prolepsis or merely "resemblance" that this may suggest, the *Yasna* is not primarily an eschatological metaphor but a self-contained ritual *sui generis*. The *pawi* is an imitation of neither the cosmogonic nor the eschatological arena, but a meeting point of *menog* and *getig* in its own right. Metaphor, as P. Ricoeur has pointed out, signifies both "is not" and "is like", but there is no such ontological ambivalence in the Zoroastrian *Yasna*. Ricoeur continues to say that we are permitted to speak of a "metaphorical truth", but "in an equally tensive sense of the word *truth*".[12] That Zarathushtra's *Gathas* abound with metaphor is a fact, but the incorporation of such metaphorical literature into the *Yasna*, its transmission of truth notwithstanding, should not be understood as implying an overriding metaphorical dimension to the ritual itself. Equally, as Kotwal and Boyd assert in relation to the *paragna*, although there is undoubtedly a symbolism in the ritual, the temptation to interpret the ritual solely or primarily in terms of its symbology should be resisted since it will lead to a unbalanced understanding of its design and nature, which is its faithful enactment *as a ritual*, and it is this which should be the main focus of any enquiry into the *Yasna*. "A defensible hermeneutic demands an understanding of rituals on their own terms", claim Kotwal and Boyd,[13] so rather than ascribe symbolic meanings to objects and actions which properly function only within their ritual context, we should avoid the danger of interpreting ritual in theological, ethical or philosophical terms, or seeing ritual objects and actions as physical representations of metaphysical realities. Ritual for the majority of Zoroastrians is an independent and unique source of religious insight and experience, and not an adjunct to theology. As Williams and Boyd note, "just as art is not a decorative addition to ritual, so ritual is not a decorative addition to religious belief and practice".[14] Of course it is recognized that ritual cannot have meaning unless it is related to a doctrinal core. At the same time however, ritual neither interprets nor supports theology nor does it lend itself to that investigative process which is the province of theological speculation. Theology deconstructs and reassembles in its attempts to make sense of creation, but it cannot compress into two and a half hours the experience of *being* a Zoroastrian. It is only from a sincere and faultless performance of the *Yasna* ceremony carried out under the prescribed conditions of purity that all its associated benefits can flow, including, for the devout practitioner, advancement along the path of *asha*.

The two other ceremonies, the *Vendidad* and the *Visperad*, which incorporate other textual material into the *Yasna* chapters, date from a later period than the final formulation of the *Yasna* itself. The *Vendidad* ritual consists of a number of texts from the book of the same name and it is essentially a nocturnal celebration of the *Yasna* with the later material added. The *Visperad* is similarly the *Yasna* plus the *Vendidad* material plus yet more Avestan material. Both these celebrations, as with the *Yasna*, are preceded by the purificatory *paragna* ceremony.

## 2 The *Afrinagan*, an "Outer" Ceremony[15]

Not all ceremonies are restricted to a Zoroastrian audience (the term "congregation" has too many associations with lay participation to be appropriate).[16] One of the main "outer" ceremonies, which may be performed in any suitable clean place (such as a house), and which may be witnessed by Zoroastrians and non-Zoroastrians[17] alike, is the *Afrinagan*, a term derived from the Avestan *fri-*, meaning "to praise" or "to bless". Indeed the *Afrinagan* is a liturgy celebrating the abundant blessings that Ahura Mazda bestows upon the world and praising him for his bounty. Fruit, wine, milk, eggs, flowers and water all form part of the ritual, as well as the ever-present fire. It is usually performed by two priests, *zot* and *raspi*, but suitably qualified laity are also permitted to conduct this ceremony. There is no preparatory ritual or *paragna* to the *Afrinagan*, but the officiants ritually wash and dress themselves in the appropriate vestments whilst reciting prescribed prayers.

The area in which the *Afrinagan* is to be performed consists of a large white cloth placed over a rug on the floor, and the priests sit at opposite ends, with the fire vase between them, the main celebrant facing east. In front of the *zot* there are trays containing fruit, eggs, three cups of wine, water and milk, other offerings and eight flowers. Twenty-four flowers are used in all, so 16 are set aside on another tray for use during the liturgy. The *raspi* must attend the fire at regular intervals, ensuring that it is kept burning by feeding it with sticks of sandalwood which are laid on a tray to his right.

The most striking visual and symbolic action in the ritual (which is a short ceremony of no more than half an hour) is the triple exchange of flowers accompanied by chants from the Avestan scriptures. At regular intervals three sets of eight flowers will be exchanged between the *zot* and the *raspi*; the flowers are said to represent different *menog* beings, and indeed in former times different flowers were ascribed to the various *yazatas* – beings worthy of worship – honoured in the ceremony. J. J. Modi writes that the flower exchanges also symbolize "the exchange of lives between this world and the next", in a visual representation of birth and death. Since the *raspi* stands in different positions according to which set of flowers are exchanged, this demonstrates the soul's relocation into the *menog* realm after death.[18]

As well as taking part in the exchange of flowers the *raspi* must also attend to the fire. He must do this at prescribed times, during the recitation of specific prayers, but he will also need to make additional offerings of sandalwood if it appears that the fire is to burn out, though this is highly unlikely. Since this is a liturgy which can be performed outside of the *pawi*, it is not unusual, as the *Afrinagan* ritual proceeds, for members of the laity to approach the ritual area with gifts of sandalwood which will be accepted by the *raspi* and offered to the fire.

After the three cycles of flower exchanges and fire offerings have been performed, the *Afrinagan* is brought to a conclusion by three sets of benedictions, to the holy guardian spirits, to the ancestors in the faith and to the Amesha Spentas. This is followed by four shorter prayers which mark the officiants' departure from the liturgical space.

The *Afrinagan*, as with all Zoroastrian ritual, serves primarily to strengthen and maintain the connection between the two created worlds, the *menog* and the *getig*. It is also a request for the blessings of the Wise Lord to be conferred on members of the community, living or departed, or on the larger community of the faithful. As with a *Yasna*, its performance will be sponsored, the benefits of the ritual often accruing first to the sponsor, though always with blessings for the community in mind. These blessings are symbolized chiefly in the food and drink that play such an important visual role in the liturgical apparatus of the *Afrinagan*. These articles are not merely decorative, but the outward signs of Ahura Mazda's generosity and care for the well-being of his people.

The *Afrinagan* can be celebrated as a single ceremony on its own, or it can form part of a larger cycle of celebrations known collectively as *Jashan* (a word derived, as with *Yasna*, from the root *yaz-*, to worship or sacrifice). In this case, a *Yasna* may also be celebrated as part of the cycle, but the *Afrinagan* is indispensable to the overall ritual combination, and may even constitute the *Jashan* by itself if no other rituals are to be performed. Thus the *Afrinagan* is not necessarily restricted to the fire temples of Iran and India.

## 3  Birth and Early Infancy

Birth seems to evoke an ambivalent reaction in Zoroastrianism, since on the one hand it is meritorious to bring a new person into the world to fight against the Ahrimanic forces and the *Vendidad* states that Ahura Mazda is said to be more pleased with a person who has children than with one who is childless.[19] Yet on the other hand a considerable amount of blood is lost at childbirth and thus it is seen to be a cause of impurity. There are a number of rituals to deal with this second matter, but no specific rituals accompany pregnancy itself, and the Avesta is silent on the subject other than to recommend practicalities such as the husband's maintaining a distance from his wife in most marital matters and she guarding herself against the threat of pollution.

After the fifth month of pregnancy has passed it is customary to hold a day of thanksgiving in which a lamp is lit in the expectant mother's house, but this is not always observed and in any case it seems to be a more social than religious tradition today. No prescribed format accommodates the procedure. The same custom may be observed following the seventh month, and following a successful delivery the lamp is lit again and kept burning for three days, ostensibly to guard against demonic forces which may try to attack child and mother.

Following the birth, it is traditional to keep the new mother, with her baby, in confinement for a period of forty days – sufficient, it is thought, to allow the impurities she has contacted to disappear.[20] Included in the prohibitions associated with this period of solitude was one forbidding the woman to leave her house, but city life has made rigorous adherence to these practices impossible, particularly for Parsis in such places as

Bombay as well as in the west. A compromise has therefore been reached whereby the new mother will eat separately from the rest of the family, and all those who do come into contact with her – including her gynaecologist and other medics, if they are Zoroastrians (which is often the case) – must undertake simple purification rites after each period of contact. After the forty days she takes a ritual bath which allows her to rejoin the community at large. Formerly this bath would be consecrated by a priest but this practice is not so common now as then, though strictly orthodox families, despite their living in the large cities, will observe the spirit of the law as far as possible when circumstances prevent the letter from being fulfilled. Finally, the clothing and bedding used by the mother during her confinement should be destroyed, but Modi reports that in this present century "that injunction is not strictly followed" and that the unwanted items are sometimes "given away to sweepers".[21]

One practice which is encouraged is that of giving the new baby a strengthening drink, and wherever possible this should be the residue of the consecrated *hom* preparation from a *Yasna* celebration. It is not always possible to obtain this and in that case the parents are recommended to make a drink using *hom* twigs and pomegranate leaves mixed with water which should then be given to the baby. The first birthday of the infant is an important occasion for the Zoroastrian family, and although there are no rules governing its celebration, one of the more commonly observed customs, for those who can do so, is to present the child at a nearby Atash Bahram for ashes from the ritual fire to be sprinkled on its forehead.

## 4 Initiation – the *Navjote* Ceremony

During the first few years of a Zoroastrian child's life, there is little in the way of ritual that will apply to him or her. Some of the simpler prayers will be taught, and attendance at such liturgies as the *Afrinagan* may be encouraged, but there are no specific religious duties which the child must perform beyond the recommended prayers. In fact Zoroastrianism, in common with many other religious traditions, does not recognize a child as being capable of making any informed decisions until the age of seven, and thus she or he is incapable of "sin" until that age.

Upon reaching the age of seven, then, the child is deemed to be sufficiently responsible to be admitted to the Zoroastrian fold by a ritual known as the *Navjote*. In cases where children, for whatever reason, have not developed sufficiently to be able to recognize the implications of the ceremony, it is recommended that it is deferred to a later time, and the *Navjote* may be performed on initiates up to the age of fifteen, and in extreme cases on adults.[22] In Iran the ceremony is rarely performed on a child of less than eleven. Modi likens the ceremony to the Christian sacrament of Confirmation,[23] and indeed it does convey an impression of affirmation and fortification.

The main purpose of the *Navjote* is affirmation of the candidate's belief in the Zoroastrian religion accompanied by the investiture with the sacred garment and sacred cord, and it is these two items which give the ceremony its name. The *Sudre* is a thin white garment worn under the outer clothing, and for orthodox Zoroastrians once donned it is kept on constantly other than in circumstances such as bathing. Its colour represents purity and innocence. The *Kushti*, or sacred cord, which should be made of wool, consists of 72 threads, in imitation of the 72 chapters of the *Yasna*. Once again this is worn at all times except during such circumstances as already mentioned in relation to the *Sudre*. It wraps around the body three times as a reminder of the Zoroastrian ethical injunction of good thoughts, good words and good deeds.[24]

Each child presented for the *Navjote* will have spent some time learning some of the main Zoroastrian prayers in Avestan, which he or she will be expected to recite with the priest during the ceremony, in the presence not only of family and friends, but also the sacred fire. Before the ceremony begins she or he will have taken a purifying ritual bath known as the *Nahn*. The initiate will also have to make a profession of faith publicly, and as part of the rite will be dressed in a new set of clothes including, for the first time, the *Sudre* and *Kushti* which should have been specially made for the occasion. The priest will bless the new Zoroastrian and sprinkle rice on the candidate's head; afterwards, family and friends will gather together for a party and meal. Attendance at a *Navjote* ceremony is open to anyone, Zoroastrian or otherwise. During the ceremony itself it is not unusual to see guests coming and going, walking around and taking photographs, and quite often there will be considerably more people at the meal than at the religious ceremony itself. This is not irreverent behaviour, though, but merely an expression of the "normality" of religion in everyday life, a feature more characteristic of eastern than western traditions. The many presents given to the child on this occasion will not necessarily be "religious" items, and will more often than not consist of gifts of money.

Throughout life thereafter the Zoroastrian treasures his or her *Sudre* and *Kushti*. Five times a day a small ritual will be enacted whereby the Zoroastrian unties and reties the *Kushti*, reciting prescribed prayers.

## 5 Initiation and Vocation – The Zoroastrian Priesthood

Initiation into the Zoroastrian priesthood, to which only the male members of priestly families are admitted, is a lengthy process. There are two principal grades of priestly initiation, the *Navar*, which enables the priest to perform "lesser" ceremonies and the *Martab* which equips him for the higher or inner ceremonies such as the *Yasna*.

The procedure for becoming a priest as practised today is almost certainly substantially that undergone by Zarathushtra himself when he assumed the priestly role and functioned as a *zaotar* for his community. Now as then preparation starts at an early age, with the memory of extensive ritual texts and accompanying ritual action and gesture being paramount and treated as the priority. The two grades demand lengthy preparation, both academic and spiritual. In addition to the ritual requirements which the would-be priest must learn, there is also training given in languages (mainly Avestan and Pahlavi), theology, history, and, since the priest's life in the training school, or *madressa*, begins so early, his general schooling will often also be conducted there.[25] However, many of the boys and men who go through the *madressa* system do not take up the priestly occupation full time, but go on to further education and other vocational pursuits, content to don the priestly attire as and when needed rather than making the priesthood their only profession. A few scholar-priests have devoted their lives to the research and production of academic material relating to the religion.

A stringent purification rite, called the *Barashnum i-no shab*, must be undertaken before the ordinand is admitted to the priestly order; this ritual, itself an intricate and time-consuming process, will also be observed at other times through the priest's life. The candidate for the priesthood undergoes it twice before his first *Navar* ordination, and once again before the *Martab*. In fact the *Barashnum i-no shab* was, in earlier times, considered a necessary ritual for *all* Zoroastrians, but its complex nature and the length of time it takes to complete has meant that more recently its regular observance has become almost totally confined to members of the priesthood. Even so, devout orthodox Zoroastrians will generally want to undergo the rite at least once during their lifetime. The details of the ritual itself will be discussed later in this chapter.

Priestly activity is almost entirely dedicated to ritual. Indeed to equate the Zoroastrian priesthood with any western "equivalent" is seriously misleading. There is no "pastoral" work as such undertaken by the Zoroastrian clergy, particularly in such matters as regularly visiting the sick, since the threat to priestly purity in such situations would be too great.[26]

As far as priestly titles are concerned, we should be aware of the following. A man who has proceeded to the first grade of priesthood is known as an *Ervad*. This priest is entitled to perform certain of the "lesser" ceremonies but not generally qualified to perform "higher" or inner ceremonies such as the *Yasna*. The second grade of priest is called *Mobed,* and this priest may perform the inner as well as outer ceremonies. Admission to the second grade requires further purification rituals including a repeated *Barashnum i-no shab*. The title of *Dastur*, as already noted, is conferred upon priests who have excelled in learning or administrative duties, and have proved themselves to be of deep spirituality. This is an honorary title, however, and does not imply additional qualifications as far as liturgical functions are concerned. There are also titles which apply solely to liturgical functions. Two of these we have seen already, being *zot* (or *zaotar*) and *raspi*, the two priests who together perform the *Yasna* ceremony. The *Nirangastan*, an Avestan text concerning priestly rituals (which is generally coupled with the *Herbadestan,* another text concerning the priesthood and its organization and functions), lists a total of eight priests required for the *Yasna* ceremony, with their functions. They are as follows:

*Zaotar*: the leading priest who chants the *Gathas*.
*Havanan*: the priest who prepares the *haoma*.
*Atarvakhsh*: the priest who tends the ritual fire
*Fraberetar*: the priest who presents the offerings, such as the wood for the fire.
*Anstar*: the priest who strains and washes the *haoma*.
*Rathvishkara*: the priest who mixes the milk and the *haoma*.
*Aberet*: the priest who brings the water (the function which the prophet may have been carrying out when he first met with Vohu Manah).
*Shroashavarez*: the priest who oversees the ritual.[27]

According to this text, the *zot* recited the *Gathas* whilst the seven subordinate priests performed various other functions now shared between the *zot* and *raspi*. Although today the personnel is greatly reduced, the ceremony is evidently much the same to judge by the functions of these seven assistant priests.

Finally, perhaps mention should be made at this point of the thesis proposed by the contemporary scholar A. Jafarey, that Zarathushtra was not in fact a priest.[28] The author states that the prophet never describes himself as a priest in the *Gathas*, and his contention is that Zarathushtra was a *manthran* (a "thought-provoker"), a term which the prophet does use of himself and his intended followers (for example at Y.32:13 and Y.50:6) and which indeed he was, but Jafarey also maintains that at Y.33:6 Zarathushtra is distancing himself from the established sacerdotal order. In condemning the pre-Zoroastrian priesthood at Y.32:14, continues Jafarey, no substitute is offered. The term *zaotar* is interpreted by Jafarey as meaning one who "pours out his heart to have a divine vision" and he continues this process of desacerdotalization by asserting that "Zarathushtrian doctrine . . . has its own simple and sublime way of communicating with Ahura Mazda".[29] Thus, argues Jafarey, direct communication with the Wise Lord obviates the need for a ritually proficient institutional priesthood (although this has not prevented Jafarey from arguing in favour of a non-hereditary gender-inclusive priesthood whose function is not principally to perform rituals but simply to interpret and expound upon the doctrine and the texts, in particular the *Gathas*). Yet if the hymns of the prophet (which are Jafarey's main witnesses in the matter) are sublime, they could hardly be called simple, and neither is the path they propose nor the doctrines they embody. Furthermore Zarathushtra does not condemn the *office* of the priesthood, merely its abuse. As already mentioned in chapter I, his compositional skill was one which could only have been acquired through a priestly education, and his allusions to ritual in the *Gathas* suggest a familiarity with *and approval of* the liturgical functions of the priesthood. We are on far safer ground in agreeing with M. Boyce that although Zarathushtra's "wide-ranging and complex thought rises to metaphysical and prophetic heights far above the realities of the ritual . . . these realities appear to have remained constantly present to him, having become part presumably of his instinctive life and thought" and that the *Yasna* in particular is "central to the faith he taught".[30] The conclusion, as Professor Boyce notes, is that today's Zoroastrian clergy are the successors to Zarathushtra in the priesthood,[31] and genealogies tracing priestly lineages back to post-Sassanian times have been at least partially successful in supporting this claim.[32]

## 6 Marriage

That Zarathushtra devoted an entire hymn (Y.53) to extolling marriage and encouraging his daughter on the occasion of her wedding is an indication of the high value which he placed upon the institution, and the Zoroastrian tradition has maintained this attitude ever since. Indeed, as we have already seen, the *Vendidad* speaks of Ahura Mazda favouring a married man over one who is unmarried, and Zarathushtra's own wedding hymn exhorts his daughter to "choose with your generous (groom) the holiest (things) of right-mindedness" (Y.53:5). Marriage, then, provides an environment within which the couple might grow together in righteousness and good thought, and it also creates the correct and stable conditions for producing children and maintaining property.[33] The *Vendidad* compares a fruitful marriage to the earth yielding a rich harvest.[34]

Zoroastrians are traditionally endogamous – that is, they do not normally marry outside their own fold. However, a trend towards marrying non-Zoroastrians has developed lately, and there are arguments favouring or disapproving the practice which can be approximately equally persuasive and certainly uniformly heartfelt. Zoroastrians originating from Iran on the whole tend to be more liberal in this (and other matters), as they have a marginally more vocal presence in the affluent west which seems to evoke a degree of sympathy not always enjoyed by the more traditionalist and often (though not invariably) ideologically "Indianized" Parsis[35] (despite the fact that the British influence on the Parsi community is, for obvious historical reasons, much more visible). The diaspora has, inevitably, contributed to this break with matrimonial custom. The issue, tightly linked to the controversy over conversion, is complex, and the debate continues at practically every level in the community. Appeals to scripture and tradition on the one hand are met with not only Gathic refutations but sociological and demographic arguments on the other – in short that the religion will die out without a massive increase in numbers, and that endogamous marriage is not producing sufficient children. We should merely note that the orthodox or traditionalist view strongly recommends that a Zoroastrian marries a Zoroastrian. It is therefore not uncommon for matrimonial partnerships to be sought by such means as advertising in the Zoroastrian press. A typical such advertisement might read along these lines:

Alliance invited from decent, home-loving Parsi girl for graduate son, aged 30, serving in a reputable bank in Bombay.[36]

The notice may also carry details of salary, prospects, whether or not the prospective groom or bride has accommodation and so on. If this all seems rather business-like, devoid of any "romantic" element or "emotional" content, it must be said that forced marriages rarely occur, and that the perceived need to preserve the community's heritage is what is really at stake for a good number of these Zoroastrians. Moreover many marriages today take place not by this sort of arrangement but by the propitious meeting of two people who happen to be Zoroastrians and decide to marry, but this is rarely done without parental approval, encouragement and involvement.

It is argued that marriage to another Zoroastrian is one important way of preserving the integrity of the community, and one which has proved supremely successful, so that by seeking and/or marrying a partner in this manner the continuance of the tradition is, for the orthodox, assured. This line of reasoning has not satisfied others, though, and 1991 saw the creation of the Association of Inter-Married Zoroastrians, a body set up to support women who have "married out" of the community and to campaign for their acceptance by the community as a whole as true Zoroastrians with all appropriate rights and privileges.

Zoroastrian wedding ceremonies in India generally take place just after sunset, a custom which Modi notes suggests the joining of two lives, just as night and day unite at twilight[37] but which was in fact imposed upon the immigrant Zoroastrians who arrived in India from Iran in 936 CE. M. Boyce reports that a similar tradition is observed in Iranian Zoroastrianism, with weddings in that country taking place at midnight.[38] It is customary for the ceremony to be performed at the bride's family home, but as this is not always possible it will certainly take place in public where a large group can gather. A group is necessary to witness the marriage, and there must be at least two Zoroastrians present to act as witnesses; these will usually be family or close friends of the couple, and will generally be themselves married people. Some time on the day of the wedding the bride and groom will each have taken the *Nahn* ritual bath in consecrated water, just as they will have done prior to their *Navjote* ceremony. One or two hours before the hour appointed for the wedding ceremony, the bride, with her entourage and family, will go in procession to the groom's house and offer gifts to his family before returning to the bride's house. After this, the groom with his family and friends and with the priests who are to officiate at the wedding go to the bride's house and all but the groom enters. The groom waits outside while he is greeted with traditional symbols of welcome, such as coconuts and eggs, and his head is marked with a red vertical mark which is said to represent the sun. In the meantime the bride will have a similar marking placed on her forehead, representing the moon. This symbolism of opposites is said to denote the joy and grief that the bride and groom will be expected to share throughout life, and derives its impact partly from the twilight hour at which the wedding occurs. The groom is then invited into the house and the wedding itself commences. As with all major rites, fire will be present, and a lesser functionary will maintain the fire vase. When the groom enters he is greeted with a song and he will join his bride on chairs which will be facing to the East; they will initially be divided by a curtain, which will be removed – dropped to the ground – as a sign of two separate people becoming joined together and the couple will sprinkle each other with rice, as will the officiating priest – another ritual action familiar from the initiation rite of *Navjote*. During the ceremony, which will be extremely joyful and full of noise and activity, there will be prayers and blessings and the officiating priest will ask if the bride and groom are ready to accept each other, in a manner similar to western wedding ceremonies. The couple's hands are joined and a symbolic tying of a knot will be performed by the senior priest. He will then direct them with words of encouragement and admonition,[39] and offer a final benediction and prayer which asks Ahura Mazda to maintain the couple in righteousness. The wedding rites, as with many Zoroastrian ceremonies of this nature, will be followed by a joyful gathering of family and friends.

## 7 Death and Funerary Rites

Death was never part of Ahura Mazda's plan for humanity. It is only due to the incursions of the hostile spirit into the good creation of the Wise Lord that this, the ultimate pollution, has been introduced into the world. Yet as we have seen, by introducing death into the world, and by first slaughtering the Primal Bull and the First Man, Gayomart, Ahriman has unknowingly secured his own defeat. Death may be a temporary occurrence, but it is still a most powerful and inevitable force, and one which is to be dealt with while the influence of the Hostile Spirit is still permitted to be active.

Because death is the most powerful sign of Ahriman's influence on creation, its treatment in Zoroastrianism has evolved as a response to not only its effect on the individual but also to the effect it has upon creation itself. The guarantee of the perfection which will be conferred upon creation at the *frashokereti* is no guarantee against the polluting effects of death in the present age of *gumezishen* (mixture), and so all precautions are taken to prevent the pollution that attends death from spilling out into the *getig* realm. We have already seen what Zoroastrianism teaches about the fate of the individual after death; now we shall look at the mechanism for dealing with its presence in this world.

Death can be defined by once again using the term we have applied to Ahriman's effect on creation as a whole, *ajyati* – "not-life", or the appropriation of the essence and substance of life for "anti-life" purposes. In fact death is the most powerful expression of *ajyati* that humanity encounters during the age of *gumezishen*. So, given that Zoroastrianism celebrates and venerates life, as it is a fundamental expression of Ahuric benevolence, death is treated with equivalent disdain. This is not to say that bereavement is not important, or that Zoroastrianism is not sympathetic to those who have suffered a loss; in fact a consequence of the ritual process is that its design not only protects the world from attracting pollution from death but also that it eases the passage of the soul into the next world and thus offers comfort to those who grieve the passing of a relative or friend. However, since death is the last word in impurity, and a deceased corpse is potentially the most dangerous of pollutants,[40] the task of caring for the corpse is given to specially appointed persons, known as *nasarsarlas*, who carry out the task of preparing the body for the funerary rites. *Nasarsarlas* have been identified as being a "sub-caste" within the larger Zoroastrian community, though this may be a somewhat pejorative description. It is believed that a Zoroastrian corpse is much more open to Ahrimanic threat than that of a non-Zoroastrian, and that the quality of life of the deceased determines how much pollution will be attracted – the holier the person, the greater the pollution. This is because Ahriman is said to instruct a larger number of demons to inhabit the body of a pious person than that of someone not so pious in the belief that it is a greater victory for the hostile spirit to infect those most discernibly righteous. Thus the *nasarsarlas*, given their particular role, must undergo a rigorous programme of purification if they wish to rejoin "normal" society after their funerary duties are over.[41] Since a corpse is said to be immediately inhabited by the "demoness of death", it is imperative that it does not come into contact with the Ahuric elements associated with Zoroastrian ritual:

It is so stated that one cannot cause dead matter to be carried to water or fire.[42]

Upon death, and after any formal medical procedures have been completed, the corpse is taken to a building called a *bungli*, part of the area set aside for the disposal of corpses. It is washed in unconsecrated bull's urine (*gomez*), since this is a powerful antiseptic agent and plays a major role in Zoroastrian purity rituals,[43] and dressed in clean, though not new, clothes (including a *sudre*), and the sacred cord (*kushti*) is tied three times around the body. The body is then removed to a specially prepared area of the room where it has three circles drawn around it, to prevent pollution from entering the rest of the area. The soul is said to hover around the body for three days, and so three days and nights of prayers are performed in the presence of the corpse. A dog is brought out to "gaze" upon the body. This rite, known as *sagdid*, in a sense confirms that the body is dead. A dog was thought in earlier times to have the power of discerning between life and death; a dog is also said to be a favoured Ahuric creature, capable of slaying three thousand demons in a night.[44]

After the three-day period, the pall-bearers will take the corpse to the place where it will eventually lie to be devoured by vultures; this place is known as the *dakhma* or "tower of silence". While this happens, the priests will begin to recite suitable prayers, and to reinforce their purity, they, and others in the procession, will hold a piece of white cloth called a *paiwand*[45] between them as they walk in pairs to a place near the steps of the tower. *Dakhmas* are large round structures, open to the elements, with three sets of concentric chambers, also unenclosed, in which men, women and children will be laid, men on the outer circle, women in the middle circle and children in the innermost.[46] Only the *nasarsarlas* are permitted to enter the *dakhma* with the corpse. Once inside, the *nasarsarlas* lay the body in its chamber and leave. It is thought that the vultures which inhabit the complex can strip the corpse of flesh within twenty minutes. A central well containing quicklime ensures that the body is disintegrated, though the *nasarsarlas* may be required to ensure that this process is carried out.

These *dakhmas*, which are only found in India and Iran, have aroused in approximately equal measure admiration and derision from non-Zoroastrians. In earlier times these structures were found in the deserts and countryside, but now the growth of urban culture has meant that they are often seen in populated areas, such as the famous *dakhma* complex in Bombay. To western sensibilities the Zoroastrian method of disposing of the dead has often smacked of irreverence, disrespect and disregard for hygiene. Yet many medical authorities have confirmed its value as a sanitary way of dealing with a corpse; and from a theological viewpoint, it totally conforms to Zoroastrian beliefs on the nature of death and pollution. The body, having served its purpose, is now given back to nature so that creation itself may benefit from it, and once again, as happened at the beginning when life sprang from death, this Ahrimanic invention is turned against the hostile spirit. Furthermore its social value is attested by an anthropologist who writes that

> as a non-religious person I believe that the Zoroastrian way of disposing of the body is the most correct and sanitary way. It is also of importance that the morbid and wrong feelings by frequent visits to the graveyards are avoided by the way Zoroastrians dispose the body.[47]

M. Monier-Williams refers with approval to the "more rapid rather than lingering operation" which the devouring vultures execute in contrast to what occurs at burial, and Professor J. Hinnells remarks on the absence of morbid feelings, often associated with western cemeteries, which he experienced when visiting the Bombay *dakhma* complex.[48] Reports of circling vultures depositing portions of putrefying human flesh into the laps of *al fresco* diners on the balconies of high-rise Bombay apartments are perhaps apocryphal, if not malicious.

In the west, where *dakhmas* cannot be constructed, Zoroastrians have been reluctantly forced to make do with alternatives such as burial or cremation. In the latter case, cremation is by electric means rather than fire.

Only a Zoroastrian is entitled to consignment in the *dakhmas*. Some orthodox Zoroastrians even consider that women who marry out of the community forfeit their right to traditional death rituals, though as with conversion and intermarriage itself the community does not have a unified view on the matter.[49]

## 8 Purification: the *Barashnum i-no shab*

The *Barashnum i-no shab* is the highest and most efficacious of all the purification rituals an individual is likely to undergo. It is also the longest, taking nine days and nights to complete. It prepares the priests for the execution of their duties prior to their ordination, and is repeated at intervals during the priest's life, particularly when, for whatever reason, he has contracted impurity and could not otherwise enter the *pawi* or perform any other ritual duty. The *Barashnum i-no shab* has been subject to a number of modifications over the centuries, though its purpose has remained constant; we shall briefly examine the modern practice here. It is conducted by Irani and Parsi Zoroastrians with only minor differences between them.

The *Barashnum i-no shab* rite comprises a series of three ritual baths which are attended by two priests as assistants. In addition, the candidate for the rite must perform other ablutions and spend time in prayer and meditation. Unconsecrated and consecrated bull's urine, *nirang*, will be used in washing a total of eighteen times, and a dog will be presented to the candidate thirteen times. Other elements in the ritual include the application of water and sand as cleansing agents. The ritual is not considered complete until a nine-night retreat has been undertaken by the candidate.

In the case of a candidate for the priesthood who has to undergo the rite, if it is vitiated more than three times this is taken to be a sign that the candidate is not to be admitted to the priestly order. Vitiation can arise for a number of reasons connected with both physical and spiritual or moral purity. Among them, Modi lists the eating of food cooked by non-Zoroastrians and long journeys. Even the white priestly turban falling from the candidate's head is deemed sufficiently serious to warrant the rite being started again from the beginning.[50] Other reasons that the rite might be invalidated include if the area in which the *Barashnum i-no shab* takes place itself contracts impurity, even if this happens through no fault of the candidate. Ordained priests will perform the rite to sustain their own purity.

J. Choksy has noted this rite's resemblance to the Hindu Brahminical practice of *Diksha*, in which a man prepares himself for the celebration of the *soma* ceremony. Both rites, according to Choksy, "prepare the postulant for access to the deepest zones of sacrality".[51]

## 9  The Instrumental and Expressive Functions of Zoroastrian Ritual

T. Luhrmann has suggested that "in some sense Zoroastrianism is no more than a ritualistic commentary on purity and pollution",[52] which is incorrect, particularly since although ritual may indeed express theological truths (though not in the metaphorical sense), it also has an *instrumental* function. It is this that creates the conditions within which the timeless truths and qualities which the good *menog* beings embody are able to intersect the spatially and temporally finite world in such a way as to enhance it and attract the worship which is rightfully theirs, and thus no major ritual – and indeed many "lesser" – may take place without the presence of the sacred fire, the sign of the divine presence of *asha*. In other words, ritual makes possible an interface between *menog* and *getig* in which both realms benefit. Hence the priesthood's insistence on the *Yasna* contributing to the world's welfare, or, as has been suggested, actually holding the world together. By the same token, physical purity, the essential requirement for ritual, deflects Ahrimanic activity and prevents it from increasing. So when Luhrmann writes later that "rituals are customs", implying their dependence on social and cultural factors, and claims that "they have no power in themselves",[53] she is somewhat wide of the mark, at least as far as orthodox or "traditionalist" Zoroastrianism is concerned. Rituals do not merely express, represent or symbolize doctrine; they go further than that by not only providing the framework within which doctrine is given concrete (physical) form, but they actually are an embodiment of Zoroastrian teaching, and it is this that gives them their purpose. As Choksy has written, "for Zoroastrians the rites . . . are meaningful because they are manifestations of the faith".[54] In attaching an exclusively expressive function to Zoroastrian rituals a grave disservice is done to understanding their purpose, since doing so denies their inherent power which strengthens the world and connects *menog* to *getig*.

## 10 Holy Days, Holy Months and a Disputed Calendar

In common with many other traditions, Zoroastrianism observes the custom of dedicating each day to a particular divine being or significant event. Each month of the calendar is also given over to a particular divine being. Since the Zoroastrian calendar is solar rather than lunar, it contains 360 days, and so five *Gatha Days* are also celebrated, bringing the total to 365. Each 30-day period or month thus enables the tradition to acknowledge, on a regularly recurring basis, one of thirty divine beings per day, twelve of which are also celebrated with their own "month". Many of the beings recognized in this way will be by now familiar to the reader – such *menog* beings as Sroash and Mithra (*Mihr*), as well as the Wise Lord himself. Additional festivals and memorials are also celebrated – the prophet's birth and death being of particular importance, and also the feast of "all souls" (*Hamaspathmaedaya* or

*Farvardingan*), when the departed members of the family are remembered with offerings of sandalwood, and, where location permits, flowers at the *dakhmas*. There are also six special "holy days of obligation", known as *Ghambars*.

Zoroastrians also celebrate the new year (*Navroze*) with great festivity, but the time leading up to it is set aside particularly for commemoration of the departed. During these ten preceding days, many Zoroastrians undertake additional observances – not, though, in the spirit of "penitence" such as in the Christian season of Lent, it must be added – during which they recite the entire collection of Zarathushtra's *Gathas*. Since there has been historical disagreement among Zoroastrians as to the precise rotation of the calendar, there are in fact three celebrations of this throughout the year, by three different groups of Zoroastrians. One group, the *Qadamis*, observes the ancient calendar, one, the *Rasimis* or *Shenshais*, a "reformed" version of this which follows the ancient calendar but one month behind, and there is a third which bases its observances on the modern Iranian calendar. This has a knock-on effect on all major festivities as well, so, for example, the Mithraic *Mihragan* festival, a particularly popular Iranian observance, is, strictly speaking, a festival of crops[55] and thus originally appointed to be celebrated during what is today September, but it can now be found taking place during the season of spring.

## 11  A Worshipping Community and Three Zoroastrian Prayers

For the Zoroastrian, praying is an essentially private, personal matter. Although Zoroastrians are encouraged to gather together at such celebrations as the *Afrinagan*, and thus ritual plays an important role in the lives of many members of the faith, there is also within the tradition a strong and ancient culture of what in western terms might be called "private devotion" (although this, as with everything else, is a limited comparison) and which in the past has sat comfortably alongside ritual activity, complementing rather than replacing it. But it would be wrong to think of a Zoroastrian "praying" or "worshipping" at a ritual in the same way as we understand a member of the Christian faith to do at, say, a eucharistic celebration. Ritual for the Zoroastrian is something to be witnessed or experienced, but there is no sense of the priest and laity engaging in communal prayer or "offering" a ritual together. The importance of ritual to the Zoroastrian lay person is precisely in this experiential, rather than participatory, engagement. However, many of today's Zoroastrians, deprived of access to regular ritual worship, have of necessity adopted this element of private prayer as one of their most beneficial and rewarding religious exercises. For some, minimal attendance at ritual functions has always been the practice although they would still identify themselves as strongly Zoroastrian, praying five times a day and observing other customs, for there is no hard and fast rule stating how often one should attend a public religious celebration, either in Iran, India or elsewhere. More recently, still other Zoroastrians have developed a religiosity which has almost entirely ceased to be dependent upon rituals, looking instead practically exclusively to the revealed words of the prophet for religious inspiration and meaning in their lives. Whatever the prevailing ideology or circumstances determining an individual's attitude to worship, it is fair to say that there are three particular prayers which will never be far from the devout Zoroastrian's heart and mind. Although these three prayers traditionally precede the *Gathas*, they are frequently used independently of that body of hymns, in ritual or otherwise.

The first of these prayers, and the one most sacred to a Zoroastrian is known as the *ahuna vairya*.

> Since He is (the One) to be chosen by the world
> therefore the judgement emanating from truth itself
> (to be passed) on the deeds of good thought of the world,
> as well as the power, is committed to Mazda Ahura whom (people)
> assign as a shepherd to the poor.[56]

This has been called the "Zoroastrian Pater"[57] and it is probably no exaggeration to say that this prayer occupies the same position in Zoroastrianism as does the Lord's Prayer in Christianity. It has also been called a "talisman",[58] since it is said to be most powerful in warding off evil and creating an environment of sacrality, and many Zoroastrians, and others, believe it to have been composed by the prophet himself, since it is in the Gathic dialect. This is the first prayer a young Zoroastrian learns, and is therefore his or her first experience of the Avestan tongue which is itself considered to possess sacred properties. This remarkable little composition in fact sets out the Zoroastrian notion of choice; it is a confirmation of the free will that the Wise Lord grants his created people. So right at the beginning of life, when a child begins to learn speech, she or he will be introduced, through the manthric power of the sacred Avestan language, to the injunction to think good thoughts, to say good words and to perform good deeds. Throughout his or her life it reminds the Zoroastrian that constant and correct discernment between the ideals of *asha*, truth and righteousness, and the characteristics of the *drug*, destruction and deceit, is crucial to the well being of the world, and that the success of the *frashokereti* is, despite its guarantee, dependent on the choices an individual makes in emulation of the proto-choice made by the Holy Spirit of Ahura Mazda as revealed in the *Gathas*. That Zarathushtra's followers are those who will renew the world means that they are the ones who will adopt the way of *asha,* and judge rightly between good and evil.

Another powerful prayer, also considered by many to be of Zarathushtrian authorship, is the *ashem vohu* (which we have already learned is recited by the priests at the commencement of rituals):

> Truth is best (of all that is) good.
> As desired, what is being desired
> is truth from Him/him who represents best truth.

This short prayer is a meditation upon *asha*. There may be a deliberate ambiguity in the identity of the object in the second phrase which this translation indicates by the use of alternative upper and lower cases.[59] Such a device would not be uncharacteristic of Zarathushtra, and in this instance it may suggest the co-operation that is necessary between Asha Vahishta and the *ashavan* if truth and righteousness are to be implanted in the world. Being almost certainly from the prophet's own mouth, this prayer harmonizes perfectly with the *ahuna vaiyra*.

The third of these short prayers is the *yenhe hatam*. Since it is composed in Younger or Standard Avestan, its authorship cannot be ascribed to Zarathushtra. It suggests that all good *menog* beings are worthy of worship, and furthermore those men and women in the *getig* realm who bear witness to the principle of *asha* in their lives are to be duly honoured.

> In accordance with truth Mazda Ahura knows the man among the
> existing,
> as well as the women, whose better (attitude is seen) at worship.
> Those men and women we worship.

Even when gathering for ritual worship, the actual process of praying – that is, communicating with the *menog* beings or meditating upon them – remains a largely solitary activity. What many Zoroastrians do believe is that by experiencing the rituals they encounter the divine in a uniquely intimate – and a uniquely Zoroastrian – way.

Truth is best (of all that is good). As desired, what is being desired is truth for Him/him who (represents) best truth.

(Y.27:14 – the Ashem Vohu prayer)

Bright things are (in store) for the munificent one, who already possesses them in his thought. Through good power he holds truth in word and action. He shall be your most welcome guest, O Mazda Ahura.

(Y.32:22)

It is your power, O Mazda, through which you will grant what is better to the poor person living decently.

(Y.53:9)

# VII

# A Living Faith – Zoroastrian Ethics

## 1 Good Thoughts, Good Words, Good Deeds

Zoroastrian ethics is based on the code of "good thoughts, good words and good deeds". This is simple in itself, of course, and it proceeds naturally from the Zoroastrian concept of ethical dualism, which is a logical development of the cosmic dualism first encountered in the Gathic verses concerning the two primal spirits and systematically expounded in the later literature. At its most fundamental, then, it is the human participation in the cosmic tension that persists between the Ahuric and the Ahrimanic. It is also bound up with the notion of choice that the *ashavan* is called upon to make: the initial, or fundamental choice to follow the path of truth (*asha*), and the individual choices that must be made throughout life. In chapter I we discussed how the choices made by the two spirits were the models, or "proto-choices", setting the pattern for humans when they make their choices to be followers either of truth (*ashavans*) or deceit (*drugvants*). The sprits of the Gathic passage in question (Y.30) have also been interpreted as two mentalities or ethical attitudes, and it was suggested in chapter I that these spirits provide a paradigm for human conduct. Now, having looked in some detail at the development of the Zoroastrian faith, and having seen how, for many (though not all) Zoroastrians, ritual is a major component in the expression, actualization and maintenance of the faith, we shall see how ethical behaviour brings it into everyday life, since Zoroastrianism does not reside solely in the *pawi*, or even in a book of *Gathas*. But first, a recapitulation of key features which underpin ethics as understood by the Zoroastrian religion.

Just as the good spirit of Ahura Mazda, *Spenta Mainyu*, and the hostile spirit, *Angra Mainyu*, are independent of each other, having no connection either conceptually or in any fundamental or primal sense (in that they share no common origin), so evil and good in this world are also completely separate to the degree that one is not only the ideological but also the physical antithesis of the other. All that is good, that which we call Ahuric, is a positive quality emanating from the Wise Lord whereas all that is bad is the result of Ahriman's intrusion into the Ahuric domain, and is in fact a deprivation of the good, a destructive incursion into the created order. That is why the Ahrimanic is sometimes referred to only by what it is not – hence the term *ajyati*, "not-life". Since the *frashokereti* is to be the event at which *getig* creation will be perfected, and since only the Ahuric creation shall enjoy the benefits of the *frashokereti*, there is a distinction between good and evil which is absolute and which operates on all levels of existence and experience, and not least in this is the physical level.

It is, in a sense, inappropriate to discuss Zoroastrian ethics and Zoroastrian theology as if they were two distinct disciplines or subjects, since Zoroastrianism so closely identifies the Wise Lord with his creation that any discussion of or investigation into the nature of Ahura Mazda is *ipso facto* an investigation into the nature of his creation. In fact many Zoroastrians would claim that their religion is primarily a way of life, an ethical system which imposes upon its adherents, once they have chosen to identify themselves with the way of *asha*, behavioural norms that are far more important than theological considerations. Since humanity is the crowning achievement of Ahura Mazda's creation, he identifies himself most intimately with his human creatures. The choice made by the holy and augmenting spirit of Ahura Mazda, Spenta Mainyu, is in reality no more than the choice that humans are invited to make. It is the choice which, as we have seen, reverberates throughout our human history and is constantly present through the synergistic relationship of mythic and cosmic time, united in the psychological dimension of the human person.

The freedom to make this choice, however, is a basic right of the human, and Zoroastrianism, in common with such traditions as Christianity, acknowledges the right of the individual to choose a path not in accordance with that of God. Zarathushtra himself recognized this, and in his great hymn of the choice, to which we must inevitably return, he counsels his listeners:

Through the radiance (of the fire) contemplate with your thought the preferences of decisions . . . (Y.30.2)

Of course he continues to warn that a wrong choice will lead to "long-lasting harm" (v. 9), but even so he is clear on the matter of individual freedom. Freedom to choose right or wrong is a key concept in Gathic and later Zoroastrian ethics, and to implement the decision-making process five tools are provided to humans by Ahura Mazda. As F. Mehr has observed, they are all to be found within the *Gathas*, and are: Mind, Desire, Conscience, Perception or Insight and Wisdom, and they lead to recognition of Truth (*asha*). Truth, though attainable by humans, cannot be seen in this context as a faculty as it belongs more properly to the Ahuric domain and is only recognized and appropriated by humans, but is not innate to them; otherwise the notion of freedom of choice would be obsolete.[1] This apparent paradox, in which the greatest of the Ahuric creations is not automatically granted the quality of *asha*, is thus solved by the notion of free will which puts the onus on men and women to choose either truth or falsehood.

## 2 The Five Faculties and Truth

The first faculty with which we have been endowed is the Mind, since it was through the Good Mind, *Vohu Manah*, that Ahura Mazda motivated his creation. It is therefore through a correctly instructed application of our minds that we are motivated to choose the right and reject the Lie. The mind receives the instruction which comes from the prophet's words and from the teachings of the good religion.

The Avestan term *man* provides the root for both Spirit and Mind, but on its own it is neutral. Only when it is preceded by a qualifier is it ethically relevant. Thus Spenta Mainyu and Angra Mainyu are in constant opposition, as indicated by the adjectives; Vohu Manah is similarly identified with the Ahuric plan.

In the *Gathas*, Zarathushtra often uses the term *man* and its derivatives without a qualifier, which suggests that he wants his intended followers to make a decision for themselves based on his message, though without any coercion. It may also suggest that many have yet to make the choice since they have not yet had the truth of his message revealed to them.

It is important that a person should consciously want to be numbered among the Ahuric warriors, or the *ashavans*. To this end Ahura Mazda grants each human with the second faculty of Desire, and the implementation of this faculty is the beginning of the process of discernment. "We desire your fire" (Y.34:4), pleads Zarathushtra, and, with an eye to the end of time, "may we be those who make existence brilliant" (Y.30:9). The desire for fire is a request to receive the truth of the message which has been revealed to the prophet and which he now proposes to deliver to his contemporaries.

The third faculty is Conscience, the *daena*. It is the *daena* which takes up the task of enabling this revelation to be understood. Earlier we saw how the *daena* was probably understood in two related ways – as the innate religious sense in the individual, and as the eschatological figure who would meet the soul at the Chinvat Bridge. Since Zoroastrianism sees no real distinction between theological and ethical categories, this religious sense must inevitably incorporate an ethical component. It is Conscience which enables men and women to do two things: to accept (or reject) the revelation which Ahura Mazda first granted to Zarathushtra through the medium of the prophet's mind – and then to continue working in concert with the Wise Lord to usher in the *frashok-ereti*. It is important to note that Ahura Mazda implants a faculty in humans which enables them to reject his invitation. The judgement that we receive at the Chinvat Bridge when we are met by the *daena* will be based upon our success or failure in this respect, in accordance with the revelation we have received.

Closely linked to Conscience is Insight. This is the noetic faculty which Ahura Mazda grants those who have chosen to follow the truth. The term *noetic* derives from the Greek *nous*, which can be translated as "intuition". It is something which the augmenting spirit confers upon those who wish to receive it, which in reality should mean all those who aspire to be *ashavans*, and it supplements that quality of innate intellectual ability which the mind already guides. Intuition is dependent upon but deeper than knowledge or understanding obtained through the exercise of the intellect, important and Ahura-given though this may be. All *ashavans*, as a result of their decision to choose the Ahuric path, are automatically given the faculty of the Good Mind (and are thus entitled to be identified with *Vohu Manah*), and certain circumstances permit this to be developed to a deeper level. One valuable opportunity for this is ritual, and Dastur Kotwal has made the observation that constant exposure to ritual increases insight:

> When you approach (a ritual) fresh, it is alive all the time. You learn something new, though you perform it hundreds of times.[2]

Of course ritual is not the only means whereby such growth in insight can occur, and a similarly frequent exposure to, for example, the Gathic literature, if carried out in the spirit of good thoughts words and deeds, will produce equivalent results; indeed for those who are unable, or do not wish, to experience ritual on a regular basis, Gathic recitation and study, and similar practices, can constitute the main mechanism for noetic enhancement.

Once this is set in motion, and provided the impulse is maintained, Wisdom is acquired. Wisdom, as Aristotle has remarked, is "intuition and scientific knowledge of the most valuable things",[3] a definition, as it is applied to humans, with which few Zoroastrian metaphysicians would wish to quarrel. Wisdom of course is the eponymous attribute of Ahura Mazda which he exhibits above all else, unparalleled and perfect in its nature. The wisdom which we as humans acquire is a result of our application of insight and intuition, granted once our minds have been set on the correct path in accordance with Vohu Manah.

The chronology of creation which we can glean from the *Gathas* is thus reflected in the individual, just as the individual's passage from pre-natal *menog* to transfigured post-apocalyptic *menog*, endowed with and seamlessly united to *getig*, is reflected in the stages of cosmic history. Wisdom is the Ahuric quality which is most necessary to establish the good dominion, since growth towards wisdom involves a parallel growth towards truth, and truth, or *asha*, is the underlying universal principle, which opposes falsehood and deceit as much as light and fire stand in opposition to darkness, and we have seen how the prophet links wisdom and the kingdom verbally in his *Gathas*. For this reason of all the qualities which constitute Ahura Mazda's being, wisdom is the one by which he is most appropriately addressed.

The acquisition of wisdom by the *ashavan* (who, as the name denotes, has already elected to live by the laws of *asha* and thus will lead as righteous and virtuous life as he or she is able), will naturally bring about a refined and correct sense of ethical behaviour. Even the desire to increase in this virtue is sufficient to ensure that one's ethical behaviour will be in accordance with that of *asha*. Some Zoroastrians maintain that perfection itself is attainable in this world, but for others the question is open. What is important is that we must be constantly moving in the right direction.

## 3 Justice

"Turn the other cheek" is a mandate with which the Zoroastrian is not especially familiar, since it overturns the implications of ethical dualism by inviting an un-Zarathushtrian passivity in the face of evil. Zarathushtra's own understanding, modified at a later stage in the religion's history, was that destruction was the price for evil deeds. Although the prophet's sense of finality in the matter of the evil person's fate, as expressed in Y.46:11 ("they will be guests in the house of deceit for all time"), is understandable for its time and permissible given the culture within which it was expressed, it gave way to a more lenient belief concerning the destiny of those who died with their bad deeds outweighing their good. What was not lost, however, was the sense of justice which Zarathushtra wove into his eschatology. Zarathushtra's anger with the sinful person and with evil in all its forms, coupled with the concept of "reward" which he had inherited from traditional Iranian religion, inspired his rigorous teachings on the notion of unremitting punishment and even utter destruction for evil actions. Some contemporary Zoroastrians may find alarming the suggestion that their prophet could be credited with such an apparently harsh doctrine, but many of those would also recoil at the suggestion that he also engaged in animal sacrifice as a religious activity. The conclusion from the available evidence, however, is that he did indeed teach the one and practise the other,[4] and in both he was impelled by an unshakeable sense of religious duty. Even though the original teaching on the fate of the evildoer gave way to a doctrine which in effect provided a second opportunity for salvation, such a modification may well have had more to do with the theological need to sustain the principle of perfection in the renewed creation rather than one of release from punishment – in other words, it safeguarded the integrity of creation which could only be attained if all humans were united at the *frashokereti*, when, to paraphrase the *Bundahishen*, they come together as one family.[5]

But the concept of justice, and its concomitant, judgement, still remained, and remain today. One major area in which Zoroastrianism has both suffered and triumphed is that of social conditions. Persecution, first under Alexander and then in Iran during and after the Arab conquest has no doubt heightened the modern Zoroastrian sense of justice in the social arena.[6] Today the creation of a just society, which includes care for the planet's ecological system, is more than merely a Zoroastrian ambition, but it is a demand made upon all who claim to be *ashavans*. For these it is an eschatological precondition, a glimpse of the *frashokereti* and a manifestation of the divine heptad which operates ecologically and economically, and thus, it is not far-fetched to say, of soteriological significance at both the personal and universal levels.

## 4 The Unbreakable Nature of the Contract as an Ethical Paradigm

According to the fourth chapter of the *Vendidad*, if someone breaks a contract or promise it is answerable down to the ninth generation that succeeds the person who reneged, and, depending on how this text is interpreted, the debt shall be paid three hundred, six hundred, seven hundred, eight hundred, nine hundred or even a thousand times over, in accordance with the nature of the contract. Alternatively the figures could refer to the amount of time (in years) the souls of the offender's progeny, or his own soul, should languish in hell, which is how the *Rivayats* understand the passage.[7] The precise meaning is not really relevant in the present context, but this section of the *Vendidad* does highlight the importance Zoroastrianism places on truthfulness, fidelity and honour. (The text, incidentally, continues to stipulate the number of lashes due for similar offences.) The earlier *Mihr Yasht*, recited in honour of the deity who presides over Contract, corroborates this, averring that

> The knave who is false to the treaty, O Spitamad, wrecks the whole county, hitting as he does the Truth-owners as hard as would a hundred obscurantists.

But

> To those who are not false to the contract grass-land magnate Mithra grants (possession of) fast horses . . . (Yt.10:2–3)[8]

It is notable that the anonymous author of the *Mihr Yasht* identifies the contract-breaker with the *drugvant*. On a more theoretical level, but again with the eschatological dimension of Zoroastrianism kept in mind, the purpose of "contract" is in a sense to anticipate that time when all people will "come together" as stated in the passage from the *Bundahishen* mentioned earlier in this chapter. A contract or pact is binding, just as the universal family is intended to be bound together in the fight against Angra Mainyu. Zoroastrianism, as a life-enhancing religion, does therefore not encourage such practices as monastic-style isolation or celibacy; indeed asceticism of any kind is discouraged, since such customs are deemed to have a deleterious and weakening effect. Part of the relationship – another term suggesting contract – that Ahura

Mazda has with humanity is that the latter should enjoy and benefit from creation, and draw strength from it, corporately diminishing the opportunities for the Ahrimanic assault. Furthermore, since asceticism is invariably connected with atonement or expiation, there is no need for it in a religious tradition whose theology has no room for notions of "original sin" or universally shared inherited guilt, as it would imply an imperfection on the part of the creator. Zoroastrian liturgies do not apologize for wrongdoing or ask for forgiveness for sin, but concentrate on praising Ahura Mazda and his *menog* beings and on purifying, or renovating, the good creation where it has been invaded by Ahriman. In fact a Zoroastrian who deliberately chooses to practise asceticism is in effect rejecting Ahura Mazda's creation, denying its benefits. The Zoroastrian attitude to marriage is perhaps the most obvious example of this. We have already seen in the last chapter how highly prized is marriage, and that the *Vendidad* praises the married man over the unmarried. Marriage is thus something of a metaphysical *paiwand* which increases the purificatory bond between two people; it is an unbreakable contract wholly Ahuric and, as Zarathushtra suggests in his wedding hymn, reminiscent of the relationship between Ahura Mazda and humanity:

> Mazda Ahura, valuing the bonds of friendship, grants a sunny harvest of good thought to the Good Religion for all times. (Y.53:4)

And just as Ahura Mazda cannot break his contract with humanity, which is promised in this hymn, so all other contracts are intended to be kept.

It is no accident that "good thoughts" is at the top of the ethical triad. The mind is the first gift to humanity, the first of our five faculties and the echo of Spenta Mainyu's indissoluble relationship with Ahura Mazda, which is itself *the* paradigmatic contract. The *ashavan* who thinks good thoughts constantly will be impelled to say good words and to do good deeds.

### 5 Putting it into Practice: Charity, Benevolence and the Parsi Zoroastrians – an Example from the Modern Era

Chang Asa, who was responsible for the establishment of the great *Atash Bahram* at Navsari, was also a man of great philanthropic virtue. A wealthy man, he is reported to have been as generous to those outside his own fold as he was to those within it, and he remains a striking example of that well-known Zoroastrian quality of charitable giving and hospitality. It is a quality which has never been absent from Zoroastrian culture, and it is carried out corporately and individually as a religious duty. It is intrinsically connected to the Zoroastrian notion of justice, for if a Zoroastrian perceives injustice to be evident – for example, where poverty is incurred through no fault of the community or person concerned – it must be challenged and corrected. Justice must always be brought to an unjust situation, for injustice is Ahrimanic since it is the opposite to justice, a facet of truth and righteousness (*asha*). This is another area where insight and perception can be deepened, for carrying out acts of charity as a religious observance and in the spirit of benevolence increases innate religiosity and counts towards the accumulation of good deeds based upon which judgement will be reckoned.

Charity, though, begins at home, and this maxim is no more evident than in the foundations and establishments set up by the Parsis for their own flock. J. Hinnells, in his survey of Parsi attitudes in this matter,[9] notes that the main task, as far as the Bombay and Gujarat based Zoroastrians of the nineteenth and early twentieth centuries were concerned, was the foundation of a number of fire temples and *dakhmas*, set up to cater for the spiritual needs of the Zoroastrian population of north-west India. In this, of course, they were doing no more than following the example set by Chang Asa centuries before, but it seems that they were also encouraged by the Irani Zoroastrians who had maintained a tradition of building new religious complexes for some time; and, as Hinnells adds, the increased wealth of many Parsis enabled them to employ servants who, since they were often non-Zoroastrians, brought impurity with them into Parsi society, making the need for pure areas set aside for worship even more urgent.[10] The Parsis' growing presence in the commercial life of India led to geographical expansion, and soon other cities began to enjoy a sizeable Zoroastrian presence. Consequently further building work was done and temples were set up in Calcutta, Delhi and smaller towns. Fire temples continued to be built usually out of the pockets of wealthy benefactors, so that these temples, of varying grades, came to be identified by the names of those who had endowed them. Priests, though often employed by families, were always available to serve the community at large. At the same time charitable bodies, known as *anjumans*, began to be founded independently of individual activities of the wealthy Parsi families, and these became responsible mainly for the *dakhmas*. *Dakhmas* were by and large paid for by subscription, and administered by committees.

Another important example of Zoroastrian charitable enterprise was the creation of colonies, or *Baugs* as they came to be known. This was Parsi charity at its most visible. These colonies – essentially concentrated apartment blocks – were set up for the most part in response to the needs of the poorer members of the Zoroastrian community – mainly farmers – who had been forced through sporadic but effective persecution from a small hostile section of the Hindu population (motivated politically rather than on religious grounds) and the resultant economic hardship, to leave the rural areas in the 1930s, and the colonies provided cheap but serviceable and comfortable accommodation in the city for those who were unable to acquire property of a more prestigious kind, and even today funds are administered to assist the Gujarat farming community from money collected all over the Zoroastrian world.[11] *Baugs* had originally been conceived as public meeting areas attached to the fire temples, where Zoroastrian social and religious activity could be conducted. For example, such occasions as marriages or *navjotes*, being open to non-Parsis, and because of the purity regulations, would never take place in the restricted areas of the *pawi* but often in the open air (and both these occasions tend to be "seasonal" – that is, they rarely occur during the monsoon period). As the rural-dwelling Parsis moved to the cities due to economic need, family dwellings were a natural extension of this, and today the colonies resemble miniature villages, often with shops including dairies and dispensaries, and invariably having a resident priest.[12] Today the accommodation is sometimes extended to non-Zoroastrians associated (usually) by employment to the Parsis, and visiting western scholars have often found a temporary home in one of the apartments.

Iranian fortunes were also, during this period, looking up. A Zoroastrian population which, at the turn of the century had been largely rural was now beginning to find its way into the cities. Inspired by the Parsi success in India and encouraged by the comparative safety the city afforded (whereas persecution was still taking place in the rural districts) the Irani Zoroastrians were also influenced by Parsi architecture, for, as M. Boyce remarks, the new temple which was established in Tehran was based on the Parsi model. And so despite their having persuaded the Parsis in the first instance to build temples, they now appeared to look to their Indian counterparts for guidance in the matter.[13]

The creation of schools and a Parsi hospital in Bombay gave the Zoroastrians there a further presence in their adopted country, and was a welcome addition to the visible manifestation of traditional Parsi charity and benevolence. At the same time a steady supply of alms had been finding its way to Iran via the Iranian *Anjuman*, founded in 1917 and administered in Bombay for the poor and oppressed in the homeland where, for example, schools and medical facilities were set up, all bearing the names of Parsi benefactors.[14] Bodies such as the Bombay-based Zoroastrian Studies continue to afford help to those impoverished Iranis who need it.

But if charity begins at home, for the Parsis it does not have to stay there, and Hinnells notes the efforts made this century in working "with churches and Institutes in Higher Education in India".[15] Parallel with this trend of joining in charitable endeavour with non-Parsi bodies is the representation of Zoroastrians on interfaith platforms, and for the past century local and international inter-religious gatherings have benefited from a Zoroastrian presence, which can only have helped to bring Zoroastrian charitable activities to the attention of the world at large.

In the midst of this admirable activity, however, theological and ideological controversy have now entered the community's agenda to an extent never before experienced in the faith's entire history. This is the subject of the next chapter.

The person who is best to the truthful one, by family, being a member of the same community, by tribe, O Ahura, or by caring zealously for the cow, that person will be in the pasture of truth and good thought.

(Y.33:3)


. . . the good Law of the worshippers of Mazda will come and spread though . . . all the earth.

(Yt.13:94)

# VIII

# *Identity, Unity and Disparity – Zoroastrianism Today*

---

## 1  Who is a Zoroastrian?

Zoroastrianism in the contemporary world finds itself at a crossroads. As with any religious community, the pressures and ideals of the modern world have entered its culture to the extent that there is now much questioning of traditional values and practices, and an unprecedented contact with members of other faiths, spurred on largely by the electronic age, fast frequent transport and mass communication, has encouraged many Zoroastrians to embark upon a reappraisal of hitherto accepted theological, cultural and liturgical norms. Already in this book we have had occasion to touch upon the most controversial issues of all that face Zoroastrianism today, conversion and intermarriage, but there are a number of other, related, subjects which we should now examine.

First, though, let us consider an alarming statistical point: one of the most obvious and worrying features with which the modern community has to contend is its diminishing numbers, a trend which some Zoroastrians believe will only be arrested by allowing conversion into the faith. It has been estimated that there are only between 129,000[1] and, at a slightly more generous guess, 150,000[2] Zoroastrians in the world today. The difficulties inherent in taking a census have prevented a more accurate figure from being reached, and this estimate will not include the many "hidden" Zoroastrians who may live in small settlements and villages in such countries as Tadjikistan and Uzbekistan, in whose sanctuaries the sacred flame of *asha* may burn undimmed but unknown to the outside world, and whose faith and practice has departed in some details from that of Iran and India but whose fidelity to the spirit of the prophet and the tradition he reformed and invigorated is nevertheless evident.[3] Nor of course could it include those few westerners who have adopted the identifying garments of the faith – the *sudre* and *kushti* – as the outward sign of their religious faith (it making little difference to the figures anyway), and nor will it ever as far as the orthodox Zoroastrians are concerned, since the orthodox community, in contrast to the "reformist" movement, does not recognize the possibility of conversion. Such an estimate, in any case, can only be approximate and the difference between the lower and higher figures is such that its only real value is that it indicates the extent of the problems met in attempting to define who is and who is not Zoroastrian. And at the heart of the problem is the question of identity.

Who is a Zoroastrian? This is the question which Kersey Antia asked when he performed the *navjote* ceremony on Joseph Peterson.[4] This is the question addressed by the scholar-priests of Bombay when they issued their condemnation of Antia's actions. This is the question which was addressed when Roxanne Shah was refused the *dakhma* facilities following her tragic death,[5] and, not least, this the question addressed by the Parsi or Irani who lives in London or New York, surrounded by images of a western culture infused with two millennia of Christianity (a tradition, incidentally, which most Zoroastrians recognize as honourable), but denied on the whole those comfortable and reassuring symbols of his or her native faith. It is a question, however, that the devout Zoroastrian priest answers in the first person when he enters the *pawi* and dons the *padan* to begin his *Yasna* ceremony. It is a question the child in Bombay similarly answers when, for the first time, he or she puts on the *sudre* and *kushti* and affirms an identification with a living religious tradition that has its origins some 3,500 years before. Yet it is also a question that the North American engineer, or the college student in Australia, feels able to answer with equal pride and conviction despite the fact that he or she may long ago have abandoned the wearing of those garments; it is a question which evokes a resounding "*I* am a Zoroastrian" from the Canadian lawyer who sees no value in ritual, or in the Avestan language, but looks to the latest English translation of the prophet's *Gathas* for spiritual guidance and perhaps meets with a few similarly-minded Zoroastrians three or four times a year for informal prayers and a discussion group.

For many, ethnicity and religion are intrinsically united. Indeed for some, ethnicity seems more important than the details or even profession of religious belief, and this is apparently not a new phenomenon. J. H. Moulton recounts the case of Dhanjibhai Naoraji, a convert from Zoroastrianism to Christianity and one of the two products of J.

Wilson's missionary campaign in India during the first half of the nineteenth century. Naoraji had presented himself for ordination and eventually took up the vocation of Christian minister. What is particularly interesting, however, is that he never renounced his Parsi identity, and Moulton records that he retained the affection and esteem of those of his former co-religionists he seemed to have deserted. With Naoraji's profession of Christianity, his subsequent ordination and simultaneous self-proclamation as a Parsi, the ethnic identity of "Parsi-ness"(*Parsipanu*) seemed for the first time in the Indian chapter of the religion's history to be wider than confessional Zoroastrianism. This cannot have been anything but immensely gratifying to Moulton who had no wish to jeopardize the relations which had built up between himself and the Zoroastrian community with which he was ingratiated, and indeed Moulton seems particularly cautious in relating his case, even proclaiming that Naoraji's death was his entry not to any Judeo-Christian "heaven" but to "the House of Song", confirming for his Parsi readers the convert's retention of his Zoroastrian roots.[6] This example, though extreme, does draw attention to what for many is the overriding importance of ethnic identity, so much so that the Zoroastrian religion becomes almost a secondary consideration. It is an attitude which, whilst not dominant, does exist today, and yet it seems countered by the equally infrequently manifest notion that religious conviction displaces ethnic considerations, so that Zoroastrianism, as a creed, is seen to be open to all who wish to profess it regardless of birth, which is precisely what Peterson affirmed at his *navjote*.

So the question remains: who is a Zoroastrian? Is it just the person born of Zoroastrian blood, who ties the *kushti* three times around the waist and says the prescribed prayers? Is it just the person who seeks his or her life partner from a dwindling Parsi or Irani stock, and who says the *ahuna vairya* in Avestan and who will, at the end of life, be consigned if at all possible to the Towers of Silence? Or is it the person who is merely content to act according to the injunction of good thoughts, good words and good deeds, and to read the *Gathas* infrequently but devoutly, and yet who has not participated in or witnessed a ritual for many years if at all, and who would welcome into the fold anyone who expressed a desire to proclaim themselves followers of the prophet? Is it, indeed, one of a number of such persons who, having been, for whatever reason, dissatisfied with his or her religion of birth has, after careful reflection and study, chosen this religion freely? Or is it all of these? Is there sufficient room for a plurality of interpretations in this tiny religious community which is none the less decidedly cosmopolitan?

## 2  The Europeans and the Zoroastrians: Orthodoxy and Reform, Text and Praxis

It may in fact be possible to speak of "Protestant" (and by extension "Catholic") Zoroastrianism, in much the same way as some scholars like to speak of "Protestant" Buddhism.[7] Allowing for such a distinction (and maintaining for convenience, for the time being, the use of these terms), we could argue that the "Catholic" (or "orthodox") wing is represented by those practitioners of Zoroastrianism who maintain fidelity to the wealth and intricacy of ritual, and who recognize an unbroken tradition of faith transmitted through the texts from the time of the prophet onwards, so that such literature as the *Vendidad* and the later Pahlavi writings, whilst perhaps not on a par with Zarathushtra's utterances, nevertheless reflects an evolving religious system. And, these "Catholics" might continue, the rituals performed today are the logical continuation of the devotion and intensity of Zarathushtra's own ritual practice, and the later texts (many of which were incorporated into the rituals) legitimate developments and expositions of Zarathushtra's original thinking, and in some cases, divinely inspired documents which supply the answers to questions that the prophet, for whatever reason, left unconsidered.

"Protestant" Zoroastrianism, in keeping with the historical experience from which the analogy is borrowed, is a later development and arose as a reform of what was seen by many to be an over-fastidious reliance on ritual and a dependence on texts which were themselves thought not only to be unhelpful but also an impediment to a truly fruitful religious life. It was argued that only by concentrating on the earliest texts – the *Gathas* – could the religious spirit of the prophet be re-introduced into the tradition. The reformists were initially inspired and encouraged in this by the arrival in India of the western scholars and missionaries in the nineteenth century, who set about the task of exposing what they saw as the incoherent and inconsistent nature of much of the non-Gathic Avestan corpus and the Pahlavi literature which, they claimed, had departed from the theology of the *Gathas*. In other words, the Europeans who had come to India were now suggesting that modern Zoroastrianism was being unfaithful to its prophet by concentrating on meaningless ritual, and teaching a corrupt doctrine which was expressing not Zarathushtra's thoughts but ideas which came after him.

J. Wilson, it seems, was particularly preoccupied with the *Vendidad*, and he had no hesitation in denouncing it as fraudulent religious propaganda, questioning not only its integrity but its intelligibility:

> It is utterly impossible for a Parsi, of any considerable intelligence, to peruse it with that perception of its accuracy which inquiry will undoubtedly impart, without coming speedily to the conclusion, that . . . both in style and substance (it is) destitute of all claims to be considered as a revelation from God, but that it is from beginning to end most singularly despicable as a human composition. The information which it gives on the most important subjects, – as the character of God, the nature of his providence and law, and the method of his grace, and the responsibility and destiny of man, – is extremely meagre and unsatisfactory, and most frequently unreasonable and erroneous to the greatest extent; and those who make it the rule of faith and obedience, are not only involved in most distressing doubts, but in insuperable difficulties.[8]

Of course Wilson was quite unfair when he contrasted a text such as the *Vendidad* with the Christian Gospels,[9] since the two are so dissimilar in style and purpose as to render such a comparison fruitless if not wholly nonsensical. Additionally, Wilson was able to use the *Vendidad* to fashion out of Zoroastrianism a Zurvanite religion, proclaiming that heresy as its true character, not only suggesting that the Zoroastrians were being unfaithful to their own tradition by not recognizing the authority on this matter of the text he so roundly condemns elsewhere, but at the same time denouncing them for making a subordinate deity of Ahura Mazda,[10] whose attributes as creator he apparently is willing, at least in this instance, to acknowledge (but only since it suits his polemical purpose to do so) and partially to identify with the God of Christianity. He believes that this Zurvanite basis to Zoroastrianism is corroborated by other writers, and he notes that

> The testimony of several Armenian writers . . . conclusively proves that they believed that the Parsis reckon Hormazd (=*Ahura Mazda/Ohrmazd*) and Ahriman to be beings of opposite character and principles, who were coetaneously produced by Time. This testimony quite accords with the less extended one of Theodorus of the fifth century, that Zaruam (=*Zurvan*) offering a libation to engender Ormisdas, produced both him, and Satanus (=*Ahriman*).[11]

As if this were not sufficient, Wilson also directs against the Zoroastrians a further charge of "extensive polytheism",[12] noting the "impropriety and sin of making them (the "angels and archangels" – ie the *Yazatas*) objects of worship",[13] an argument he attempts to justify philologically.[14] An attack on all fronts indeed! But to a community which had heard little of the ways and means of textual criticism and had had scant experience of western rhetoric, the techniques employed by Wilson seemed sophisticated and assured, and, perhaps more significantly, they carried the stamp of authority, and they certainly demanded an extensive response.

What was not realized by Wilson, and not addressed by his opponents, was that Zoroastrianism, in common with other traditions, is not merely what the texts say it *should* be but that it is also the development and continuity of its practices as they have accumulated throughout history, and that the true *locus* of a religious tradition does not necessarily reside exclusively in one particular form or expression, such as the textual, where this is contradicted or otherwise challenged by historical and contemporary evidence.[15] And because of this, since Wilson was unable – or unwilling – to grant to Zoroastrian practice the same status he evidently believed the Zoroastrians should have accorded their texts, he was able to compare and contrast their theology, of whose details they were revealed to be lamentably uncertain, with the well-ordered theology he believed derived from the scriptural repository of his own tradition, and then, finally, to characterize Zoroastrianism as a whole as inconsistent if not incoherent.

Although the conclusions that Wilson (and others) drew from his study of and debates with the Parsis of Bombay were ultimately rejected by them, the seeds he and other western scholars had sown found a fertile soil in the minds of some Zoroastrian intellectuals, and an already gathering impetus towards reform – which meant, in many instances, simplification – was given further stimulus.[16] And whereas it would be unwise to attribute to western scholarship completely the trend in some contemporary Zoroastrian circles to promote the faith as a pure monotheism, it is fair to say that an appreciation and assimilation of non-Zoroastrian philosophical and theological learning, together with a newly discovered acquaintance with textual criticism as well as a rediscovered enthusiasm for Avestan and Pahlavi studies, has contributed a great deal to a move in that direction.

"Protestant" Zoroastrianism also found a voice and allies in Iran, and in particular in the work done on the *Gathas* and other Avestan texts in the 1920s by the Islamic scholar Ibrahim Pur Davud, who interpreted the prophet's verses in uncompromisingly monotheistic terms, much to the delight of many of the reformists in both countries. Though it seems that he never sought formal admission to the Zoroastrian fold, Pur Davud was clearly troubled by his own tradition's emphasis on an almost passive attitude towards the divine will (*islam* means "submission to Allah"), and he found in the prophet's teachings a more satisfactory understanding of the nature of humanity's struggle against evil, with its demands on a practical and conscious opposition to all that is wrong. Furthermore he recommended such an outlook to his own co-religionists. More importantly for his Zoroastrian friends, he rejected dualism as being completely un-Zarathushtrian. To find such support outside the tradition was a great boost to the Zoroastrian morale in Iran, but the beneficial effects of Pur Davud's work were also felt in India, where an English language version of his work appeared in 1927.

In the meantime the more traditionalist practices and values were steadfastly being maintained in the rural parts of both India and Iran, but particularly in the latter, where, for example, the custom of blood sacrifice at certain important feasts was still observed, whereas it had all but died out in the cities and in India. In areas such as these the fruits of theological speculation were hardly likely to penetrate in any significant way and so the old traditions and beliefs could continue undisturbed for a while, and indeed attempts to impose some of the newer ideas onto these old communities were at least initially strongly resisted, but mainly for cultural reasons; therefore it is probably meaningless to ascribe any label at all to the practitioners living in these non-urban regions since the opportunity for any deep scrutiny of the theological bases of the proposed reforms did not arise.

But in the urban setting, where but a few decades earlier the backlash had been against the encroaching missionaries with their alien creeds, the lines were now being more tightly drawn between the traditionalist adherents and the reformists. The traditionalist Zoroastrians, with their arguments based firmly in the historical development of doctrine and practice, made ever increasing appeals to the generational transmission of the faith over the centuries and the supremacy of ritual as the chief means whereby *menog* and *getig* unite and Ahura Mazda and the *menog* beings are glorified. In contrast to this, the reformists looked more and more to the original *Gathas* (whose Zarathushtrian authorship had been confirmed for them by the European M. Haug) as their sole authority in matters of religion, and simultaneously distanced themselves from the ritual-centred activities of the priests, perhaps on occasion only reluctantly acknowledging the debt they owed to the priesthood in the matter of receiving the *Gathas* intact.

Significantly, a few years before Pur Davud's work appeared, J. J.

Modi had published, in 1922, his authoritative work on the ceremonies of the Parsi Zoroastrians,[17] which describes in great depth the requirements and liturgical details of all the major Zoroastrian rituals as carried out in India, noting also the minor variations that obtained in the Iranian tradition. Such a publication was bound to be a comfort to those who had feared that the anti-ritual movement that was gaining support in both Iran and India was about to eclipse the community. Modi, who had attained the priestly rank of *Ervad*, was evidently sensitive to the background of conflict against which he wrote the book, for his attempts to reconcile ancient and modern liturgical practice betokened a parallel *rapprochement* between orthodoxy and reform. Although he recognizes that, for example, some of the more archaic purification rites were in need of revision and simplification, at the same time he is aware of the danger of needlessly dispensing with all forms of ancient practice which, he complains, is precisely what some Parsi Zoroastrians seemed to be doing. In point of fact Modi's book ultimately identifies its author with the orthodox and the ritual tradition; nevertheless his work, apart from being a definitive volume which satisfies equally the needs of student and practitioner, goes some way towards showing to its future readership "what was the good that was heedlessly thrown off and what was the bad that was properly thrown off".[18] This sentiment is, arguably, faintly echoed by Antia when, defending his decision to receive Joseph Peterson into the North American Zoroastrian community, he writes that "we will therefore be well advised and well prepared to offer our future generations something that will still rightfully secure their allegiance to Zoroastrianism, even though in so doing they will move further away from ritualism and purity laws".[19] Discussing the situation as it obtains in the contemporary west, R. Writer has remarked that "the Parsi predilection for the *Vendidad*, with its emphasis on purity laws, are (*sic*) emphasized by orthodoxist practitioners whereas the 'liberal' Zoroastrian of North America would wish to consciously remove such accretions to the faith, thereby making it more amenable to his adoptive environment".[20] It seems from this that for some Zoroastrians a situation has been reached whereby the "adoptive environment" is a crucial factor in determining the community's identity – either that or the identity itself is no longer deemed important.

But experience shows that the struggle to create and maintain a unique identity is felt as keenly by many of the so-called reformists as it is by the orthodox. The difference is that whereas for the orthodox this identity already resides within defined and visible ethnic boundaries but is now threatened from outside, for the reformists it needs to be fashioned anew by the introduction of fresh blood, and with it fresh ideas.

However the exclusive identification of liberal with the west and orthodox with the east is, as remarked previously, untenable, and so the identity issue is one that affects all Zoroastrians. Nevertheless the encounter of the Zoroastrians with European philosophical and theological thought and methodology, together with an exposure to western forms of higher education and general cultural attitudes particularly with regard to such matters as conversion and intermarriage, has been at least partially responsible for this trend to question traditional ideologies and, on occasion, to break completely with established practice and the received wisdom of earlier times.

## 3  The Status of Women in Contemporary Zoroastrianism

One of the more evident manifestations of this departure from conventional ideology is the attention now given to the position of women in Zoroastrianism which, despite the profoundly egalitarian message that the *Gathas* send out on this matter, has consistently been, until recently, the traditional one of wife, mother and homemaker and not one of prominence in either the liturgical or public scholarly life of the community. J. Rose has suggested that this is partly due to the introduction of the fire temple at around the time of Artaxerxes II.[21] Until then the home had been the main focus of religious life. This meant that in addition to their traditional roles women had the further task of teaching and maintaining religious practice, ensuring that the family's living space was adequately prepared both physically and spiritually for religious activity to be carried out in a spirit of fidelity and devotion. Further back still, in pre-Zarathushtrian times it would appear that the woman's role was solely that of serving the men, who would in return hunt and provide the food and shelter and protect the homes and villages from raiders. This is a possible explanation of the mythology surrounding the figure of the *daena* who, as we have seen, was initially envisaged as receiving only the souls of the departed males at the Bridge of the Separator. In accordance with Zarathushtra's implicit drive for equality the role of women was considerably widened, at least for a time, in the society his vision helped to fashion, and the woman of the household seemingly assumed the responsibility for religious instruction and conduct. With the advent of the fire temples in around 400 BCE, the attention was shifted away from the home, and the priesthood, which was always exclusively male, assumed the role of teacher to a far greater degree. As a result of this the woman's position reverted to that of wife and mother, caring only for the immediate material well-being of the family although by this time the paradise which had been previously denied her was secure.

That such a situation was maintained more or less undisturbed for over two thousand years is on the one hand testimony to the endurance of Zoroastrianism as a religious environment capable of supporting a viable social structure, albeit one fashioned according to a specific set of cultural norms. On the other hand, however, the question is raised (and it is one which could also be asked of a number of other religions) about the precise ways in which women are perceived in the Zoroastrian tradition as a whole. It is a question which begins to be answered in the twentieth century.

It is in the matter of education that the male-female division was felt most keenly. Even if the priesthood, until the *madressas* were established, was not over-generously supplied with men of great erudition,[22] at least the priests' familiarity with ritual and religious behaviour seemed to give them the intellectual edge over their female co-religionists. It was by and large an unquestioned system, and it was quite plainly even more accentuated by the men who were not of priestly families (or those who were but chose not to pursue a priestly vocation, often because the alternatives were more attractive!) and who made strides in business and other ventures. In both cases the women were left by the wayside (although J. Rose notes an interesting irony in the close affinity enjoyed by the priests and the women since they were seen as those most under threat from Ahrimanic pollution – the priests due to their ritual functions which demanded greater attention to maintaining purity and the women due to their physiology which demanded a greater reliance on purificatory procedures).[23]

The secondary role assumed by women in Zoroastrianism was challenged with the arrival of western-style education in the mid-nineteenth century, and since that time women have increasingly asserted themselves in the Parsi and Irani communities as much as they have anywhere in the world. (It is perhaps an irony that to a large extent the Parsi Zoroastrians were partly introduced to western education by those with a missionary agenda in the hope that they may eventually adopt Christianity, and not that they might use these methods to regenerate their own intellectual tradition.) As far as the orthodox are concerned, women even now still have no place in the "higher" ritual life of the faith, but even staunch traditionalists have been heard on occasion to remark that there is no reason why they should not take up the work of scholars and educators (perhaps in a more formal acknowledgement of their ancient role in this second area) which had historically been largely the province of the priesthood. Indeed today a number of Zoroastrian women are at the forefront of Zoroastrian educational projects, engaging with their students in as competent and successful a manner as their male colleagues. What is more, this now takes place on an official and recognized basis rather than informally in the setting of the family.

Turning to the physiological dimension, we might note that the ambivalence surrounding such matters as childbirth will never disappear as long as the tradition maintains its stance on the precise ramifications of women's physiology *vis-à-vis* purity, and it shows no signs of relinquishing this position since it is at the heart of a lengthy period of Zoroastrian theological development. But even this may eventually be seen to be a detail, and details are always negotiable.[24] Such laws as there are concerning the purity of women were formulated during a time when the biological sciences were not at their most sophisticated, and menstruation, for example, came to be seen as the kiss of Ahriman on the head of whore-demoness *Geh*,[25] which was introduced into humanity to further arrest the battle against evil. The important point is that even despite the durability of this view the educated Zoroastrian woman is now welcomed as an asset to a global community which many believe to need all the help it can get as far as maintaining an intellectual power base is concerned. The religion is in some circles beginning to develop a new and practical quasi-theology of gender equality and complementariness which many modern Zoroastrians believe has been absent at least from the time of the Achaemenians (though conceivably earlier), but which, it is possible to show, has Gathic precedent. This does not mean that women are beginning to stampede the doors of the seminaries demanding admission to priestly orders (although some modern Zoroastrians would no doubt welcome such a move). But it does mean that women are beginning to be accorded a dignity and standing in the community above and beyond that very great dignity which comes with marriage and motherhood which Zoroastrianism has always recognized. It also means that a theological reappraisal is taking place within Zoroastrianism which recognizes that the soteriological significance of activities carried out by the male priests is complemented, enhanced and even equalled by those tasks which are only – and can only be – carried out by women in the fight against the Ahrimanic forces. Functions necessarily reserved to women such as bearing children thus take on a new religious significance and can arguably claim a status commensurate with that of the priestly functions in the Ahuric plan, since the emphasis on human-divine co-operation is one of its defining characteristics.

This, however, is a young theology, and it has not yet matured. Resistance to such thinking is inevitable, given the sociological and cultural environment within which it must develop, and nor does the achievement of equality in one sphere imply that it will occur in another. As Ketayun Gould writes of the current Parsi Zoroastrian situation, "enlightened attitudes towards women in one of these arenas is not a precursor of automatic changes in the traditional models of thinking in the other arena",[26] so there is an uneven progress. Jenny Rose sees the problems surrounding the position of women in the tradition as paradigmatic of those facing the community as a whole, and hints that by solving such dilemmas many other questions which the community faces may also be addressed positively:

> In the future, it may be that the dominant male ideology will not automatically be accepted as representing a complete view of what any religion is about. Within Zoroastrianism, women are increasingly learning to evaluate themselves positively and to realize the significant contribution they make to the religious life of their community, particularly through their 'alternative' ways of experiencing religion . . . The task now facing the Zoroastrian community is to determine which elements of the faith are traditions without any present religious or social relevance and therefore should be allowed to lapse into obsolescence (the prohibitions on the initiation of children for mixed marriages and conversion might fall into this category) and which traditions actually preserve vital elements of the faith and therefore need to be retained or reinstated if the faith is to continue to prosper.[27]

## 4  Other Issues in Contemporary Zoroastrianism and a Glance to the Future

The contact with western values has also had an impact in areas apart from those we have discussed in this chapter and elsewhere. Dress, particularly for the younger Zoroastrians, is one obvious way in which visible identification is made with contemporary values not considered by many to be intrinsic to the community, but other predominantly western habits such as using tobacco, condemned by all orthodox Zoroastrians due to its perceived abuse of fire, are now common particularly amongst that section of the community.[28] Many of these younger

Zoroastrians have also abandoned the *sudre* and *kushti*, or only wear them for religious occasions and on occasions when not doing so might cause distress or offence to parents or relatives. The priesthood is once again failing to attract young men, and few Zoroastrians of university age choose to take up the study of their tradition as an academic career either exclusively or within the larger context of religious studies.

Attitudes towards Zoroastrian ritual life have followed the same pattern of rationalization first encountered in the nineteenth century with regard to such matters as the *menog* beings and dualism. Rather than view these rituals as efficacious in themselves by virtue of their ritual identity, a number of Zoroastrians are now interpreting them as no more than human-centred actions, at best perpetuated and at worst invented by the priesthood, whose sole purpose is externally to express obsolete mythologies for those who require this kind of reinforcement. Thus rituals are no longer believed by some modern Zoroastrians to have an instrumental function capable of affecting the world, and the *menog* realities they invoke and honour are understood as no more than psychological constructs, or the residues of a bygone age whose culture and categories are seen as an embarrassment to the sophisticated mind. The enormous strides in scientific discovery in the twentieth century, coupled with a parallel philosophical leaning towards neo-empiricism, have also been put at the disposal of the educated Zoroastrian rationalist. A process of "demythologization" (to use R. Bultmann's term) has been established, the results of which posit that Zarathushtra was merely dealing with human ethical behaviour within a specific social context. This has not only encouraged in some quarters a blanket rejection of the later purity regulations, but it also challenges the dominance of ritual worship with its implication of (and therefore dependence upon) a heavenly hierarchy. This has inevitably meant that for many contemporary Zoroastrian intellectuals the religion must now be defined as a pure monotheism rather than as a cosmological dualism, a theological shift which can at least partly be attributed to western influence.

Others have been a little more conservative in their appropriation of the sciences, and J. M. Whitehurst cites the case of M. D. Karkhanawala who "tries to show that the discovery of anti-matter provides proof that Zoroastrian dualism is scientifically tenable".[29] Dissatisfaction with traditional expressions of the faith have led in other directions, and some Zoroastrians, possibly inspired by a western preoccupation with mysticism, have dabbled in occultism, and particularly in the *Ilm-e-Khshnoom* movement, which grafts theosophical concepts onto orthodox Zoroastrianism and promotes concepts such as reincarnation which are totally alien to the tradition. On the other hand, there has been a resurgence in Gathic studies amongst many modern Zoroastrians, encouraged by the number of excellent modern translations and commentaries which have appeared in recent years. The attention given to the *Gathas* by groups in the west has often been at the expense of an equivalent enthusiasm for the later literature, an omission naturally regretted by the advocates of doctrinal continuity. This familiarity with the *Gathas* in translation has also, arguably, had an effect on belief in the manthric character of the Avestan language which, within the ritual context, is thought to possess inherent sacred properties (though M. Dhalla in the first years of this century was keen to see the provision of Gujarati and English versions of scripture for the laity), and calls for a vernacular liturgy have lately increased.

Most telling of all, some western-born Zoroastrians are ceasing to see India and Iran as their national (i.e. ethnic) or religious (i.e. spiritual) homelands. This however is not a universal perception and, curiously, for some Iran rather than India is seen as "home", even those who would be technically classed as of Parsi origin. Perhaps this more than any other factor illustrates the complexity of the problems surrounding Zoroastrian identity. Our enquiry at the beginning of this chapter was "who is a Zoroastrian?". Clearly no one answer will satisfy all. And when, as R. Writer has reported, one Zoroastrian can affirm with conviction that she is "British", and another that he is "Iranian",[30] despite their living in the west, it goes some way to demonstrating the extent to which identity has been confused if not eroded. No wonder then that the orthodox insistence on ethnic solidarity and exclusivity is being challenged, since it has no meaning for many of those who have never known a social structure other than that found in the cities of Europe and the United States. And although it is hardly the fault of the traditionalists that this identity is threatened, their demand for a revitalization of Zoroastrian unity centred on ritual and traditional belief to confirm this identity, and the intensity with which they argue in its favour, is indicative of their fears about the consequences of the diaspora may be for the community as a whole.

Indications, however, are that the future may see a more formal acknowledgement of the divisions which are in evidence today in that, as with other religious traditions, there may grow out of historical Zoroastrianism a new parallel movement which wishes to adhere to the prophet's fundamental message but which finds itself unable to subscribe to all that has since been gathered along the way. It may then, in the future, be permissible to speak of "formal" and "material"

Zoroastrians – in fact it may be possible to do so today, if by "formal" is meant those who have been born into the faith and by "material" those who have chosen to follow the teachings of the prophet but are unable, for some reason, to be accepted into the traditional community whose boundaries are irrevocably defined. Ethnic identity would thus be preserved for those who wish it, and a new, looser identity created for those who do not recognize its importance. In this connection the French scholar Paul du Breuil, who had often expressed a desire to become a Zoroastrian but shied away from such a step since he was reluctant to cause pain to his Parsi friends, recognized the possibility of proceeding somewhat along these lines. For he was able to write in 1984 that

> beyond human religions ruled by tradition and ritual, there is a meta-physical and universal community acting as an ecumenical and invisible Church of all righteous *Fravartis* of men and women having the best thoughts, words and deeds. They cannot be known as direct followers of Zarathushtra, yet they are praised in the *Farvardin Yasht* (Yt.13) chapters 17, 21, 94, 143. They are those who fight against evil powers and whose sacrifices bring on Earth a Fire of new light and hope. They are those who work for the transfiguration of the world as requested by Zarathushtra. The faithfulness of Irani *Zarthoshti* and of *Parsees* to their cultural identity, to preserve and protect it as such, is not incompatible with a wholesome though selective opening of their religion to the world as an example of human dignity, of courage and of universal ethics".[31]

There are clear signs that this is happening now, but whether what this implies is enthusiastically embraced as providential or merely accepted as inevitable is a matter for future Zoroastrians to determine. What we can say with certainty, however, is that Zoroastrianism has something, even today, to teach us all, something of great value over and above the legacy that we have inherited from its more visible presence earlier in our history. Humanity, despite the progress which it is supposed to have made, and indeed perhaps because of it, has urgent need for a vision such as that of Zarathushtra; it needs to hear messages of hope and consolation, and even, at times, to be reassured of its inherent worth. It is, perhaps, not too fanciful to suggest that the world would be a poorer place were the noble (and ennobling) voice of the prophet of Iran never to be heard again above the din and clatter of our wayward times.

# Appendix 1: Zoroastrianism, Judaism and Christianity

There are so many features that Zoroastrianism seems to share with the Judeo-Christian tradition that it would be difficult to deny some relationship between them. Historically the first point of contact that we can determine is when the Achaemenian Cyrus conquered Babylon in Mesopotamia and released the Jews[1] from captivity, in 539 BCE. Although many Jews had risen to prominent positions and had enjoyed relative security in Babylonian society during the exile, they had been denied access to the *locus* of their religious activity, Jerusalem, where they believed Yahweh resided in an almost exclusive way. As the psalmist puts it: "how can we sing the song of Yahweh in an alien land?" (Psalm 137:4). This was because their god, Yahweh, was, prior to the exile and during its early years, understood very much as a "tribal" god, concerned only with the lives of his people. Therefore to characterize pre-exilic Judaism as "monotheistic" is in fact erroneous since we have clear evidence that the existence of other deities was acknowledged – hence, for example, the "sacrificial contest" between Elijah, the prophet of Yahweh, and the priests of Baal as recorded in 1 Kings 18:20–40. The years of exile and those immediately following it formed what was in all likelihood the most significant period of theological activity in the entire history of Judaism. The exile had meant that the Jews were for the first time separated from their god, and so as their captivity continued they began to reconsider how they should understand him. Because it would be unthinkable to suggest that he had completely detached himself from them, the Jews began to view him in more universalist terms, ceasing to confine him to one geographical area and even questioning his exclusive identification with one ethnic group. Since Cyrus brought at least some Zoroastrian beliefs with him into Babylon (where, incidentally, he was also influenced by Babylonian practice), it is highly probable that the Jews were in some way affected by his religious beliefs in this and other matters. The great god of Cyrus, Ahura Mazda (or *Ahuramazda* as many inscriptions dating from the period have it), was certainly a universal deity, acknowledged by his worshippers as the creator of all things. Cyrus himself was hailed by the Jews as the "Lord's anointed" (Isaiah 45:1), a title which would be more usually associated with messianic figures from within the Jewish tradition itself; it is therefore significant that a Jewish author could associate a non-Jew with a figure who had until then been perceived as a tribal deity but who was now emerging as a universal god. Isaiah goes on to define Yahweh in unmistakably monotheistic terms, by saying "I am Yahweh, and there is no other god but me" (Isaiah 45:5). Since the section of Isaiah from which this verse is taken was written after the exile, when Persians and Jews had enjoyed considerable contact, it is likely that, in the period leading up to its composition, their awareness of *Ahuramazda*'s universal nature had conditioned their perception of Yahweh, about whom they had already begun to think in more universalist terms as a response to their captivity. Not only did Cyrus liberate the Jews from Babylonian rule, he also encouraged them in their religious customs and allowed them to return home. Furthermore, although Cyrus had permitted those Jews who so wished to go back to Jerusalem (where a new temple was eventually built with Persian funds), many decided to remain in Mesopotamian territory where they continued to prosper under the Achaemenian empire. As the two cultures mingled, ideas on the natures of their respective religions will have been exchanged between them. The Jews, who by now were well on the way to being monotheists, will have recognized in the religion practised by their Zoroastrian compatriots a similar, though not of course identical, expression of the divine person to that which they were beginning to adopt. In fact it appears that the Jews went even further than the Persians in acknowledging one god alone, for, unlike the Persian Zoroastrians who could attribute the evil in the world not to *Ahura Mazda* but to an independent hostile power, the Jews could ascribe to Yahweh the claim that "I make the light and I create the darkness, I make well being and I create disaster" (Isaiah 45:7), a saying that is often considered an early Jewish refutation of Zoroastrian dualism.

Another area where Zoroastrian influence on Jewish religion may have occurred is eschatology. Prior to the exile there had been among the Hebrew peoples no real interest in the afterlife, which was seemingly discussed only in the vaguest terms. In fact pre-exilic Judaism was distinctly non-eschatological, content to speak of a shadowy and ill-defined place called *Sheol*, where a static kind of existence continued indefinitely. This is reflected in an earlier passage from the book of Isaiah (written by a different author from the later passages which we have just discussed) which says "I shall be held at the gates of Sheol for the rest of my days; . . . I shall never see Yahweh again in the land of the living" (Isaiah 38:10–11). It seems that, following the conquest by Cyrus, the Jews had progressively adopted the Zoroastrian belief in the matter of eschatology, for the ideas of reward and punishment following death begin to appear in Hebrew literature from this period, and, later still, the concept of complete separation of good from the evil – familiar from the Zoroastrian *Gathas* – is one that figures prominently in some Christian texts concerning eschatology. (It is also interesting that one word for heaven – "paradise" – which begins to appear in Jewish literature at this time, and is also found in the writings of the early Christians, derives from the Persian word for "garden".)

Linked to this eschatological notion of heaven, hell, reward and punishment is that of a coming saviour. We know that Zarathushtra proclaimed a series or group of saviours or "bringers of benefit" who would "heal the world" and "make existence brilliant" (Y.30:9), and that he believed himself to head this group. Similarly, although nearly one thousand years later, as their exile drew to a close the Jewish people began to develop a belief in messiah-type figures who would re-establish their fortunes. Initially it seems that any number of such figures was anticipated, and so the messianic title could be granted to anyone who was thought to be sent by Yahweh, and that such figures were not necessarily to be born of Jewish blood – hence Cyrus' designation as the "Lord's anointed". Over time this messianic character began to shed his humanity and become almost divine, eventually merging into a "son of man" figure as expressed in the writings of Daniel, who speaks of one on whom "was conferred rule, honour and kingship . . . (which) . . . will never come to an end" (Daniel 7:14). There is in this "kingdom" more than a passing resemblance to the Zoroastrian *frashokereti*.

As far as Satan is concerned, although a figure of that name does appear in the Hebrew scriptures, in the book of Job, he is not to be thought of as the author of evil. Rather he appears there as one of God's agents whose task it is to test Job's sincerity. There is certainly no indication that he is meant to be understood as the enemy of God, and although some early rabbinic writers attempted to identify Satan with the evil inclination in humans, the idea was never incorporated into mainstream or "normative" Jewish theology (although a truly "unified" Judaism has yet to emerge). It is not possible, therefore, to detect any overt Zoroastrian influence on Jewish satanology. However Satan reappears in the Christian scriptures, but even in Mark's gospel (the earliest to be composed) he is initially presented merely as one who comes to test Jesus (Mark 1:12–13), much in the same way as he tested Job. Matthew though presents a different picture. In a passage parallel to Mark's brief allusion to the "tester", Matthew clearly speaks of Jesus being tempted by "the devil" (Matthew 4:1–11). Matthew's gospel continues to present the figure of the devil as one whose goal is to frustrate the divine plan and seduce humanity away from God, and here we can see a much clearer resemblance to the Zoroastrian figure of Ahriman. Towards the end of the gospel, in the passage known as the "eschatological discourse" (Matthew 25:31–46), the evangelist writes of the absolute separation of good and the evil people ("sheep and goats"). The Greek term he employs in this passage suggests a physical separation rather than an ideological one. In the *Gathas* Zarathushtra had used a term which carries the sense of physical separation, as well as of judgement and discernment, as in the phrase *Bridge of the Seperator*. The suggestion in Zarathushtra's hymns is that those who have followed the evil path will languish for ever in the House of Lies, having chosen to follow the hostile spirit. Although it is unlikely that Matthew will have been familiar with the *Gathas* themselves, it is not impossible that he would have been acquainted with the idea of final and eternal separation, originally a Zoroastrian rather than Jewish doctrine. This idea may have come to him through Zoroastrian contacts. In his infancy narrative, Matthew gives a prominent place to the *magi*, who travel to Bethlehem having seen a star which they believe to be a sign of an auspicious birth (Matthew 2:1–12). Since *magi* was a contemporary term for the Zoroastrian priestly class (the Greek geographer Strabo, writing roughly at the same time, uses the word in his work when referring to the Persian priesthood), it is thought that the "wise men" of Matthew's gospel were Zoroastrian priests. If this is the case, we should consider the possibility that Matthew will have been aware of the Zoroastrian myth predicting the virginal conception of future *Saoshyants*, or at least that such figures were awaited by the Zoroastrians, an expectancy he may have wished to suggest as having been fulfilled in the child of Bethlehem. Other possible Zoroastrian allusions can be detected in the gospel, such as the injunction to "let the dead bury their dead" (8:22),[2] possibly a cryptic acknowledgement of Zoroastrian funerary procedures.

Finally, we should note that at 4:24 the evangelist remarks that knowledge of Jesus "spread throughout Syria". This seems at odds with other references in the gospel in which the extent of Jesus's activity, and that of the disciples, is limited to Israel, such as "do not make your way into gentile territory, and do not enter any Samaritan town; go instead to the lost sheep of Israel" (10:5–6) and "I was sent only to the lost sheep of Israel" (15:24). As there were Zoroastrian communities in Parthia, Cappadocia and Armenia,[3] it is probable that the trading opportunities offered by neighbouring Syria would have meant that a Zoroastrian presence would have been felt there also, and some scholars have suggested that Antioch in Syria was the place where the gospel may have been composed (or reached its final form). This being the case we can further speculate that Matthew may have partly targeted his evangelistic energy at the Zoroastrian community in the Syrian region, recognizing in its beliefs elements similar to those of his own; hence Syria's appearance in an otherwise geographically restricted gospel. Another possibility is that the gospel was composed in roughly two stages, or that it reflects two stages in the life of Matthew's community, the group for which he was writing and of which he was a member, possibly its "spokesperson". The first stage approximately corresponds to a period in which the community understood itself to be geographically and ideologically restricted to Palestine, and the later stage to a break with this territorial and ideological bond in which missionary activity demanded the expansion of the community's ethnic composition. If this is so any Zoroastrian community in Syria might have seemed a potentially fruitful target for evangelism. Either way, the appearance of the *magi* in chapter 2 of the gospel may have a more specific significance than has generally been recognized, since in introducing these figures Matthew may have not only been subtly acknowledging a cultural and theological interdependence between his tradition and one adjacent to it, but also establishing in his opening passages a definite evangelistic purpose to the book. For the same reason the Syrian reference at 4:24 and the "hard saying" at 8:22 may have been inserted to act as signposts for those outside the Israelite fold, in this case the Zoroastrians.[4]

# Appendix 2: The Roman Mithraic Mysteries

One of the most elusive and hotly debated issues in the study of Zoroastrianism is the precise nature of the connection between the Iranian deity Mithra and the military Roman Mithraic mystery cult, a connection which seems on the one hand so conclusive[1] and yet on the other so disturbingly remote. Even the historical problem of the manner of Mithra's arrival on the Roman scene remains unanswered. Some scholars have suggested that the conscription of Persian soldiers into the Roman army may account for it; others believe that Roman Mithraism was in fact a totally separate religion from its inception and was merely given a Persian "gloss" to make it attractive to a population obsessed with the cryptic and inscrutable east. Still others connect the Roman cult with Anatolia, where Mithra was known to be venerated in the company of other deities familiar to Zoroastrianism such as Anahita. There is little we can say about its journey west with any certainty, since it was evidently a cult which seemingly functioned without the need for texts (there are none remaining which, given the geographical area covered by the cult at its most popular, strongly suggests that none were ever written down), and the few inscriptions that do survive often merely illuminate the subjects of the carvings they accompany, revealing nothing substantial about the cult's origins. The cult which venerated Mithra in Roman circles (where he is traditionally known as *Mithras*), and which enjoyed a life of nearly 400 years, was esoteric, confined to male members of the Roman military and political elite (though traders and even slaves may have been eligible for membership), and demanded a series of seven graded initiation rites.

The basic doctrine of Mithraism, as far as can be told, is that Mithras was a god who was born from a rock and destined to secure the salvation of the world; to do this he was commanded by the god Apollo (through the intermediary agent of a raven) to slay the Bull from the region of the Moon, which was said to represent the fullness of life. Mithras was reluctant to do this but acquiesced in deference to the divine will; in the ensuing struggle between god and bull, other animals joined in – the dog, and scorpion and the snake. After Mithras was successful a quarrel broke out between Mithras and Apollo, but they were reconciled and celebrated a banquet. Much of this seems to be reflected in the iconography, the seven grades and what we know of the rituals of the Mithraists.

**Mithraic Grades (in order of ascent)[2]**

| Grade | Zodiacal Sign | Emblem (worn or carried) |
| --- | --- | --- |
| *Corax* (Raven) | Mercury | Wand, beaker |
| *Nymophus* ("Bride") | Venus | Crown, lamp, veil |
| *Miles* (Soldier) | Mars | Helmet, spear |
| *Leo* (Lion) | Jupiter | Thunderbolt, "fire-spade" |
| *Perses* (Persian) | Moon | Persian sword, scythe |
| *Heliodromos* (Sun-runner) | Sun | Crown, torch, whip |
| *Pater* (Father) | Saturn | Ring, staff, cap |

What is particularly interesting and most immediately obvious, however, for the student of Zoroastrianism, is the iconography of this cult, which contains so many tangible references to the Iranian religion as to prevent ruling out at least some connection and is the most direct evidence we have of Mithraic practice and teaching. Most striking of all is the central image of the slaughter of the bull. Reliefs on the many Mithraic altars scattered around Europe invariably show the god Mithras killing the "Bull of Heaven", a scene clearly echoing that of the slaughter of the uniquely-created Primal bull by Ahriman and recounted in the *Bundahishen*. (It also resembles a similar Mesopotamian myth from the Gilgamesh epic.) What is more, this scene contains other imagery which is also identifiably Zoroastrian, such as the dog who leaps up in apparent approval of Mithras' deed; the dog, we know, is an important creature in Zoroastrianism, essential to certain death rites. The snake, an Ahrimanic creature, which can be seen under the bull's body, is shown attempting to prevent the fruits of the sacrifice, the blood of the bull, from making contact with the earth and giving it life.

Mithraic temples were conceived in imitation of the "world cave" in which the god was supposed to have captured and killed the Bull of Heaven and secured for himself the title *Mithra Tauroctonus* (Mithra the Bull-Slayer), from which the term *tauroctony*, or "slaying of the bull", is derived. According to the early Mithraic historian Euboulos (cited by Porphry),[3] the first *mithraeum* was supposed to have been conceived by Zarathushtra himself, but given the prophet's silence of the subject of Mithra, subsequent attributions to him of Mithraic doctrine, such as it can be determined, are also best discounted, and the lengthy *Mihr Yasht* included in the later Avestan literature is almost certainly the work of Mithra enthusiasts within the Iranian tradition who were keen to ensure that their favoured deity should not go unnoticed.

Temples dedicated to Mithras (*mithraea*) were generally subterranean structures which consisted of a series of small rooms and a larger area set aside for communal liturgy where the altar is housed; it is possible that the smaller enclosures were where the seven stages of initiation were conducted. From the signs around the frame of the reliefs we can conclude that the seven stages of initiation were connected to the zodiac (see table above) which are in turn related to the four seasons. Some scholars today interpret Mithraism wholly in terms of these signs, since the main figures on the reliefs are also associated with the zodiac.[4] Since Zoroastrianism knows of no esoteric societies comparable with that associated with Mithras (Roman Mithraism has been likened to freemasonary), the development of such an association within the larger Roman socio-religious context, if it owes anything at all to the Persian religion, is a source of some bewilderment for many scholars, and some deny that such a connection exists. In fact one hallmark of the religion of Zarathushtra is its openness and accessibility to its people, with no room for sub-groups forming around any particular cultic figure. Roman Mithraic liturgies, hidden away from the gaze of the population, were a far cry from the open-air ceremonies conducted by the prophet of Iran and the priests of his class and even today, despite the culture of exclusivity that many orthodox Zoroastrians advocate, there is nothing to compare with the secretiveness of Roman Mithraism. Nor are we assisted in our investigations by informative texts other than the inevitably biased accounts of outsiders, whose reliability cannot always be guaranteed. Among such texts, however, those by the Christian writers Tertullian (who may at one time have been a Mithras worshipper) and Justin have been instrumental in reconstructing some details of Mithraic liturgy, and we can be sure that, in addition to the initiation process, a form of "communion" rite was celebrated, even if the inevitable bias of the Christian authors has meant that their interpretation of such rituals as diabolic inversions of Christian liturgies must be treated with scepticism.[5] It is also known that a banquet was regularly held as part of the ceremonial, in imitation of the reconciliatory feast shared by Mithras and Apollo.

It is impossible to say with any certainty how many adherents of the Mithraic cult there were, even in its heyday. Given the extent of excavated *mithraea*, one might suppose many thousands over the four centuries of its life. Even if only twenty people could meet at a time (an assumption based solely on the size of excavated *mithraea*), we do not know how often a ritual would take place, nor if the same people would attend on each and every occasion over a given period. The tendency to think of religious observance as a weekly event, as is the general "Sabbath day" custom with, say, Judaism or Christianity, has often conditioned our interpretation of the practices of other traditions, and in fact in the case of Mithraism, with its obvious zodiacal connections, we would be entitled to suggest that a more frequent gathering of the faithful may have been the norm.

Each Mithraic chapter, which will have been attached to a particular *mithraeum*, seems to have been autonomous, with no centralized government taking responsibility for the overall behaviour of the cult's members. It is all the more remarkable, then, that there was apparently such a uniformity of practice, though no doubt this is a testimony to the intense sense of discipline felt by men associated with and responsible for maintaining a power such as that which resided in Rome.

The question of the connection of Roman Mithraism with Zoroastrianism has so far remained unanswered, despite a century of research. Given the great distance between the two traditions in doctrine, architecture and practice, and the lack of evidence on the Roman side for a definite Iranian link, other than a possible transformation of the iconography as the cult was brought from Persia to Rome (a thesis that has been severely criticized recently), it seems that a number of options are still open to the scholar. The Roman Mithraic Mysteries may have been an "invention" by a high-placed Roman citizen (or group) who had some knowledge of Iranian Mithraic religion and who was fascinated by the mythological possibilities suggested by bull slaughter; it may have been a result of Roman assimilation of an attractive cult followed by the Persian people, although why Rome should adopt a deity of its major enemy is yet another question. It may indeed have been imported from Persia, somehow arriving in Rome unaccountably altered but still retaining a superficial resemblance to the Zoroastrian teaching; similarly, it may have been a refashioned non-

Zoroastrian Mithraic cult which somehow survived alongside Zoroastrianism and found its way west. It may, as has been more recently suggested, owe nothing to Zoroastrianism at all, being rather an astrological movement whose iconography represents not a cosmic struggle but an elaborate star chart. There is clearly much work to be done, but unless a totally new piece of concrete evidence is discovered, which will solve the Iranian problem once and for all, the issue will remain forever in the realm of speculation.

**Chart 1  The historical relationship between Zoroastrian and Judeo-Christian religion**

| | | | | |
|---|---|---|---|---|
| pre-Zoroastrianism (a) | Zarathushtra......Zoroastrianism................................................ | | | Parsis (g) |
| | | | 400 BCE (c) | |
| | | | Christianity.................. | |
| Ancient Israel | | Judaism............................. | | |
| 2000 BCE | 1400 BCE (b) | 539 BCE (d)   331 BCE (e) | 651 CE (f)   1,000 CE | |

(a) Mithra, Haoma, "polytheism", Vedic: Varuna, Soma, Agni etc.
(b) Zarathushtra's date disputed by some scholars who put it at c. 600 BCE.
(c) Fire temples introduced by Artaxerxes II (probably in response to Babylonian custom).
(d) Cyrus. Temple rebuilt in Jerusalem under Persian instructions.
(e) Alexander of Macedon and the destruction of Persepolis.
(f) Arabian invasion of Iran.
(g) Migration of Zoroastrians to India. The Zoroastrian community has now dispersed world-wide; there are major Zoroastrian communities in Canada, North America, Britain (mainly London), as well as smaller settlements in Hong Kong, Japan, Australia.

**Chart 2    The possible thematic relationships between Vedic, Zoroastrian and Judeo-Christian religion**

| Vedic | Zoroastrian | Judeo-Christian |
|---|---|---|
| | | |

Creation:
*Purusa-sukta*

*Bundahisen* (Gayomart)

7 stages of creation

Genesis

*Soma*

*Haoma*

*Indra*

*Indra* (*daeva*) (inverted – *Vendidad* 10:9 & 19:43)

Gathic

*Saoshyant* (cf. virginal conception) "son of man": Parousia/Judgement

*rta* (regulating law later supplanted by *dharma*) Varuna

**Ahura Mazda** *asha* ("righteousness")

opposing spirits

Qumranic & Inter-testamental literature

**Chart 3  Ahura Mazda, Spenta Mainyu and the Amesha Spentas**

| AMESHA SPENTA (AVESTAN) | ENGLISH | CREATION | REPRESENTATION IN YASNA | 7 HOLY DAYS OF OBLIGATION | OBSERVANCE IN EVERYDAY LIFE |
|---|---|---|---|---|---|
| *Khshathra Vairya* | (Desirable) Power Dominion The Kingdom (of God) | The sky of stone; later thought of as metal | The stone pestle and mortar; flint knife Later metal implements | Mid-spring *Maidhoizaremaya* | Exercising proper authority whether king or householder; honesty, thrift, charity |
| *Haurvatat* | Wholeness Health | Water | Consecrated water used in sprinkling | Mid-Summer *Maidhyoshema* | Keeping water unpolluted; Temperance, self-discipline |
| *(Spenta) Armaiti* | (Holy) piety Devotion | Earth | The ground of the *pavi* | Bringing in corn *Paitishahya* | Tilling and enriching the soil; being patient, enduring, productive |
| *Ameretat* | Long Life Immortality | Plants | *Haoma* and pomegranate wheaten cakes, strew of grass | Homecoming (of herds) *Ayathrima* | Nurturing plants and trees; Evergreen trees especially reverenced Temperance, self-discipline |
| *Spenta Mainyu/ Ahura Mazda* | Holy Spirit of God | The just man | The priest | All Souls *Hamaspathmaedaya* | Looking after one's own physical and moral well being |
| *Asha Vahishta* | (Best) Right, Truth Order | Fire | The ritual fire | New day *No Roz* | Keeping fire unpolluted; Justice and righteousness in thoughts, words and actions so *asha* remains |

(adapted with permission from Sarah Stewart, 1993)

# *Notes*

## Chapter I    Ancient Faith: Zarathushtra – Prophet and Priest

1   In keeping with contemporary practice I have used throughout this book the abbreviations "BCE" (Before the Common Era) and "CE" (Common Era) rather than the ideologically loaded "BC" and "AD".

2   I have used the proper name *Zarathushtra* throughout the book, in preference to the westernized *Zoroaster* which arrived in the English-speaking world through the Greek commentators. However, rather than use the term *Zarathushtrianism* in preference to *Zoroastrianism*, I have retained the latter since this is the choice of most Zoroastrians of my acquaintance. (This convention is, of course, discarded if I am citing the work of another writer such as in the title of G. Cameron's paper "Zoroaster the Herdsman".) *Zarathushtrian*, as an adjective, means something belonging to or emanating directly from Zarathushtra as in "a common Zarathushtrian literary/oral device"; *Zoroastrian*, on the other hand, means something pertaining to the faith or it means a person *of* the faith. Neither the term *Mazdaism*, nor any of its derivatives, is used here.

3   Higher (or *inner*) Zoroastrian religious ceremonies, such as the *Yasna*, may only be celebrated in India and Iran due to the fact that it is not possible to take the purified (*alat*) ritual objects over sea. This does not mean of course that the recitation of the *Gathas* is confined to priests resident in these countries. Indeed many of the priests throughout the world recite them (or portions of them) regularly, as do many laity.

4   This word does not appear in Zarathushtra's *Gathas*. It is a coalescence of two Avestan words meaning "wonderful" and "to make".

5   I. Gershevitch has noted that the term is the result of an amalgamation of two Indo-Iranian words whose meanings were "he who performs the libation" and "he who calls the gods". See I. Gershevitch, *The Avestan Hymn to Mithra* (Cambridge, 1967), 272.

6   See, for example, the (later Middle Persian) Pahlavi *Dinkard* Book 7, chapter III, 51ff. Zarathushtra is collecting water for the *Haoma* ceremony.

7   The commonly used term *Younger Avestan*, a term traditionally employed to denote texts that were composed or formulated after the prophet's lifetime, should not *always* be taken to imply something which came later than the *Gathas*, for there is evidence that much of the so-called *Younger Avesta* reflects a pre-Zarathushtrian tradition. I. Gershevitch has recommended on more than one occasion that the terms *Gathic* and *Standard* Avestan be used

to distinguish the two bodies of texts, since identifying them in this way does not denote greater or lesser antiquity (e.g. I. Gershevitch, "Approaches to Zoroaster's Gathas" in *Iran*, British Institute of Persian Studies, 1995). For example, the hymns to the gods Mithra (*Mihr Yasht*), and to Haoma (*Hom Yasht*), both of them post-Gathic works, contain thematic material which is identifiably pre-Zarathuishtrian. The first of these hymns is interesting in this context since, although the worship of Mithra is definitely pre- and extra-Zoroastrian, the hymn incorporates this deity in such a way as to retain his tradition but simultaneously accord him a subordinate place to Ahura Mazda. The *Hom Yasht* similarly "Zoroastrianizes" Haoma worship by including passages in which Zarathushtra addresses the deity Haoma in a reverential fashion. It may be that these passages were composed to prevent the loss of Haoma worship entirely, which could have been the case had the Gathic passages relating to the cult been interpreted too zealously. Finally there are differences between the two languages known as Gathic and Standard Avestan, but these do not concern us here.

8   Cf. *Vendidad*, 10:9 and 19:43.

9   Haug took this one step further in his formulation of what became known as the "European heresy", when he announced that the two spirits were *united* in Ahura Mazda, resulting in the proposition that Ahura Mazda was directly responsible for good and evil. Haug taught that the two spirits were "inseparable as day and night" and "indispensable for the preservation of creation" despite their being in constant opposition. The later dualism is therefore, for Haug, an aberration. See M. Haug, *The Parsis: Essays on their Sacred Language, Writings and Religion,* 1878 (reprinted Delhi, 1978), 304–5. This monistic interpretation of Haug's no doubt owed something to Haug's familiarity with material from the Sanskrit texts he studied, but we must remember also that Haug was primarily a philologist and not a theologian, and that his understanding of the development of religious tradition was based on the only direct experience he had, with Christianity.

10  Thus the term "twin", as in Y.30:3. though invariably employed in relation to this problem, has mislead in the past; it is sufficient to say that the term should not imply a common parenthood for the spirits, but merely denotes their characteristic as primal beings.

11  See W. Malandra, *An Introduction to Ancient Iranian Religion* (Minneapolis, 1983), 39–40 for an explanation of the grammatical device used in this passage to convey this idea.

12  A fuller discussion of the presence of evil in the world according to later Zoroastrian thought will be found in chapter IV.

13  M. Schwartz, "Coded Sound Patterns, Acrostics and Anagrams in Zoroaster's Oral Poetry" in R. Schmitt and Prods O. Skjærvø (eds) *Studia Grammatica Iranica: Festschrift für Helmut Humbach* (München, 1986), 348.

14  See e.g. W. E. Hale, *Ásura in Early Vedic Religion* (Delhi, 1986), 186. On the name of the supreme deity in the *Gathas* see also F. B. J. Kuiper, "*Ahura Mazda* Lord Wisdom?", *Indo-Iranian Journal* 18 (1976): 25–42.

15  This is the opinion of, amongst others, S. Insler (*The Gathas of Zarathushtra*, Leiden, 1975), who omits the *Gatha* from his translation, and H. Humbach with collaborators (1991 and 1994). M. Boyce

(*Zoroastrianism: Its Antiquity and Constant Vigour*, Costa Mesa, 1992) argues in favour of a Zarathushtrian authorship for the *Haptanhaiti Gatha* (87ff).

16   The last two *Gathas* are almost certainly incomplete.

17   The name of this daughter of the prophet, his youngest, is *Pouruchista*, a name which means "full of wisdom". Zarathushtra, who in ascribing this characteristic to his eponymous exalted God shows that he reveres wisdom above all else, recognizes this innate quality in his daughter, urging her to "take counsel with her intellect" (cf. Y.53:5).

18   Suggestions as to its identity vary. H. Falk, in "Soma I and II", *Bulletin of the School of Oriental and African Studies* 52:1 (1989): 77–90, notes that there have been three classifications of Haoma/Soma in attempting to identify it. First, there is the hallucinogenic class, proposed by R. G. Wasson in *Soma, divine mushroom of immortality* (New York, 1968) and which is linked to a Vedic passage (RV 10:119) concerning flying and its association with shamanism, but as Falk points out, there is no Zoroastrian or Vedic shamanism. Second, it has been identified as an alcoholic drink which Falk has dismissed since he maintains that the rituals would not allow time for fermentation. Third, it has been identified as a stimulant, in particular the *Ephedra* plant., by M. Boyce, see her "Haoma Priest of the Sacrifice", in M. Boyce and I. Gershevitch (eds), *W. B. Henning Memorial Volume* (London 1970), 62.

19   *Karapan* can mean "mumbled" or "garbled" in Avestan, and so Zarathushtra may have been alluding to their slovenly performance of the liturgy. H. Riechelt suggests that the Karapans later came to be thought of as the "enemies of the nation", though in the *Gathas* the term denotes an Iranian class of priests. See his *Avesta Reader* (Strassburg, 1911), 26.

20   B. Lincoln, *Priests Warriors and Cattle* (California, 1981), 63ff.

21   M. Boyce, *A Persian Stronghold of Zoroastrianism* (based on the Ratanbai Katrak Lectures, 1975) (Oxford, 1977): 44.

22   J. Kellens and E. Pirart, *Les textes veil-avestiques*, vol. 1 (Wiesbaden, 1988).

23   "Approaches to Zoroaster's Gathas", 2.

24   "Coded Sound Patterns, Acrostics and Anagrams in Zoroaster's Oral Poetry", 381.

25   Notably by the French scholar G. Dumezil, but see also the writings of B. Lincoln cited in this book and in the bibliography. Lincoln later distanced himself from many of Dumezil's conclusions.

26   See e.g. W. Malandra, *Introduction*, 17.

27   Attempts to find references to Zarathushtra in the Vedic texts have been unsuccessful, and owe more to wishful thinking than to scientific exegesis. There is no polemic in the Vedic texts directed against Zoroastrian doctrine; on the other hand, Zarathushtra does demonstrate a familiarity with Vedic literary technique (see further chapter II).

28   Plutarch, *Isis and Osiris*: 46, cited in J. H. Moulton, *Early Zoroastrianism* (London, 1913), 399.

29   M. Boyce, *Zoroastrianism: Its Antiquity and Constant Vigour*, 32.

30   See Boyce, *Zoroastrianism: Its Antiquity and Constant Vigour*, 13ff.

31   F. Müller (ed.), *Sacred Books of the Eas*, vol. 47, trans. E. W. West, 73.

## Chapter II    Ahura Mazda, Spenta Mainyu and the Divine Heptad

1   Its first recorded appearance is in the first verse of the *Yasna Haptanhaiti*, a verse which, in addition to Zarathushtra's disputed authorship of the whole of this *Gatha*, is not considered as part of the original hymn.

2   This is slightly adapted from Humbach and Ichaporia (*The Heritage*, 83). The italics, showing the English renderings of the members of the Ahuric court, are mine. That there are eight names in what is generally called a heptad is explained by the unique relationship between Ahura Mazda and Spenta Mainyu, already considered in chapter I and to be discussed again shortly.

3   See *Vendidad*, chapter 10: 7–9.

4   The terms *getig* and *menog* are Pahlavi derivations from the Avestan words meaning "material" and "immaterial" respectively. They are used by later Zoroastrian theologians and other writers to denote the two created realms. Their use here may therefore seem anachronistic, but their convenience outweighs any inaccuracy it may suggest.

5   In grammatical terms the Amesha Spentas are either feminine or masculine in the *Gathas*; theologically they should be thought of as pure spirit and thus transcending gender.

6   This is not always the case, however, and certain texts do seem to speak of Spenta Mainyu as having been created by the Wise Lord. Quite often such texts represent no more than an individual author's opinion and so they are not to be taken in all cases as articulating a definitive teaching.

7   For example in F. Mehr, *The Zoroastrian Tradition* (Rockport, MA, 1991), 29.

8   See chapter VI.

9   This is recounted in the opening section of the *Bundahishen*. M. Boyce considers this to be part of the prophet's original teaching, bearing in mind the obvious respect he held for this liturgy. See her *A History of Zoroastrianism*, vol. 1 (Leiden, 1975), 231.

10  Since this hymn consists of rhetorical questions the apparent problem in verse 5, concerning the creation of darkness, is solved by accepting Insler's suggestion that the position of the conjunctive copulative "and" (*ca*) after light and dark (or "luminous bodies and dark spaces" in Insler) shows that these two cannot be "in equal co-ordination" and thus we can likewise distinguish their origins. See S. Insler, *The Gathas of Zarathushtra*, Leiden, 1975, 67 and 244, and see also chapter IV on the nature of Ahrimanic "creations".

11  The later practice, which survives to this day, was to have the assistant priest, known as the *raspi* (from the Avestan root *rac-*, to help) responsible for this liturgical duty.

12  See G .Cameron, "Zoroaster the Herdsman", in *Indo-Iranian Journal* 10 (1968): 261–81. This is a questionable interpretation, and is not accepted by Insler (*Gathas*, 141f) who nevertheless accepts Cameron's general thesis on the metaphoric possibilities of this animal in the *Gathas*. It is in any case a curious observation for Cameron to make in view of his earlier assertion that, despite the tendency of religious teachers to use familiar imagery, the cow would not have been a familiar figure in Iran (267f). The reality, as

Insler points out, is that the cow would not have prospered particularly well in Iran due to the barrenness of the land. *This* would most likely have been the reasoning behind the prophet's use of this image. In the context of this verse the question could well be "how will you evaluate and nourish the cow (*good vision*) I have fashioned?" in which case the idea of weighing up actions and results is still relevant.

13 J. D. Randria has suggested that "Ahura Mazda's conceiving and executing the Creation by 'thought' has been seen to be analogous to His performing the Yasna or Sacrifice. Thus the terms thought, intention, Yasna and sacrifice are not only akin to one another but are inherently creative". See J. D. Randria, "The Philosophy of the Religious Tradition of Haoma and Sacrificial Worship" in *Journal of the K. R. Cama Oriental Institute* (Bombay, 1994), 65.

14 This is a later modification to Zarathushtra's apocalyptic scenario, incorporated into the Pahlavi sources. Gathic judgement seems to be less lenient.

15 *Ashi*: see e.g. Y.34:12; Y.43:12; *Sroash*: see e.g. Y.33:5; Y.44:16.

16 See Boyce, *History*, vol. 1, 227.

17 There may, however, be an etymological connection of *atar* with the Latin *atrium* which, as Moulton discusses, may suggest a cultic dimension to fire in earlier (and pre-) Zoroastrian history. See J. H. Moulton, *The Treasure of the Magi* (London, 1917), 145.

18 For example Y.31:20; Y.44:11.

19 *The Zend-Avesta*, Part 2, *Sacred Books of the East*, vol. 23, ed. F. Max Müller, trans. J. Darmesteter (Oxford, 1882; Delhi, 1993), 24–5.

20 M. Eliade, *Myth and Reality* (New York, 1963), 95. *Deus otiosus*, a technical term in the study of religions, means, literally, "a hated god", which may be a severe definition, but which expresses in a hyperbolic way the distance that has grown between the Supreme Being and the believing community.

21 See the section on the *Yasna* in chapter IV.

22 Cf., however, Gershevitch, *The Avestan Hymn to Mithra*, 22ff.

23 This highly contentious issue is dealt with in more depth in Appendix 2.

24 See M. Boyce, "On the Orthodoxy of Sasanian Zoroastrianism", *Bulletin of the School of Oriental and African Studies* 59/1(1996), 22.

25 This is not an isolated instance of Ahura Mazda venerating other deities. In Yasht 5:17, he prays to Anahita to secure Zarathushtra's allegiance.

26 However, see, briefly, the section *Holy Days and Holy Months* in chapter VI for details on the calendar dispute.

27 For example in the *Haptan Yasht*, the Amesha Spentas are offered sacrifices but so are other beings such as *Saoka*, *Râta*, *Gaokerena* and so on.

28 There are hints at this, however. In the *Ormazd Yasht* and the *Haptan Yasht* the Amesha Spentas are listed in order; in the *Kordad Yasht* Ahura Mazda is proclaimed as the creator of *Haurvatat*. What is wanting in the *Yashts* is systematic detail. The *Gathas* refer to Ahura Mazda as the "father" of the bountiful immortals but this is understood in a metaphorical sense (cf. Boyce, *History*, vol. 1, 184, n11).

29 Boyce, *Textual Sources for the Study of Zoroastrianism*, Manchester, 1984, 23.

30 All quotation from the GBd. are taken or adapted from Boyce *Textual Sources*.

31   Humbach and Ichaporia (*The Heritage*, 13) draw attention to the presence of Ahrimanic concepts in the *Gathas*, such as *Aka Mainyu* (evil spirit), *Aka Manah* (evil thought) but a demonic heptad corresponding to Zarathushtra's cardinal virtues is not encountered until the *Bundahishen*.

32   Cf. Y.32:5.

33   Darkness may be understood in this context as an absence of light, having a negative character signified by an absence of form and substance rather than existing in any qualitative sense.

34   See, for example, the Rig Vedic hymn *Purusa-sukta* (RV Bk. 10:90). This might suggest a common proto-Indo-Iranian root for this particular mythological concept.

## Chapter III   Zoroastrian Eschatology

1    Y. 34:13; 44:2; 45:11; 46:3; 48:9; 48:12; 49:3; 49:9; 51:9; 53:2.

2    H. Reichelt, *Avesta Reader* (Strassburg, 1911), 268. Other suggestions include "one who strengthens".

3    See J. R. Hinnells, "Zoroastrian Saviour Imagery and its Influence on the New Testament" in *Numen* 15 (1969): 161–85.

4    Cf. GBd. 1:20 in Boyce, *Textual Sources*, 46.

5    The Avestan root *ci-*, as in the Gathic phrase *cinvaot peretu* means "to cut" or "to separate".

6    Bruce Lincoln has drawn attention to the similarity of Zarathushtra's role in the individual judgement as expressed here to that of Charon, the ferryman of Greek mythology, and has suggested that Zarathushtra took over an earlier version of the myth (from the hypothetical Proto-Indo-European tradition), attributing to himself this key position. Lincoln's reasoning in this is based on the etymology of the prophet's name, which he analyses as "Zarat-ushtra", the "t" in the first component replacing the usual "$\theta$"; "zarat" he sees here as the past participle of the Avestan *zar-*, meaning "to age", cognate with the Greek *geron*, "old man", the term by which Charon was most commonly described. Lincoln thus clearly believes that both the Iranian and the Greek myths of crossing over to the afterlife derive from the same P-I-E myth, and that Zarathushtra boldly inserted himself into the myth when he refashioned it. See B. Lincoln, "The Ferryman of the Dead" in his *Death War and Sacrifice* (Chicago, 1991): 62–75.

7    There is also the "Place of the Mixed Ones", for the souls of whose accumulated good deeds and bad deeds are judged are evenly balanced. Any suggestion that this place resembles the Christian notion of purgatory, since it is located midway between heaven and hell and is not intended for the "damned", is misleading. In fact the Christian notion of purgatory owes more to the Zoroastrian House of Lies since in both cases eventual "salvation" is assured.

8    Taking my cue from M. Boyce (*Zoroastrianism: Its Antiquity and Constant Vigour*: xii), and for the sake of clarity I have here retained the Avestan transliteration of the term in preference to a transliteration of the Pahlavi version of the word.

9    Boyce explains the derivation of this precise figure, fifty-seven years before

The End: "The figure 57 is apparently made up of the 30 years allotted to each of the Saviours, as to Zoroaster himself, before he embarks on his great work, followed by thrice nine, or 27 years, an auspicious number for bringing about Frashegird (*frashokereti*)" (*History*, 291). She also refers to A. V. Williams Jackson, "The Fifty-seven Years in the Zoroastrian Doctrine of the Resurrection", in *Journal of the Royal Asiatic Society*, 1928: 1–6, in which he sets out the texts relating to this figure.

10  See F. Max Müller (ed.), *Sacred Books of the East*, vol. 47 (trans. E. W. West), 28 ff.

11  F. Max Müller (ed.), *Sacred Books of the East*, vol. 23 (trans. J. Darmesteter), 202.

12  Müller (ed.), *Sacred Books of the East*, vol. 23, 202. *Spitama* is Zarathushtra's family name; the *baresma* is a reference to the bundle of pomegranate twigs used in the *Yasna* ceremony (now replaced by metal wires) – see chapter VI.

13  See e.g. Jal Dastur Cursertji Pavry, *The Zoroastrian Doctrine of a Future Life* (New York, 1926; 1965), 28ff.

14  See also Boyce, *History*, 238.

15  See also chapter VII, section 3, *Women in Contemporary Zoroastrianism*, for a brief explanation of the cultural conditions surrounding this notion.

16  See Boyce *Zoroastrianism: Its Antiquity and Constant Vigour*, 75f for a fuller discussion on this topic.

17  *History*, 244.

18  *History*, 231; 244.

19  B. T. Anklesaria (trans.), *Drayisn-I Ahraman o Divan* in *Zand-I Vohumen Yasn and Two Pahlavi Fragments* (Bombay, 1957), 133.

20  See GBd. 1:26.

## Chapter IV   The Two Existences and the Problem of Evil

1  Y.28:2 and Y.43:3.

2  See e.g. S. Shaked, "The Notions *menog* and *getig* in the Pahlavi Texts", *From Zoroastrian Iran to Islam* (Variorum Collected Studies Series), (Aldershot, 1995), II, 64–5.

3  J.J. Modi, *The Religious Ceremonies and Customs of the Parsees* (Bombay, 1922), 390.

4  Later in the chapter we shall see how the apparent "challenge" to this view in the *Vendidad* is satisfactorily reconciled with the notion of creation being essentially Ahuric.

5  F. M. Kotwal and J. Boyd, *A Persian Offering – The Yasna, A Zoroastrian High Liturgy* (Paris, 1991), 3f.

6  Cf. *Dadestan-i Denig* 37:45 in F. Max Müller (ed.), trans. E. W. West, *Sacred Books of the East*, vol. 18, 92.

7  See A. V. Williams, "The Body and the Boundaries of Zoroastrian Spirituality", *Religion*, 19 (1989): 227–39.

8  This is a problematic notion. What is meant here is that Ohrmazd is able to manifest his attributes *directly* through his good creation whereas Ahriman has to content himself with the kind of "borrowed" manifestation under discussion.

9  GBd. 1:47 (see Boyce, *Textual Sources*, 47).

10  S. Shaked, "Some notes on Ahreman, the Evil Spirit and his creation", *From Zoroastrian Iran to Islam* III, 227–34.
11  See Boyce, *History*, 201.
12  Boyce, *History*, 2 and 23.
13  See further Louis H. Gray, "The 'Ahurian' and 'Daevian' Vocabularies in the Avesta", *Journal of the Bombay Branch of the Royal Asiatic Society* (1927): 427–41.

## Chapter V  Zoroastrianism and Fire

1  See *Qur'an* Surah 9:29.
2  The three groups are also linked together as ones who believe in "the last day" (Surah 2:59).
3  Some Zoroastrians believe that the fire itself was brought from Iran, but others think this unlikely.
4  From John Chardin, *Voyages en Perse et autres lieux de l'Orient*, vol. II (Amsterdam 1753, cited in Boyce, *Textual Sources*, 126). Over the next two hundred years things were to improve so that what were apparently bribes were no longer necessary to ensure the well-being and safety of Zoroastrians in Iran. "A Fatwa on the Rights of Zoroastrians" (1910) states that to "vex and humiliate the Zoroastrian community or other non-Muslims who are under the protection of Islam is unlawful. . . ." (cited in R. Writer, *Contemporary Zoroastrians*, New York, 1994, 47). Dr Writer notes that the guarantee enshrined in these words has not been observed in all instances.
5  See F. M. Kotwal, "The Authenticity of the Parsi Priesthood", *Indo-Iranian Journal* 33 (1990): 165.
6  J. C. Heesterman, *The Broken World of Sacrifice* (Chicago, 1993), 101.
7  See also J. J. Modi, *The Religious Ceremonies and Customs of the Parsees* (Bombay, 1922), 200 ff.
8  F. M. Kotwal and J. Boyd, *A Persian Offering: the Yasna, a Zoroastrian High Liturgy* (Paris, 1991), 14.
9  See F. M. Kotwal and J. Boyd, "The Zoroastrian *paragna* ritual", *Journal of Mithraic Studies*, vol. 2:1 (1977), 41.
10  In addition to the great Atash Bahrams there are a number of temples in which "lesser" fires can be housed; these temples are generally known by the Parsi Gujerati term of *Agiary*.

## Chapter VI  A Living Faith – Zoroastrian Worship, Rituals and Other Observances

1  A few invocations are recited in a secondary liturgical language called *Pazand*, but these interpolations are recited in a lower voice in order to maintain an unbroken flow of Avestan sound.
2  Although these are now metal, in earlier times they consisted of 21 hairs of a consecrated bull.
3  R. G. Williams and J. W. Boyd, *Ritual Art and Knowledge: Aesthetic Theory and Zoroastrian Ritual* (Colorado, 1993), 29.

4 Kotwal and Boyd, "The Zoroastrian *paragna* ritual", 44.
5 Williams and Boyd, *Ritual Art and Knowledge*, 29.
6 Cf. Y.31:19.
7 Kotwal and Boyd *A Persian Offering*, 24
8 This seems to resemble the Hindu custom of *prasada*, in which the priests distribute small portions of the food offered to the gods in *puja* to those devotees who have witnessed the ritual. As far as the Zoroastrian *Yasna* is concerned, it is perhaps of some significance that the *zot* does not consume this second preparation but rather that he distributes it to creation, and W. Darrow has suggested that this is in recognition of the deferral or "delay" of the *eschaton*. To summarize and slightly expand this point, since milk, absent from the *parahom* but now introduced into the second *hom* preparation in the *Yasna*, will also feature in the *hom* preparation of the final apocalyptic *Yasna*, the priest "refuses" this eschatologically implicative drink, thus maintaining a unique position mid-way between the two cosmic events of creation and apocalypse, unwilling to make a total identification with the "fullness" of the priesthood as unveiled at the end of time. See W. Darrow, "Keeping the Waters Dry, The Semiotics of Fire and Water in the Zoroastrian *Yasna*", *Journal of the American Academy of Religion* 56/3 (1987): 417–42.
9 See Kotwal and Boyd, "The Zoroastrian *paragna* ritual", 36.
10 "Keeping the Waters Dry", 420.
11 Remark made by Dastur Kotwal in a video recording demonstrating the *Yasna* ceremony produced by Colorado State University. See introduction for details. See also *A Persian Offering*, 25. I acknowledge here the usefulness of this video recording in writing this section.
12 Paul Ricoeur, *The Rule of Metaphor* (Toronto, 1977), 7.
13 "The Zoroastrian *paragna* ritual", 33.
14 *Ritual Art and Knowledge*, 142.
15 This ceremony is also demonstrated on the Colorado State University video recording.
16 Despite the non-involvement of the laity in the higher rituals such as the *Yasna* and a distinguishing characteristic of Zoroastrianism as a religious tradition which, in its devotional life, fosters above all else the individual's communion with the Creator and the *menog* beings through private recitation of the Avestan prayers and other spiritual aids, there has recently been interest expressed in gathering the community together for corporate prayers, and this venture has received approval from community leaders. In a joint interview published in the July/August 1995 edition of the popular Bombay-based Parsi magazine *Parsiana*, the two high priests, Dasturs Kotwal and JamaspAsa, together with Khojeste Mistree, director of the Bombay-based Zoroastrian Studies, and the economist Fredie Mehta, all supported the suggestion of introducing for the community a regular series of meetings which would be partly worship and partly instruction. Modelled, it is recognized, on the Christian and Muslim practice of regular gatherings of the faithful rather than on an established Zoroastrian custom, this innovation would, it is hoped, help the Parsis to "instil . . . a spirit of devotion and reverence towards their religion", as JamaspAsa notes in the *Parsiana* interview.

17 A non-Zoroastrian is sometimes referred to as a *juddin*. This is a neutral term merely meaning a person of another religion (as opposed to a *bedhin*, a follower of the Zoroastrian religion) but to the distress of many members of the Zoroastrian community, it has, over time, acquired pejorative associations in some circles.

18 *The Religious Ceremonies*, 376–7.

19 Cf. *Vendidad*, 4:47.

20 A similar confinement is also technically demanded of women during their monthly period, although it is often difficult to impose it today. In earlier pre-urban times when the village was the usual environment, such women would be sent away to small huts which were constructed outside the confines of the village so that the pollution they carried would not infect the remainder of the community. This custom is still practiced in the remoter parts of Zoroastrian Iran. In such societies a woman is said to be *bi-namaz*, or "without prayer", a euphemism which does not prevent her contemporaries from regarding her mere glance as "contaminating". See M. Boyce, *A Persian Stronghold of Zoroastrianism* (Oxford, 1977), 100.

21 *The Religious Ceremonies*, 7.

22 Since orthodox Zoroastrians do not entertain the idea of conversion into the faith, and very few "cradle" Zoroastrians would need to wait until adulthood for their initiation into the fold, this is very rare indeed, but isolated examples of conversion have occurred in the west recently, with adults receiving the *Sudre* and *Kushti*, to the deep consternation of many traditionalist members of the community. Arguments favouring conversion (or "acceptance") point to the initial wave of converts that Zarathushtra himself must have produced to propel the religion onto the Iranian scene, and in particular to the first of those converts, his cousin Maidhyoimah, who accepted the religion ten years after Zarathushtra began his ministry, and a little later King Vishtaspa who, with his family, is traditionally said to have accepted Zarathustra's religious message in the prophet's forty-second year, a result, it seems, of the prophet miraculously curing the king's favourite horse. Arguments against the practice claim that there were no such "conversions" from outside the ethnic group, merely that modifications of the existing religious tradition were adopted by Zarathushtra's first adherents, and indeed the orthodox hold inviolate the characteristic ethnic identity of Zoroastrianism which, being as much part of the heritage as the doctrinal element of the faith itself, cannot be diluted by outside influence. Two recent, and somewhat contrasting, examples may illuminate the extent and complexity of the problem. In 1983 the *Navjote* ceremony of Joseph Peterson, an American of the Judeo-Christian tradition, was performed in New York, to the great dismay of the orthodox. Among the officiating priests was Dr Kersey Antia, who, as a consequence of this and his general policy on conversion, produced a privately printed document *The Argument for Acceptance* (submitted to *Parsiana* 1984, published 1985) which received substantial circulation and incurred the wrath of the scholar-priests of Bombay who published their own riposte entitled *Antia's 'Acceptance' – A Zoroastrian 'Armoigih' (Heresy)* (Bombay, n.d.). One of the chief arguments against Peterson's acceptance was that he had not been born into the faith; Antia's philological expertise was also called into ques-

tion, the verb translated as "to convert" being particularly problematic. The scholar-priests who had denounced Antia's actions, Dasturs Kotwal, Mirza and JamaspAsa, prompted a controversy of their own when they became involved with the case of Neville Wadia, an octogenarian of Parsis descent who had been raised in the Church of England but who now wished to return to the faith of his ancestors. After much theological and historical debate Wadia was eventually returned to the Zoroastrian fold since, it transpired, he was a Parsi Zoroastrian by both descent and conviction despite his Anglican background, but his *Navjote* ceremony did not take place until a great deal of divided opinion had been engendered throughout the community. As noted on other occasions, the issue seems, on a general level, to be Parsi rather than Irani concern. More detailed discussions of the Peterson case may be found in R. Writer, *Contemporary Zoroastrians*, 213–6. A text from the Sasanian period may suggest that during that period at least conversion was not discouraged: "Cease, therefore, to harass the Christians, but exert yourselves diligently in doing good work, so that the Christians, and adherents of other religions, seeing that, may praise you for it and feel themselves drawn to our religion" (from *a letter by Hormizd IV [579–90] to leading magi* in Boyce, *Textual Sources*, 115), although this may be interpreted as merely a general plea for tolerance. On the subject of conversion see also the brief discussion on intermarriage in this chapter. I am indebted to Dr Antia for providing me with a copy of his paper, and for his permission to refer to it in this book.

23 *The Religious Ceremonies*, 170.

24 The *Kushti* thus seems to be reminiscent of the sacred cord worn by the "twice-born man" in Brahminical religion; quite possibly the two customs, if related, derive from a common Indo-European practice.

25 The modern form of the *madressa* is dated back to the latter part of the nineteenth century, the first having been established in 1854 partly in response to the intellectual onslaught of western Christian scholarship largely introduced into India by the missionary movement. Such men as John Wilson, who had studied in Europe, were able to display a knowledge of Zoroastrianism far greater than that of the majority of Zoroastrians themselves, and even when this learning was defective or its conclusions misguided, as was sometimes the case, they were able to turn this learning to their advantage in their quest to denounce Zoroastrianism and replace it with Christianity. It was felt that a revitalized and much more learned Zoroastrian priesthood was essential in refuting the missionaries' arguments. The establishment of such seminaries was one contribution to the creation of new indigenous Zoroastrian scholarship which is still active – and enjoys a deservedly high reputation – today.

26 This was pointed out to me by Khojeste Mistree of Zoroastrian Studies, Bombay, January 1996. A priest will sometimes be called in to recite the Zoroastrian creed when a person is known to be dying, after which he will repurify himself with appropriate rites. Priests also have a role in death rituals, but they maintain a physical distance from any dead matter, and observe extra precautions against impurity whilst engaged in funerary duties.

27 See Reichelt, *Avesta Reader*, 180f.

28 See A. Jafarey,"The Zoroastrian Priest in the Avesta" in *World Zoroastrian Organization Conference on Zoroastrian Religion, Culture and History, Chicago, 1987* (London, 1990): 24–33. J. H. Moulton makes a similar point in *The Treasure of the Magi*, 14–15, but, I think, from different motives; moreover Moulton does not deny the existence of a priestly institution.

29 "The Zoroastrian Priest", 25.

30 See M. Boyce, "Zoroaster the Priest", *Bulletin of the School of Oriental and African Studies* 33:1 (1990): 22–38.

31 "Zoroaster the Priest", 38.

32 See, for example, F. M. Kotwal "Initiation into the Zoroastrian Priesthood: present Parsi Practice and an old Pahlavi Text" in *A Green Leaf, Acta Iranica* 28 (Leiden, 1988): 299–307, for a further discussion on priestly initiation and an example of a priestly genealogy (at note 4).

33 Cf. *Vendidad*, 3:2–3. It must be recognized that these texts, even in translation, reflect a patriarchal society, similar to that which produced the Hebrew scriptures. Today the move towards gender equality has encouraged the belief that a man's wife is no longer deemed subordinate to his dog or his cattle.

34 Cf. *Vendidad*, 3:25.

35 This is a useful generalization, but it is not set in concrete. See for example Writer, *Contemporary Zoroastrians*, 206 on the matter of the Parsi-Irani debate on "conversion".

36 Taken (with modifications) from *Parsiana*. The magazine carries a number of these advertisements in practically every issue.

37 *The Religious Ceremonies*, 20.

38 See M. Boyce, *A Persian Stronghold*, 172 ff. Modi notes that it is traditional for a Parsi wedding rite to be repeated at midnight in imitation of this old Persian custom (*The Religious Ceremonies*, 40).

39 When the marriage takes place in India (or is of Indian Zoroastrians in the west) part of this address may be in Sanskrit, a custom deriving, it seems, from the earliest days of the Parsi Zoroastrians in Sanjan. It has no religious significance, being simply a gesture to history.

40 As Dastur Dr K. M. JamaspAsa has written: "Dead matter is a pollution, hence a dead body is contaminated and a source of disease to the living." Short essay in the booklet *Towers of Silence*, The Trustees of the Parsi Punchayet Funds and Properties (Bombay, 1994), 9.

41 Today, at least in the major cities, the expectation is that a *nasarsala* will undergo a modified and shortened version of the rite that was practised in earlier times – another example, it seems, of urbanized living.

42 Cf. Question and Answer 104, *Pahlavi Rivayat of Aturfarnbag and Farnbag-Sros* (2 vols) trans. B. T. Anklesaria (Bombay, 1969), 101.

43 *Gomez* is also believed by Zoroastrians to confer immortality. This is probably due to an identification of a consecrated form of the urine with the proto-sacrificial Primal Bull, but it must be noted that urine, consecrated or otherwise, from a bull that is not owned by a Zoroastrian cannot be considered to have sacred properties. See also the section on the *Barashnum i-no shab* rite.

44 For further information on the dog in Zoroastrianism see e.g. *Vendidad* Fargard XIII in Darmesteter, ed. Müller, *Sacred Books of the East*, vol. 4,

1887, 151 ff.

45    A. Williams has noted that this Pahlavi term carries a number of meanings associated with "connection", among them "tradition", "kin" and relationship. It is used literally and figuratively in Pahlavi literature. See A. V. Williams, "Medieval Texts in a Modern World", *World Zoroastrian Conference, July 1986 Souvenir Issue* (London, 1986), 56.

46    In ancient Iran the practice was merely to deposit the dead corpse on the hillside, away from the villages.

47    L. Jemt, Doctoral Student in Social Anthropology in the University of Uppsala, Sweden, cited in *Towers of Silence*, 32.

48    *Towers of Silence*, 31 and 32.

49    The most notable recent example was in the case of Roxanne Shah, a Parsi woman who had married a non-Zoroastrian and after whose death was refused the *dakhma*. This caused a now infamous exchange of letters in the Parsi press and beyond. See T. Luhrmann, *The Good Parsi: The Fate of a Colonial Elite in a Postcolonial Society* (Harvard, 1996), 158ff for a detailed account of the debate; also F. M. Kotwal, "The Divine Laws of God Must Prevail" in *Parsiana*, Sept. 1990 and so on.

50    See *The Religious Ceremonies*, 141.

51    J. Choksy *Triumph over Evil: Purity and Pollution on Zoroastrianism* (Texas, 1989), 49.

52    *The Good Parsi*, 101.

53    *The Good Parsi*, 162.

54    *Triumph over Evil*, 114.

55    In the *Mihr Yasht* Mithra is addressed as a "grass-land magnate"; see Gershevitch, *The Avestan Hymn to Mithra, passim.*

56    The translation of this and the two other prayers in this section are also taken from Humbach and Ichaporia, *The Heritage.*

57    S. Insler, "The *Ahuna Vairya* Prayer", *Acta Monumenta HS Nyberg* (Leiden, 1975), 409.

58    D. McIntyre, "The Talisman", *Proceedings of the Second North American Gatha Conference* (FEZANA Journal of the Research and Historical Preservation Committee, vol. II), ed. Saroash J. H. Maneckshaw and Pallan R. Ichaporia, Womelsdorf, 1996:153–69.

59    See further Humbach's earlier English version (in collaboration with J. Elfenbein and P. O. Skjærvø) in *The Gathas of Zarathushtra and Other Old Avestan Texts* (2 parts) (Heidelberg, 1991), part 1, 115 (with commentary in Part 2).

## Chapter VII    A Living Faith – Zoroastrian Ethics

1    Cf. F. Mehr, "Zoroastrian Ethics", *The 1st World Conference on Zoroastrian Religion, Culture & History, London 1984, Souvenir Issue* (London, 1984), 89. Mehr notes four of these faculties, not mentioning Desire, though, with due respect to Professor Mehr, I believe I am right in identifying Desire as a further faculty. The question, of course, is begged: is "Desire", strictly speaking, a faculty? In the present context I believe it can be justified to call it such, or at least to say that as a human impulse it is

absorbed into this group of human attributes, since it can be understood as an Ahuric provision intended to assist the advancement of the Zoroastrian along the path of *asha*. Desire, of course, is also innate to humans.

2 Quoted in *Ritual Art and Knowledge*, 78, from Boyd, 1989, field notes.

3 Timothy A. Robinson, *Aristotle in Outline* (Indianapolis, 1995), 39.

4 M. Boyce points to a similar blind spot in Christianity, stating that Jewish Christians of the first generation would in all probability have maintained the custom of sacrificing animals until the fall of the Temple in 70 CE, alongside their meeting together for Christian worship, a suggestion not generally well received by today's Christians. See M. Boyce, "*Atas-zohr* and *Abzohr*", *Journal of the Royal Asiatic Society* (October 1966), 110.

5 Cf. *Bundahishen* 34.10 ff in Boyce, *Textual Sources*, 1984, 52.

6 Though it seems that some Zoroastrian rulers in history were not above indulging in a little persecution of their own. Shapur II (309–379 CE), for example, had two Christian bishops killed for refusing to acknowledge the Zoroastrian religion's superiority to their own, yet such conflicts were not always one-sided. The Zurvanite intrusion into Zoroastrianism, picked up perhaps a little too eagerly by some Christians, is no doubt partly responsible for identifying Ahura Mazda with the devil during the Sasanian years, which led to a blanket abjuration of all things Zoroastrian. Of course such persecution as occurred, by whoever was the instigator, would always be seen as necessary for upholding orthodoxy. See further M. Boyce *Zoroastrians, Their Religious Beliefs and Practices* (London, 1979), 118 ff.

7 The orthodoxy of this interpretation is questionable since it harmonizes neither with Zarathushtra's eschatology nor that of the later Pahlavi texts.

8 I. Gershevitch, *The Avestan Hymn to Mithra*, 75.

9 J. Hinnells, "The Flowering of Zoroastrian Benevolence: Parsi Charities in the 19th and 20th Centuries", *Papers in Honour of Professor Mary Boyce* (Leiden, 1985), 261–326.

10 "The Flowering of Zoroastrian Benevolence", 266.

11 For example by the World Zoroastrian Organization.

12 For a fictional but realistic account of life in a Parsi Colony which is alternately amusing and tragic, see Rohinton Mistry's *Tales From Firozsha Baag* (*sic*) (Penguin, Canada, 1987; London, 1992).

13 *Zoroastrians*, 218.

14 "The Flowering of Zoroastrian Benevolence", 283. It is worth remarking, I think, on the Parsi custom of naming its religious foundations not in honour of spiritual or divine beings (as is the general Christian practice) but rather after the people who endowed them, suggestive, possibly, of the Zoroastrian belief in the supreme religious duty of helping one's fellow humans, in contrast to presuming on divine assistance at all times.

15 "The Flowering of Zoroastrian Benevolence", 289.

## Chapter VIII   Identity, Unity and Disparity – Zoroastrianism Today

1 Boyce, *Zoroastrians*, 227.

2 R. Writer, *Contemporary Zoroastrians*, Introduction.

3 See e.g. Khorshed F. Jungalwala, "Historical Evidence of Avestan Culture and The Apparent Zoroastrian Beliefs in Modern-Day Tadjikistan" in *The*

*Journal of the Research and Historical Preservation Committee* 1 (Federation of Zoroastrian Associations of North America, Hinsdale Illinois, 1995): 29–51.

4  See chapter VI, note 22.

5  See chapter VI, note 49.

6  See J. H. Moulton, *The Treasure of the Magi*, 214. Moulton had followed Wilson into India some decades later, and seemed to have a much softer attitude towards the Parsi community than Wilson, characterizing the latter's writings as being "fierce", and yet even the Victorian elegance of Moulton's prose, which again and again expresses admiration for the prophet and the Zoroastrian community, can barely conceal its author's deeper purpose: the rescue, as he saw it, of the Parsi from error. He concludes this second study of the Zoroastrian religion with the following exceptional paragraph:

> A waning crescent moon hung over the harbour of Bombay and faintly illuminated the beautiful city that slept upon its shore. The borrowed radiance faded as the dawn drew on, and vanished, not destroyed but outshone, as the great sun leapt into the sky. Even so, sooner than perhaps we have dared to hope, shall the Sun of Righteousness arise on India, with healing in his wings. (253–4)

It is also worth noting that Naoraji's success in producing converts were apparently even less spectacular than his mentor's, for the one Parsi he persuaded to receive baptism, one Nuserwanji Maneckji, returned to the faith of his ancestors but a few days later, though seemingly without harbouring any ill feelings against the Christians. See further Susan Stiles Maneck *The Death of Ahriman: Culture, Identity and Theological Change Among the Parsis of India* (Bombay, 1997), 224 ff.

7  See e.g. R. Gombrich, *Therevada Buddhism* (London, 1988), chapter 7, who uses the term throughout; see particularly Gombrich's reference (p. 173) to the Anglican Bishop of Colombo writing in 1892:

> There are two Buddhisms now in Ceylon: the residuum of the old Buddhism of the past centuries, as it lingers on the put-of-the-way places, and as it has shaped the habits and ways of those who are not under European influence; and a new revival, much more self-conscious and artificial, which aims indeed only at reviving what Buddhism always professed to be, but which has been influenced, in its estimation of that profession, very largely by Europeans.

Substituting "Zoroastrianism" for "Buddhism" in the above passage, and allowing for other minor modifications, the analysis seems to hold good for the modern Zoroastrian situation.

8  J. Wilson, *The Parsi Religion as Contained in the Zand-Avesta, and Propounded and Defended by the Zoroastrians of India and Persia, Unfolded, Refuted and Contrasted with Christianity* (Bombay, 1843), 342.

9  See e.g. Wilson, *The Parsi Religion*, 69 (and *passim*); M. Boyce (*Zoroastrians*, 197) suggests that a fairer comparison would have been with the book of Leviticus.

10  *The Parsi Religion*, 112–13.
11  *The Parsi Religion*, 147.
12  *The Parsi Religion*, 272.
13  *The Parsi Religion*, 274.
14  *The Parsi Religion*, 268 ff. This western tendency to identify the good *menog* beings – particularly the Amesha Spentas – with angels needs to be challenged, since in western religious thought angels are generally understood as being "messengers" and not worshipped as such, whereas the *yazatas* are clearly objects of veneration and praise in their own right whose purpose is not to carry instructions or exhortations from the Wise Lord but to assist men and women in their work towards the *frashokereti* and to receive the praise and honour which is their due.
15  This approach was not, of course, confined to the study of Zoroastrianism; I was grateful for the opportunity to discuss this with Dr W. J. Johnson within the context of a separate religion tradition.
16  It is worth mentioning here the experience of Maneckji. Dhalla, a noted priest and erudite scholar, author of the still respected *Zoroastrian Theology* (1914), who was sent by the reformists to America to study with the renowned Iranist A. V. W. Jackson. He remains a singular example of a fusion of "Protestant" and "Catholic". When he first went to America he was a devout traditionalist, but after his contact with western scholarship his attitude towards a number of issues changed, and on his return to Bombay he was a strong advocate of reform, espousing such causes as conversion and questioning the value, or at least the supremacy, of ritual. He was also unsteady on the matter of dualism, preferring to adopt what might be described as a neo-Zurvanite stance on that particular doctrine. Yet he continued to venerate the *menog* beings throughout his life, and on the whole he was a unique blend of orthodoxy and reform, seeing no problems with the inconsistencies he represented, and his heart was unswervingly Zoroastrian.
17  See chapter VI for references to this work.
18  *The Religious Ceremonies*, ix.
19  K. Antia, *The Argument for Acceptance* (Bombay, 1985), 6.
20  *Contemporary Zoroastrians*, 205.
21  Jenny Rose, "The Traditional Role of Women in the Iranian and India (Parsi) Zoroastrian Communities from the Nineteenth to the Twentieth Century", *Journal of the K. R. Cama Oriental Institute* (Bombay, 1989), 1.
22  J. Wilson, for example, cites the case of the Zoroastrian priest who believed the *Bundahishen* to be a false document composed by an "enemy" of the religion. See Wilson, 1843, 37.
23  "The Traditional Role of Women", 81.
24  D. McIntyre has drawn attention to the *Vendidad's* proscriptive words concerning those who allow hair to fall to the ground without protective rituals, but rather wryly observes that in modern times "religious facilities have not been denied to Zoroastrians who patronize barber shops and hairdressing salons" ("What heritage must we preserve?", *Parsiana* vol. 13:1, May 1991), 29. The principle on which protective rituals were required in the matter of dead hair is substantially that concerning blood-loss, in that *any* dead matter is polluting.

25 Choksy, *Triumph over Evil*, 95.
26 Ketunam H. Gould, "Status of Women: Sacred and Secular 1", *Parsiana*, vol. 18, 3, October 1995, 24.
27 "The Traditional Role of Women", 83–4.
28 At a recent (1997) international Zoroastrian Youth Congress held in London a number of delegates were smoking, to the consternation of many others; the example set by arguably the most famous "young" Zoroastrian of recent years, the late Freddie Mercury of the rock band Queen, who was invariably photographed with cigarette in hand (or mouth), is bemoaned by the traditionalists. It can be doubted whether Mr Mercury was aware of his responsibility in the matter.
29 J. M. Whitehurst, "The Zoroastrian Response to Westernization: A Case Study of the Parsis of Bombay", *Journal of the American Academy of Religion* (1969) 37:3, 233.
30 *Contemporary Zoroastrians*, 227.
31 P. du Breuil, "New scope on some aspects of Zoroastrian history and philosophy" *The 1st World Conference on Zoroastrian Religion, Culture & History, London, 1984, Souvenir Issue* (London, 1984), 70 (du Breuil's spellings in this extract have been retained).

## Appendix 1: Zoroastrianism, Judaism and Christianity

1 The terms "Jew", "Jewish" etc. are used here in a general way. Strictly speaking of course Judaism did not come into existence until after the exile.
2 This was suggested to me by Revd. Richard Spencer, New Testament tutor at St Michael's College, Llandaff.
3 Basil of Caeserea complains about the presence of Zoroastrians in his diocese up to at least 377 CE. See F. R. Trombley, *Hellenic Religions and Christianisation c.371–529*, vol. 2, Leiden, 1994, 123.
4 I thank Dr Christine Trevett of the Department of Religious and Theological Studies, Cardiff University of Wales for her help in clarifying some points in this Appendix.

## Appendix 2: The Roman Mithraic Mysteries

1 F. Cumont argued for a solid connection in his many writings, especially in *The Mysteries of Mithra*, originally published (in French) in 1902 which set the standard of Mithraic studies for many years after its publication. His arguments have been strongly questioned in more recent times (see bibliography for details of the English language version).
2 See J. Hinnells, *Persian Mythology*, London, 1973, 1985, 84–5 for a more detailed and illustrated explanation of these grades.
3 *De antro Nympharum* in L. A. Campbell, *Mithraic Iconography and Ideology* (Leiden, 1968), 6.
4 See e.g. D. Ulansey, *The Origins of the Mithraic Mysteries: Cosmology and Salvation in the Ancient World* (New York, 1989).
5 See further Luther H. Martin "Roman Mithraism and Christianity" in *Numen*, 36 (1989): 3–15.

# Glossary

---

*Note*: This glossary consists of Avestan (Av.), Pahlavi (Phl.), Arabic (Ar.), Gujarati (Guj.), Persian (Pers.), Latin (Lat.), Greek (Gk.) and Sanskrit (Skt.) terms used in the text and commonly employed in Zoroastrian studies

| | |
|---|---|
| *Afrinagan* (Av.) | An "outer" religious ceremony of praise celebrating *Ahura Mazda's* abundant blessings. |
| *Agiary* (Guj.) | A "lesser" fire temple. |
| *Ahuna Vairya* (Av.) | A short prayer frequently recited by many Zoroastrians. |
| *Ahura Mazda* (Av.) | The omniscient Wise Lord, Creator, and the exalted God of Zoroastrianism. Later known as *Ohrmazd* (Phl.). |
| *alat* (Ar.) | Purified ritual equipment. |
| *'amal* (Ar.) | A priest's ritual power which enables him to perform ceremonies. |
| *Ameretat* (Av.) | Immortality; the *Amesha Spenta* exemplifying this attribute and represented by vegetation in ritual. |
| *Amesha Spenta* (Av.) | "Bountiful Immortal"; one of the six aspects of Ahura Mazda's divine personality, representative of theological and ethical virtues. Later associated with primal creations, and represented as such in the *Yasna* ceremony. Later known as *Amahraspand* (Phl.). |
| *Anahita* (Av.) | Goddess associated with the waters, invoked in the *Yashts*. |
| *Angra Mainyu* (Av.) | The hostile spirit; the custodian of deceit, the "devil". Later known as *Ahriman* (Phl.). |
| *Asha* (Av.) | "Righteousness"; the divine aspect of truth. |
| *Asha Vahishta* (Av.) | The *Amesha Spenta* exemplifying truth, represented by fire in ritual. |
| *Ashavan* (Av.) | "Possessor of righteousness"; a follower of the truth. |
| *Ashem Vohu* (Av.) | A short prayer used at the start of the *Yasna* |

| | |
|---|---|
| | ceremony, and recited on many other occasions. |
| *Ashi* (Av.) | Goddess of recompense, possibly invoked by Zarathushtra. |
| *Atar* (Av.) | Divinity associated with fire possibly invoked by Zarathushtra. |
| *Atash Bahram* (Per.) | A fire of the highest grade ("fire of victory"); a major fire temple. |
| *Athravan* (Av.) | A class of priest; title given to Zarathushtra in a later Avestan text. |
| *Avesta* | The sacred writings of the Zoroastrians in the *Avestan* language; two forms of the language exist, *Gathic* and *Younger* or *Standard*; the collection of texts in this language, comprising the *Gathas* and the *Yasna*; the *Vendidad*, the *Visperad* and the *Yashts*. |
| *Ayathrima* (Av.) | Homecoming (of herds) festival. |
| *Barsom* (Phl.) | Metal wires used in the *Yasna* celebration. |
| *Barashnum* (Phl.) | The nine-day and night purification ceremony performed by those to be initiated into the priestly grades. |
| *Baug* (Guj.) | A Parsi colony consisting of apartments, places of worship (including a fire temple) and, sometimes, shops. |
| *Bhakti* (Skt.) | "Loving devotion"; a movement within Hinduism, advocating a personal relationship with God, which came to prominence in the tenth century but which can be detected as far back as the *Bhagavad Gita*. |
| *Bundahishen* (Phl.) | "Creation". The texts dealing with creation and eschatology and other matters. The two texts are a short and longer version of the same composition, Iranian and Indian. |
| *Chashni* (Pers.) | Offering to laity of the *hom* mixture towards the end of the *Yasna* ceremony. |
| *Chinvat Peretu* (Phl.) | The bridge which the soul of the departed crosses to the afterlife. |
| *Dar-i Mihr* (Pers.) | "Court of Mithra"; a name given to fire temples. |
| *Daena* (Av.) | The maiden who meets the soul of the departed at the *Chinvat Peretu*; personification of the human conscience or "religious spirit". |
| *Daeva* (Av.) | Demon. |
| *Dakhma* (Av.) | "Tower of Silence"; large open structure where bodies are taken for exposure to the elements after death. |
| *Dastur* (Pers.) | Title conferred on a priest who has been exemplary in piety, learning or other qualities; |

| | |
|---|---|
| | generally given to a priest in charge of a major-fire temple. |
| *Drug* (Av.) | "The Lie"; evil counterpart of *asha*. Later known as *druj* (*Phl.*). |
| *Drugvant* (Av.) | Follower of *drug*. |
| *Duraosha* (Av.) | "Averter of death"; epithet for *Haoma* used by Zarathushtra in the *Gathas*. |
| *Ervad* (Phl.) | Title of a priest. |
| *Fargard* (Phl.) | "Chapter" or section of a longer text. |
| *Frashokereti* (Av.) | The renovation or refreshment of the universe. Later known as *Frashegird* (*Phl.*). |
| *Fravarane* (Av.) | "Creed" recited in the *Yasna* and on other occasions. |
| *Fravashi* (Av.) | Divine component of all created things; protecting spirit. |
| *Gahambar* (Phl.) | One of six festivals in the Zoroastrian calendar celebrating the six creations. |
| *Gatha* (Av.) | Hymn or song, especially those of Zarathushtra. |
| *Gayomart* (Av.) | The "first man", often called the "Zoroastrian Adam"; slaughtered by *Ahriman* in creation mythology. |
| *Getig* (Phl.) | "Material"; the physical creation; the present world (cf. *menog*). |
| *Geus Tasha* (Av.) | The "Fashioner of the Cow", Gathic metaphorical image and (possibly) divinity invoked by Zarathushtra. |
| *Geus Urvan* (Av.) | The "Soul of the Cow", Gathic metaphorical image and (possibly) divinity invoked by Zarathushtra. |
| *Gomez* (Phl.) | Unconsecrated bull's urine, used in purifications (cf. *nirang*). |
| *Gumezishen* (Phl.) | "Mixture"; the present age in which good and evil forces are locked in combat. |
| *Hamaspath-maedaya* (Av.) | All Souls' Day |
| *Haoma* (Av.) | The sacred plant (probably *ephedra*) whose juice is used in the *Yasna* and other ceremonies; also called *hom* (*Phl.*); the deity presiding over this plant who will assist *Ahura Mazda* at the apocalyptic liturgy; the "averter of death". |
| *Haurvatat* (Av.) | "Integrity, wholeness"; the *Amesha Spenta* exemplifying this attribute and represented by water in ritual. |

| | |
|---|---|
| *Jashan* (Phl.) | A liturgical service, generally an "outer" ceremony. |
| *Khshathra* (Av.) | The "good dominion" or "kingdom of God". |
| *Khshathra Vairya* (Av.) | The *Amesha Spenta* exemplifying the good dominion, represented by the metal *alat* instruments in ritual. |
| *Kriya* (Guj.) | (In the ritual context) action, rite, performance. |
| *Kushti* (Per.) | The sacred cord traditionally worn by Zoroastrians from their *Navjote* onwards. |
| *Magi* (Lat.) | Priest (from Old Persian *magu*) (Gk. μαγοι). |
| *Maidhyairya* (Av.) | Mid-winter festival. |
| *Maidhyoi-zaremaya* (Av.) | Mid-spring festival. |
| *Maidhyoshema* (Av.) | Mid-summer festival. |
| *Mainyu* (Av.) | Spirit (cf. Av./Skt. *man*, mind); a (class of) good being of the *menog* realm, worthy of worship. |
| *Manthra* (Av.) | "Sacred word," believed by some to possess talismanic properties; particularly the words of Zarathushtra as recorded in the *Gathas*, but also other Avestan literature in the ritual context. |
| *Menog* (Phl.) | "Immaterial"; the spirit creation; (cf. *getig*). |
| *Mithra* (Av.) | Zoroastrian deity associated with contract and friendship and also with the harvest; the "protector" of the homeland Iran, and later-keeper of the pact between *Ahura Mazda* and *Angra Mainyu*. |
| *Mithras* (Lat.) | Roman mystery god whose imagery and cult is probably partially derived from the Zoroastrian *Mithra*. |
| *Mithraeum* (Lat.) | A subterranean temple dedicated to the Roman god *Mithras*. |
| *Mitra* (Skt.) | Vedic deity associated with Contract; linked with *Varuna* as in ... |
| *Mitravaruna* (Skt.) | "Contract and True Speech"; custodians of the cosmic law *rta*. |
| *Mobed* (Pers.) | Priestly title denoting higher responsibilities. |
| *Navjote* (Guj.) | "New life"; the initiation ceremony whereby one is received into the Zoroastrian fold. |
| *Nirang* (Phl.) | Consecrated bull's urine, used in purifications (cf. *gomez*). |
| *No Roz* (Av.) | New Year festival. |
| *Padan* (Phl.) | Face mask worn by priests during rituals to prevent their breath and saliva from defiling the *alat* and *pawi*. |
| *Pahlavi* | Middle Persian language of the later Zoroastrian |

*Paitishahya* (Av.)          texts and in use during the Sassanian period. (Festival of) bringing in corn (harvest).

*Paiwand* (Phl.)             Piece of cloth held between two priests or laity during certain rituals, to strengthen their bond and thus maintain purity; a "connecting" ritual.

*Paragna* (Av.)              "Pre-worship": preparatory ritual performed by the *raspi* in which instruments and *pawi* are made *alat* and *parahom* prepared in readiness for the *Yasna*, *Vendidad* or *Visperad* ceremonies.

*Parahom* (Av.)              Sacramental mixture of *hom*, water and pomegranate twigs prepared during the *paragna* and drunk by the *zot* in the *Yasna* and other ceremonies.

*Pawi* (Guj.)                Consecrated and purified area in fire temples set aside for the celebration of higher liturgies; the furrows demarcating this area.

*Pazand* (Phl.)              *Pahlavi*-based language used interpolatively in some liturgies; recited at a lower voice in recognition of the sacred character of *Avestan*.

*Qissa-i Sanjan* (Pers.)     Epic narrative poem composed *c.*1600, recounting the voyage and early life in India of the migrant Zoroastrians who fled Iran during the Arabic persecution.

*Raspi* (Pers.)              "helper" (cf. *rac-*, Av. "to help"); the assistant priest at a *Yasna* and certain other liturgies.

*Rta* (Skt.)                 The law which regulates the cosmos in Vedic religion.

*Sagdid* (Phl.)              The rite of exposing a corpse to the gaze of a dog as part of the funerary procedure.

*Samsara* (Skt.)             The understanding of the world which proposes that it is "trapped" in a constant cycle of birth and death.

*Spenta Armaiti* (Av.)       "Holiness, devotion, piety"; the *Amesha Spenta* exemplifying this attribute and represented by the *hom* in ritual.

*Spenta Mainyu* (Av.)        The augmenting Holy Spirit of *Ahura Mazda*, hypostatically united to him, and represented by the priest in ritual.

*Sroash* (Av.)               Gathic divinity, possibly venerated by Zarathushtra, denoting listening to God's word.

*Sudre* (Per.)               Undergarment traditionally worn by Zoroastrians from their *Navjote* onwards.

*Vendidad* (Av.)             "Laws against the Demons"; a book containing ritual purity regulations and other miscellaneous material; an "inner" ceremony incorporating this book (also called *Videvdat*, a contraction of *Vidaeavo-datem*).

*Visperad* (Av.). "Lords of the Ritual"; a book containing a number of miscellaneous hymns; an "inner" ceremony incorporating this book.

*Vohu Manah* (Av.). "Good Mind"; the *Amesha Spenta* exemplifying this attribute and represented by dairy produce in ritual.

*Wizarishen* (Av.) The "Separation"; the era following the apocalypse when good and evil will be eternally separated.

*Yasdathragar* (Av.) Priest who "purifies creation"; *zot* or *zaotar*.

*Yasht* (Av.) Hymn in praise of a good *menog* being.

*Yasna* (Av.) "Worship, sacrifice"; high liturgy of the Zoroastrians; hymn or poem, including the *Gathas*.

*Yazata* (Av.) *Menog* being worthy of worship; in Phl. *Yazad*.

*Zand* (Phl.) Translation and commentary of Avestan texts into the middle Persian vernacular.

*Zaotar* (Av.) Priest; chief celebrant at a liturgy such as the *Yasna* (Phl. *zot*).

*Zurvan* (Av.) "Time"; a minor deity in the later Avesta; from which is derived the term *Zurvanism*, denoting a Zoroastrian heresy which states that Ahura Mazda and Angra Mainyu are twin sons of "Time". This heresy was revived and reviled by, notably, J. Wilson, in the mid-nineteenth century.

*Zurvan akarana* "boundless time".

# Bibliography

## 1 The Zoroastrian Texts

Alklesaria, B. T. (ed.), *Zand-I Vohuman Yasn and Two Pahlavi Fragments*, Bombay, 1957.

———, *The Pahlavi Rivayat of Aturfarnbag and Farnbag-Sros* (2 vols), Bombay, 1969.

Boyce, M., *Textual Sources for the Study of Zoroastrianism*, Manchester, 1984, Chicago, 1990.

Geldner, K. (ed.), *Avesta, Sacred Books of the Parsis* (3 vols), Stuttgart, 1886–96.

Gershevitch, I., *The Avestan Hymn to Mithra*, Cambridge, 1959.

Humbach, H., *The Gathas of Zarathushtra and the Other Old Avestan Texts* (in collaboration with J. Elfenbein and P.O. Skjærvø) Parts 1 and 2, Heidelberg, 1991.

Humbach, H. and Ichaporia, P., *The Heritage of Zarathushtra: A New Translation of his Gathas*, Heidelberg, 1994.

Insler, S., *The Gathas of Zarathushtra*, Leiden, 1975.

Malandra, W., *An Introduction to Ancient Iranian Religion*, Minneapolis, 1983.

Müller, F. M. (ed.), *Sacred Books of the East*:
    vol. 4, *The Zend-Avesta pt. 1* (L. H. Mills), Oxford, 1881, Delhi, 1992.
    vol. 5, *Pahlavi Texts pt. 1* (E. W. West), Oxford, 1880, Delhi, 1993.
    vol. 18, *Pahlavi Texts pt. 2* (E. W. West), Oxford, 1882, Delhi, 1994.
    vol. 23, *The Zend-Avesta pt.. 2* (J. Darmesteter), Oxford, 1882, Delhi, 1993.
    vol. 24, *Pahlavi Texts pt. 3* (E. W. West), Oxford, 1885, Delhi, 1994.
    vol. 31, *The Zend-Avesta pt. 3* (L. H. Mills), Oxford, 1887, Delhi, 1988.
    vol. 37, *Pahlavi Texts pt. 4* (E. W. West), Oxford, 1892, Delhi, 1994.
    vol. 47, *Pahlavi Texts pt. 5* (E. W. West), Oxford, 1897, Delhi, 1994.

Reichelt, H., *Avesta Reader*, Strassburg, 1911.

## 2 Works consulted and cited on Zoroastrianism

Antia, K., *The Argument for Acceptance* (Bombay, 1985).

Boyce, M., "Atas-zohr and Ab-zohr", *Journal of the Royal Asiatic Society* (October 1966), 100–18.

———, "On the Sacred Fires of the Zoroastrians", *Bulletin of the School of Oriental and African Studies* (1968) 31:1, 54–68.

———, "On Mithra's Part in Zoroastrianism", *Bulletin of the School of Oriental *and African Studies* (1969), 32:1, 10–34.

——, "Zoroaster the Priest", *Bulletin of the School of Oriental and African Studies* (1970), 33:1, 22–38.

——, "Haoma Priest of the Sacrifice", *W. B. Henning Memorial Volume* ed. M. Boyce and I. Gershevitch, 1970, 62–80.

——, "Mihragan among the Irani Zoroastrians" *Mithraic Studies* vol. 1 ed. J. R. Hinnells, Manchester, 1971, 106–18.

——, *A History of Zoroastrianism* vol. 1, Leiden, 1975.

——, *A Persian Stronghold of Zoroastrianism*, Oxford, 1977.

——, *Zoroastrians, their Religious Beliefs and Practices*, London, 1979.

——, "Priests, Cattle and Men", *Bulletin of the School of Oriental and African Studies* (1987) 50:2, 508–26.

——, *Zoroastrianism: Its Antiquity and Constant Vigour*, Costa Mesa, 1992.

——, "On the Orthodoxy of Sasanian Zoroastrianism", *Bulletin of the School of Oriental and African Studies* (1996) 59:1, 11–28.

Boyd, J and Kotwal, F. M., "Worship in a Zoroastrian Fire Temple", *Indo-Iranian Journal* (1984) 26, 292–318.

Boyd, J. and Crosby, D. A., "Is Zoroastrianism Dualistic or Monotheistic?", *Journal of the American Academy of Religion* (1978) 47:4, 557–88.

du Breuil, P., *Zarathoustra et la Transfiguration de Monde*, Paris, 1978.

——, "New scope on some aspects of Zoroastrian history and philosophy", *The 1st World Conference on Zoroastrian Religion, Culture & History, London, 1984, Souvenir Issue*, London, 1984, 63–71.

Cameron, G., "Zoroaster the Herdsman", *Indo-Iranian Journal* (1968) 10, 261–81.

Choksy, J., *Triumph over Evil: Purity and Pollution in Zoroastrianism*, Texas, 1989.

Dhalla, M., *Zoroastrian Theology*, New York, 1914.

Darrow, W., "Keeping the Waters Dry: The Semiotics of Fire and Water in the Zoroastrian *Yasna*", *Journal of the American Academy of Religion* (1988) 57:3, 417–42.

Duchesne-Guillemin, J., *The Hymns of Zarathushtra* (trans. from the French by M. Henning) London, 1953.

——, *The Western Response to Zoroaster*, Oxford, 1958.

Gershevitch, I., *The Avestan Hymn to Mithra*, Cambridge, 1959, 1967.

——, "Approaches to Zoroaster's Gathas", *Iran* (British Institute of Persian Studies), London, 1995, 1–29.

Gould, K. H., "Status of Women: Sacred and Secular 1", *Parsiana* (October 1995), 24–9.

Gray, L. H., "The 'Ahurian' and 'Daevian' Vocabularies in the Avesta", *Journal of the Bombay Branch of the Royal Asiatic Society* (July 1927) Part III, 427–41.

Hartman, S. S., *Parsism, the religion of Zoroaster (Iconography of Religions* XIV, 4), Leiden, 1980.

Haug. M., *The Parsis, Essays on their Sacred Language, Writings and Religion*, London, 1862 repr. Delhi, 1978.

Hinnells, J. R., "Zoroastrian Saviour Imagery and its Influence on the New Testament", *Numen* (1969) 16, 161–5.

——, *Persian Mythology*, London, 1973, 1985.

——, "Zoroastrian Influence on the Judeo-Christian Tradition", *Journal of the K.R. Cama Oriental Institute* 45 (Bombay, 1976), 1–23.

——, *Spanning East and West*, Milton Keynes, 1978.

——, *Zoroastrianism and the Parsis*, London, 1981 (repr. Bombay, 1996).

——, "The Flowering of Zoroastrian Benevolence: Parsi Charities in the 19th and 20th Centuries", *Papers in Honour of Professor Mary Boyce*, Leiden, 1985, 261–326.

——, *Zoroastrians in Britain*, Oxford, 1996.

Insler, S., "The Ahuna Vairya Prayer", *Acta Iranica 4, Monumentum H. S. Nyberg*, Leiden, 1975, 409–21.

Jafarey, A. A., "The Zoroastrian Priest in the Avesta", *World Zoroastrian Chicago Conference on Zoroastrian Religion, Culture and History, November 1987*, London, 1990, 24–33.

——, "Woman venerated and victimized", *Parsiana* 13:10, April 1991, 29–34.

Jungalwala, K. F., "Historical Evidence of Avestan Culture and The Apparent Zoroastrian Beliefs in Modern-Day Tadjikistan", *The Journal of the Research and Historical Preservation Committee*, vol. 1, Federation of Zoroastrian Associations of North America, Hinsdale, Illinois, 1995.

Kellens, J. and Pirart, E., *Les textes vieil avestiques* (3 vols), Wiesbaden, 1988, 1990, 1991.

Kotwal, F. M., "The Authenticity of the Parsi Priestly Tradition", *Journal of the K. R. .Cama Oriental Institute* 45 (Bombay, 1976), 24–33.

——, "Initiation into the Zoroastrian Priesthood: Present Parsi Practice and an old Pahlavi Text", *Acta Iranica 28 "A Green Leaf"*, Leiden, 1988, 299–307.

——, "A Brief History of the Parsi Priesthood", *Indo-Iranian Journal* (1990) 33, 165–75.

——, "The divine laws of God must prevail", *Parsiana* (September 1990) 13:2, 27–9.

Kotwal, F. M., and Boyd, J., "The Zoroastrian *paragna* ritual", *Journal of Mithraic Studies* (1977) 2:1, 18–52.

——, *A Persian Offering: The Yasna, a Zoroastrian High Liturgy*, Paris, 1994.

Kuiper, F. B. J., "Avestan *Mazda-*", *Indo-Iranian Journal* (1957) 1:1, 86–95.

——, "The Bliss of *Asa*", *Indo-Iranian Journal* (1964) 8:2, 96–129.

——, "Ahura Mazda Lord Wisdom", *Indo-Iranian Journal* (1976) 18, 25–42.

Luhmann, T. M., *The Good Parsi: The Fate of a Colonial Elite in a Postcolonial Society*, Harvard, 1996.

Maneck, Susan Stiles, *The Death of Ahriman: Culture, Identity and Theological Change Among the Parsis of India*, Bombay, 1997.

McIntyre, D., "What heritage must we preserve?", *Parsiana* (May 1991) 13:11, 27–30.

——, "The Talisman", *The Journal of the Research and Historical Preservation Committee* vol. 2 (Proceedings of the Second North American Gatha Conference, Houston, Texas), Federation of Zoroastrian Associations of North America, Hinsdale, Illinois, 1996, 153–69.

Mehr, F., "Zoroastrian Ethics", *The 1st World Conference on Zoroastrian Religion, Culture & History, London, 1984, Souvenir Issue*, London, 1984, 87–95.

——, *The Zoroastrian Tradition*, Rockport, 1991.

Mirza, H. K., Jamaspasa. K. M. and Kotwal, F. M., *Antia's "Acceptance": A Zoroastrian "Ahrmogih" (Heresy)*, Bombay, n.d.

Mistree, K., *Zoroastrianism, An Ethnic Perspective*, Bombay, 1982.

Mistry, R., *Tales from Firozsha Baag*, Canada, 1987, London, 1992.

Modi, J. J., *The Religious Ceremonies and Customs of the Parsees*, Bombay, 1922.

Moulton, J., *Early Zoroastrianism*, London, 1913 repr. New York, 1980.

——, *The Treasure of the Magi*, London, 1917 repr. New York, 1972.

Pavry, J. C., *The Zoroastrian Doctrine of a Future Life: From Death to the Individual Judgement*, Columbia, 1926, repr. New York, 1965.

Randria, J. D., "The Philosophy of the Religious Tradition of Haoma and Sacrificial Worship", *Journal of the K.R. Cama Oriental Institute*, 59 (Bombay, 1994), 61–78 (Lecture III in *Some Unique Concepts in Zoroastrianism*).

Rose, J., "The Traditional Role of Women in the Iranian and Indian (Parsi) Zoroastrian Communities from the Nineteenth to the Twentieth Century", *Journal of the K. R. Cama Oriental Institute*, 56 (Bombay, 1989).

Schwartz, M., "Coded Sound Patterns, Acrostics, and Anagrams in Zoroaster's Oral Poetry", *Studia Grammatica Iranica, Festschrift für Helmut Humbach* ed. R. Schmitt and P. O. Skjærvø, München, 1986.

Shaked, S., *Dualism in Transformation, Varieties of Religion in Sasanian Iran* (Jordan Lectures, 1991), London, 1994.

——, *From Zoroastrian Iran to Islam* (Variorum Collected Studies Series), Aldershot, 1995.

Stewart, S., *The Concept of "Spirit" in the Old Testament and Zoroastrian Gathas* (SOAS occasional papers 11), London, 1993.

Trustees of the Parsi Punchayat Funds & Properties, Bombay, *Towers of Silence*, Bombay, 1899, revised and repr. 1994.

Williams, A. V., "Medieval texts in a modern world", *World Zoroastrian souvenir issue (One-day seminar on Zoroastrian Religion, Culture & History, London, July 1986)*, London, 1986, 45–56.

——, "The Body and the Boundaries of Zoroastrian Spirituality", *Religion* (1989): 19, 227–39.

Williams, R. G. and Boyd, J., *Ritual Art and Knowledge, Aesthetic Theory and Zoroastrian Ritual*, Columbia, 1993.

Whitehurst, J. M., "The Zoroastrian Response to Westernization: A Case Study of the Parsis of Bombay", *Journal of the American Academy of Religion* (1969) 37:3, 224–36.

Wilson, J. *The Parsi Religion as contained in the Zand-Avesta, and Propounded and Defended by the Zoroastrians of India and Persia, Unfolded, Refuted and Contrasted with Christianity*, Bombay, 1843.

Writer, R. *Contemporary Zoroastrians*, Lanham, Maryland, 1984.

Zaehner, R., *Zurvan, A Zoroastrian Dilemma*, London, 1955.

——, *The Dawn and Twilight of Zoroastrianism*, London, 1961.

## 3 Other works consulted and cited

Cumont, F., *The Mysteries of Mithra* (trans. from second French edition by T. J. McCormack), New York, 1956.

Eliade, M., *Myth and Reality*, New York, 1963.

Falk, H., "Soma I and II", *Bulletin of the School of Oriental and African Studies* (1989) 52:1, 77–90.

Gombrich, R., *Therevada Buddhism, A Social History from Ancient Banares to Modern Colombo*, London, 1988, 1991, 1994.

Hale, W. E., *Ásura in Early Vedic Religion*, Delhi, 1986.

Heetsrman, J. C., *The Broken World of Sacrifice*, Chicago, 1993.

James, H. L. (trans.), *Strabo's Geography*, London, 1930.

Lincoln, B. *Priests Warriors and Cattle*, California, 1981.

——, *Death War and Sacrifice*, Chicago, 1991.

Martin, L. H., "Roman Mithraism and Christianity", *Numen* (1989) 16, 3–15.

Monier-Williams, M., *A Sanskrit-English Dictionary*, Oxford, 1899, Delhi, 1993.

Ricour, P., *The Rule of Metaphor*, Toronto, 1977.

Robinson, T. A., *Aristotle in Outline*, Indianapolis, 1995.

Trombley, F. R., *Hellenic Religions and Christianisation c.370–529*, vol. 2, Leiden, 1994.

Ulansey, D., *The Origins of the Mithraic Mysteries: Cosmology and Salvation in the Ancient World*, New York, 1989.

Wasson, R. G., *Soma, divine mushroom of immortality*, New York, 1968.

Weller, P. (ed.), *Religions in the UK, a multifaith directory* (second edition), University of Derby, 1997.

# Index